Getting Started in Retirement Planning

Tim Mulcahy

The Getting Started In Series

Getting Started in Online Day Trading by Kassandra Bentley
Getting Started in Asset Allocation by Bill Bresnan and Eric Gelb
Getting Started in Online Investing by David L. Brown and Kassandra Bentley
Getting Started in Stocks by Alvin D. Hall
Getting Started in Mutual Funds by Alvin D. Hall
Getting Started in Estate Planning by Kerry Hannon
Getting Started in 401(k) Investing by Paul Katzeff
Getting Started in Security Analysis by Peter J. Klein
Getting Started in Global Investing by Robert P. Kreitler
Getting Started in Futures by Todd Lofton
Getting Started in Financial Information by Daniel Moreau and Tracey Longo
Getting Started in Technical Analysis by Jack D. Schwager
Getting Started in Hedge Funds by Daniel A. Strachman
Getting Started in Options by Michael C. Thomsett
Getting Started in Real Estate Investing by Michael C. Thomsett and Jean Freestone Thomsett
Getting Started in Annuities by Gordon M. Williamson
Getting Started in Bonds by Sharon Saltzgiver Wright
Getting Started in Retirement Planning by Ronald M. Yolles and Murray Yolles

Getting Started in
Retirement Planning

Ronald M. Yolles
Murray Yolles

John Wiley & Sons, Inc.
New York • Chichester • Weinheim • Brisbane • Singapore • Toronto

This book is printed on acid-free paper. ♾

Published by John Wiley & Sons, Inc.

Published simultaneously in Canada.

Library of Congress Cataloging-in-Publication Data:

Yolles, Ronald M.
Getting started in retirement planning / Ronald M. Yolles and Murray Yolles.
p. cm.—(Getting started in)
Includes index.
ISBN 0-471-38310-4 (pbk. : alk. paper)
1. Retirees—Finance, Personal. 2. Retirement—Planning. I. Yolles, Murray. II. Title. III. Series.
HG179 .Y628 2001
332.024'01—dc21 00-042267

Printed in the United States of America.

10 9 8 7 6 5 4 3 2 1

To Julie and Elinor

Preface

THIS ISN'T YOUR PARENTS' RETIREMENT

Retirement these days is very, very different from the retirement that your father or mother knew. Even the venerable group AARP has changed. AARP, formerly known as the American Association of Retired Persons, now goes only by the acronym AARP. AARP wants nothing to do with the word "retirement" or any notion that their members are elderly. In fact, AARP's members are actually vibrant people in their fifties, sixties, seventies, eighties, and nineties.

Baby boomers (born 1946–1964) and the younger members of the World War II generation (born 1928–1945) are revolutionizing the way people think about and plan for retirement. The two Gs—golf and gardening—have been replaced by many of the following as worthwhile retirement pursuits:

- ✔ Returning to college or obtaining a new degree.
- ✔ Taking a primary caregiver and financial role in raising grandchildren.
- ✔ Embarking on a new, completely different career.
- ✔ Learning computer skills.
- ✔ Developing investment expertise.
- ✔ Starting a vigorous exercise program.

While notions of retirement are changing, surveys show that people are ill prepared for this "new retirement." Hopefully, this book will serve as a blueprint for both the financial and, perhaps more importantly, the emotional issues that you will face as you plan for retirement.

When the Social Security Act was passed in 1935, the average life expectancy in the United States was 58 years of age. This made it very easy for the government to promise Social Security benefits at age 62 or even age 65 because most people did not live that long. These days a healthy 62-year-old woman is expected to live to age 88, and many experts feel that newborns have a life expectancy of 120. By the year 2050 there will be several million people over the age of 100—enough to populate an entire major city. Clearly our notions of retirement have changed dramatically and even the word "retirement" is probably a misnomer. What we have thought of in the past as retirement should really just be thought of as either the second half or final third of a person's life.

In interviewing over 100 people and working with retirees and pre-retirees for many years, we have found that people no longer retire but rather reinvent or partially reinvent their lives after their initial careers have run their course.

Since the old ideas of retirement have become passé, the task of planning for the new type of retirement or financial freedom has become much more complex and much more difficult; however, the rewards and chances for fulfillment are much greater than in the old view of retirement. The old view of retirement meant you worked for one company until age 62 or 65, then retired, put your money into a certificate of deposit, traveled a little, and passed away at age 68. The new retirement paradigms are as varied and diverse as choices faced by anyone at any stage of life. People are either retiring or reinventing their careers at much younger ages and enjoying vigorous activities much longer in life. Increased choices and longevity create the necessity to begin planning at an earlier age how to achieve either retirement or reinvention in a second career.

Many of these issues are particularly important for women in light of the fact that the average woman lives more than seven years longer than her husband. Women have to be prepared both financially and emotionally to live a significant period of time on their own. In the group of people over the age of 85, there are currently 285 women per every 100 men. Changes in health and exercise practices should narrow this gap substantially in the years ahead.

This book is written for people of all ages. For those of you in your thirties and forties, the book can be a road map of not only how to start saving for retirement but also how to start thinking about the second half or final third of your life in the midst of raising your children and developing your careers. For those of you in your fifties, sixties, and seventies, the book will prove to be an objective source on both the emotional and psychological issues that you face as well as the financial and investment issues that you have to deal with. Finally, for the increasingly large group of people age 80 and up, the book not only covers issues that you face in the areas of investment and estate planning, but also deals with how to communicate with your spouse, children, and grandchildren about issues that are extremely important to your family and that directly affect the quality and enjoyment of your life.

Our goal for this book, which is designed to be a hands-on reference guide, is to provide you with an invaluable investment road map that will make your retirement journey smooth and comfortable.

The first step to successfully preparing for your retirement is finding a source of objective information to help you evaluate, plan, and understand alternate courses of action. Unlike other critical issues in your life, where you know whom to talk to about obtaining insightful advice, you may be unsure about how to find reliable professional investment counsel. We hope that this book will be a significant resource and clear up the uncertainty you may have about the investment world. Additionally, this book will provide you with necessary background information before you visit your financial and tax professionals.

We believe that this book is unique in several ways. We feel very strongly that most of the information that retirees and preretirees receive is inappropriate for their specific financial circumstances. In addition to presenting detailed, objective, and well-documented advice and facts, we have devoted parts of several chapters to outlining the problems that can result from conventional investment wisdom. We will show you alternative, more effective, ways to plan your overall investment and retirement program.

Perhaps more importantly, we hope to dispel myths about how retirees and preretirees should think and feel about their financial planning. When you have finished this book, we hope that our faith in the well-researched and time-tested financial principles that we have discussed will have helped you overcome all or most of your fear about retirement and financial planning.

Between us, we have more than 50 years' experience counseling clients, most of whom are retirees or preretirees. We like to say that we have been providing investment and financial counsel for over 150 years because we believe it is critical to understand at least the prior 100 years of investment and market history to provide well-informed investment counsel to our clients.

Over this long time frame, we have seen many clients who have implemented successful investment and retirement plans and also many people who have not been as lucky. We feel very strongly that one of the most valuable things we can do in this book is to point out the many problems that people run into in their investment, financial, estate, and tax planning. Hopefully, by doing this, we can share our insights into the causes of these problems. It is our sincere hope that we can help you, the investor, to avoid these situations.

In the next 12 chapters, we will explore many key issues and provide critical topical and historical information pertaining to the world of finance. We will examine why certain behavioral traits perpetually lead investors to make emotional, hasty, and harmful investment revisions to what was a well-designed, long-term retirement plan. And we will look at other investors who have the personality characteristics to make productive investment decisions.

The single most critical issue for many people is how to achieve a growing and sustainable source of cash flow to either fully or partially retire someday. We will examine the proper way, or what we call the optimal way, to broadly diversify a multimanager investment portfolio and achieve retirement investing success.

We feel that this book takes on a unique perspective. Not only do we enjoy a very close father-and-son relationship, but we are currently business associates. At various times in our lives, we have each been a client of the other in our particular specialties—tax and estate planning, law and investment management, respectively.

We believe that our different perspectives give us several advantages in illuminating points emphasized in the book. Throughout, you will see case studies of our experiences with actual clients whose circumstances may be very similar to your own.

This book is organized into four parts with examples, case studies, and definitions given throughout. Part One, which covers Chapters 1 through 4, is titled "Saving for Financial Independence." Part Two, which covers Chapters 5, 6, and 7, focuses on "Life Stage Financial Strategies" and your particular temperament and risk tolerance. Part Three, which covers Chapters 8 and 9, is titled "Preserving Your Wealth: Estate Planning." And finally, Part Four, which covers Chapters 10 through 12, is titled "Enjoying the Good Life."

In our professional capacity as wealth managers, one critical observation that we have made is that retirement planning and investment issues can be extremely upsetting and unnerving. These issues are equally unnerving to young and old. Younger people are saving for financial independence while simultaneously trying to raise and send their children to college as well as get established in their own careers. Those who have reached or are about to reach financial independence or some form of partial financial independence have to deal with the central issue of whether their money will last.

At Yolles Investment Management, Inc., we help clients, both those saving for financial independence and those who have already reached financial independence, implement financial strategies that allow them to sleep soundly at night. With this book, we plan to dispel investment myths and provide you with a level of comfort to be successful and confident enough to stick with your long-term retirement plan. Please note that this plan may have several different aspects for several different stages of your life. There will also be a certain element of flexibility built into the plan. This book will give you the tools to continue learning about investment and retirement planning throughout your entire lifetime.

We live in a complex day and age, particularly as we enter a new millennium. This makes the challenge of retirement planning both scary and exciting. Scary, in the sense that all, or many, of the rules in society are changing and changing very rapidly. For example, the Internet and Internet-based companies are replacing many long-established companies, and in many ways the investment and financial worlds have been turned at least partially upside down. Exciting but also scary is the notion that people are living to age 100 and must plan accordingly. However, we are both optimists and find the challenge and opportunity invigorating. The notion that we can spend a third or even half of our lives in some form of financial independence has to be terribly fulfilling. So read on and join us for what we hope will be a very important, insightful, and enlightening journey.

RONALD M. YOLLES
MURRAY YOLLES

Southfield, Michigan
September 2000

Acknowledgments

This book was a true collaborative effort. We received input from experts right up to publication date as potential changes in estate tax and 401(k) regulations were debated in Congress. Readers can access updates on these and other issues at the "We wrote the book" icon at our web site, www.yollesinvest.com.

This book would not have been possible without Darlene Hemker. Julie Yolles deserves significant writing and editing credit. Special thanks to our fellow members in The Council of Independent Financial Advisors (CIFA) who have helped us define, and constantly redefine, what it means to run a client-centered investment management firm. Our colleagues at Yolles Investment Management—Robert Samrah, Tim Atkinson, Maria Bertolino, Brian Weisberger, Sal Giacomazza, Meg Atkinson, and Amanda Hillman—deserve our thanks and gratitude.

Working with our editor and friend Debra Englander at John Wiley & Sons has been a pleasure. Thanks also go to associate managing editor, Mary Daniello, at Wiley as well as the staff at Cape Cod Compositors.

Richard Ennis at Ennis, Knupp & Associates provided a tremendous amount of research insights, as did Sam Adams at Dimensional Fund Advisors and Thomas Bergh, Esq., at Raymond and Prokop.

R.M.Y.
M.Y.

Contents

Introduction

If you are like most people, you probably have neglected planning some, or several, details of your financial life. Additionally, you probably have not taken the time to communicate with your spouse, or yourself, about how you feel about money and what money means to you. This book will help you work through crucial financial decisions in a systematic way that will give you both long-term peace of mind and, hopefully, complete or substantial *financial independence* at as young an age as possible.

> **financial independence** when work is no longer a necessity, but rather a choice.

In working with and interviewing hundreds of investors, we have found that planning for retirement or financial independence is as much about peace of mind and emotional issues as it is about financial issues. Too often we find that people who have done the right thing do not have the sense of comfort that they should have. Additionally, we find that too often emotions lead people to make poor financial decisions.

These emotional factors cause many preretirees and baby boomers to be overconfident about their ability to retire, and this overconfidence often leads to severe financial pain and uncertainty down the road. Surveys show that many people overestimate by a factor of three their likely investment returns before and during retirement, and because of this they grossly underestimate the amount that they will need to save for retirement.

One of our primary goals for this book is to teach you to separate fact from fiction in the investment world and rely much more on fact than on your friend Heather's advice on the golf course or your Uncle David's advice over Thanksgiving dinner about the next "hot stock" tip. A key component of anyone's financial education—and this applies to both investment professionals and individual investors—is to learn that nothing in the financial world is guaranteed or certain. Investment management and *financial economics* are not hard sciences but rather are social sciences. Anytime we discuss principles in investing we are talking about giving you the greatest *probability* of success. There is never certainty in the investment world. Mastering this single concept will go a long way toward helping you achieve financial success, and it will help you avoid hot tips that sound like sure winners. The sooner you recognize that there are neither financial gurus nor guarantees, the closer you are to making sound financial decisions.

financial economics the scholarly study of investment principles and facts.

probability the concept that nothing in this world is certain.

We've surveyed over 100 investors from ages 31 to 91 to learn how retirement feels, and we've been fortunate to have access to some very sophisticated computer programs, designed by a former NASA rocket scientist (really), which helps us look at 2,000 best-case and worst-case retirement scenarios for the individuals, couples, and families that make up the case studies used throughout the book. Certainly one or several of these case studies will nearly or even exactly match your particular fact situation so that you can use these as a frame of reference in your financial planning. The single key feature and usefulness of this book is that it should empower you before you see your professional advisers to get the financial help you are entitled to. Having background knowledge is critical before you interface with your investment adviser, your certified public accountant (CPA), your attorney, and your insurance broker, who will constitute your *financial planning team* and will be critical to your financial success. (See Figure I.1.)

financial planning team consists of your attorney, CPA, investment adviser, and insurance broker.

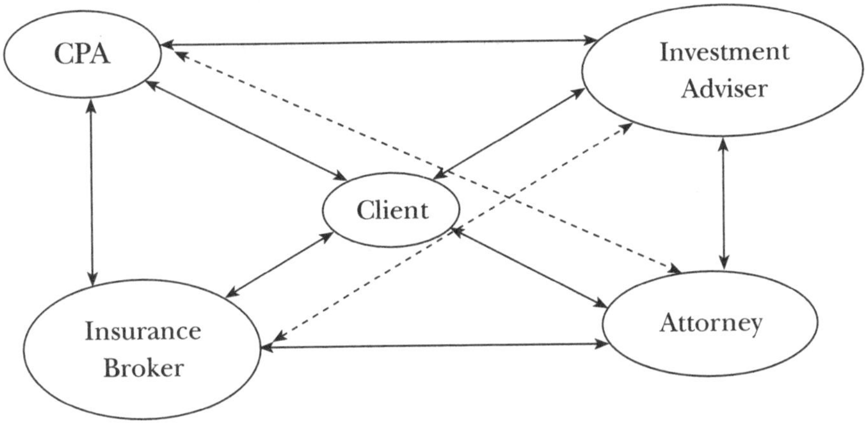

FIGURE I.1 Your financial planning team.
Source: Yolles Investment Management.

Avoid jack-of-all trades planners. Your investment adviser should be a seasoned investment professional who has at least 10 years of experience and either the Chartered Financial Analyst (CFA) designation or an MBA from a leading university.

One of the most difficult situations faced by seasoned investment professionals is helping a client who has procrastinated and fails to seek our counsel early on. This happened again recently when a friend (we'll call her Lorna) visited our office shortly after her husband Albert succumbed to lung cancer at age 72.

Although Albert worked right up until the year before his death, he and Lorna neglected their retirement planning. Now, Lorna, age 65, will have to pay the price—namely a lower standard of living and the necessity to return to work. Fortunately, though, we can still help Lorna, using many of the same techniques we will present to you in this book.

Albert and Lorna neglected all six of the following areas of their investment planning:

1. They failed to invest their assets properly and missed nearly all of the benefits of investing in sound *no-load mutual funds* or common stocks over the past 15 years.
2. They failed to evaluate sustainable withdrawal rates from their retirement accounts and therefore spent too much and saved too little.

no-load refers to a product that is bought directly without a commission (load).

mutual fund an investment company that provides professional management and research of stock and bond portfolios.

3. Their *estate plan* was outdated, which caused Lorna and their children needless probate and estate costs, hassles, and taxes.
4. They failed to evaluate and obtain *long-term care insurance*, an omission that cost Lorna $40,000 in caregiver costs.
5. Albert failed to involve Lorna in their financial decisions, which caused her utter confusion following his death.
6. Albert purchased a costly *annuity* that only provided income for his lifetime and left Lorna with an income shortfall.

Albert and Lorna's investment procrastination is one of the two most common problems that we see with retirees. The other common problem involves emotional as opposed to objective investing and decision making. This problem was exhibited by a new client (we will call her Barbara).

estate plan designed to provide funds for the individual's dependents upon the death of the individual, but also to conserve the personal assets to be bequeathed to the heirs.

long-term care insurance coverage if you require either an extended stay in a nursing home or at-home nursing care.

annuity contract between an individual and an insurance company, providing lifetime income to the person on whose life the contract is based in return for either a lump-sum or periodic payment to the insurance company.

An edgy 65-year-old Barbara called us for help in March of 1997. Although her 67-year-old husband, Freddy, had a successful advertising business, they had failed to put away enough money for their retirement. They had lost money in almost every investment, including oil and gas limited partnerships, real estate partnerships, junk bonds, and a variety of investments in small stocks that were all supposed to become the next Microsoft.

Barbara made all of their investment decisions based on hearsay and emotion with a hope of striking it rich. She was envious of her younger sister, Ellen, and Ellen's husband, Stuart, who were in much better financial shape than Barbara and Freddy even though Stuart's lifetime earnings were much lower.

Ellen and Stuart were longtime clients of our firm. We had put together a sensible long-term retirement program for them based on economic and financial facts rather than hearsay and emotion.

As mentioned, financial professionals must often help procrastinators. For some reason individuals procrastinate in getting professional counsel for their financial planning needs whereas they do not procrastinate in getting appropriate medical help or even getting professional help when their cars need an oil change. This probably happens for one of two reasons: Either people are intimidated about financial issues and have a sort of financial paralysis or people mistakenly feel that they can go it alone when doing their financial, tax, and even legal planning. More often than not, this false confidence proves detrimental to their financial health. Knowledge is power, and we hope that this book can be the source of information that allows you comfortably to get the professional help that you probably need.

Most people fall into one of three categories as to their ability as investors. Half of you are probably what we call delegators who realize that you need appropriate financial and tax help and will delegate this to professionals. Probably one-quarter of you are what we call do-it-yourselfers who are diligent students of publications like *Consumer Reports* when you're making any decisions or purchases. You apply a similar discipline, keen intellect, and sense of doing thorough research to your financial decisions and are hopefully competent in ultimately executing the proper decisions. Finally, probably one-quarter of you are what are called validators who like to do certain things on a do-it-yourself basis but want to interact with professionals for a substantial number of the key financial decisions that must be made. There will be value in this book for all three types of investors.

Young people in their 30s and 40s are among the biggest culprits in neglecting to save for financial independence and spending beyond their means. The evidence shows that Americans have one of the lowest savings rates in the developed world and that baby boomers in particular are not saving nearly enough for retirement. Equally disconcerting for these young people as they approach middle age should be the evidence that while the World War II generation will pass on trillions of dollars of wealth to their offspring, they will also spend a good part of their children's inheritances and direct large portions to charitable endeavors in their wills.

The following seven areas of financial planning neglect represent just some of the mistakes that we see young people make:

1. Failing to have updated *wills* and *trust* agreements.
2. Failure to purchase personal *umbrella insurance* coverage or *disability insurance*.
3. Neglecting to create an insurance trust to hold certain types of insurance.
4. Neglecting to put away part of each paycheck toward long-term savings goals such as children's education and financial independence.
5. Neglecting to communicate with one's spouse (it is still often the woman who is left in the dark) about the nature of a couple's or a family's saving and spending habits and needs.

will a legal declaration of how a person wishes his or her possessions to be disposed of after death.

trust something (as property) held by one party (the trustee) for the benefit of another (the beneficiary).

umbrella insurance adds a layer of protection over existing policies by increasing policy limits on certain coverages or insuring against additional liabilities not covered by the basic policy. Provided coverage if your personal negligence causes an injury to another (e.g., car accidents or not cleaning the ice off your porch).

disability insurance provides coverage if an accident or illness renders you fully or partially unable to work.

6. Failing to communicate with parents, or even grandparents, about financial planning needs that affect the entire family.
7. Neglecting to think about and determine what money means to you at a young enough age to make sure that the lifestyle and career choices you make are in concert with your feelings about money. Too often erroneous or imagined money considerations, if any at all, lead people to make bad life choices.

Among people in their 50s and 60s who are planning for retirement and financial independence, we see them making these same seven mistakes, but in addition we see them making seven new kinds of mistakes:

1. Failing to properly diversify assets so as to achieve the required rate of return with as little risk as possible.
2. Failing to evaluate sustainable portfolio withdrawal rates from retirement and other accounts. In most cases too much is spent and/or too little is saved; however, occasionally we will see people actually spend too little in retirement. They do not get as much enjoyment as they should have, and end up leaving a bigger estate to their children than either they might have expected or the children might have wanted.
3. Neglecting to communicate with children and grandchildren on estate planning issues that can have very large effects on the entire family.
4. Failure to evaluate and obtain proper long-term nursing care coverage.

5. Neglecting to create a *financial inventory* so that the surviving spouse, most often the woman, is not left bewildered by the state of financial affairs when her husband passes away or suffers some sort of injury or illness that prevents him from handling the family finances. We repeatedly emphasize that both spouses must be involved in financial planning.
6. Failing to understand the costs and penalty structures of various investments, often making investment mistakes, and buying into either costly annuities or heavily loaded mutual funds.
7. Failure to create the type of *limited partnership* known as a *family limited partnership* (FLP) both to save on estate taxes and to prepare children to assume financial responsibility.

financial inventory an exhaustive list of all key financial documents and advisers.

If you're looking for a comprehensive and objective source of information on how to structure and enjoy your financial life during retirement, this book is for you.

Too often, retirees or preretirees fail with their investments because either they do not receive truly objective financial counsel or they base their financial decisions on emotions or tips from friends, relatives, or even television or magazine gurus rather than facts.

In this book, we want to help you apply only those financial principles that have stood the test of time. Applying these fact-based principles, as opposed to hearsay and emotion, should give you the confidence to sleep at night and enjoy your retirement.

limited partnership a special partnership that has at least one general partner and at least one limited partner. General partners have broad management powers and limited partners have very limited management powers. General partners have unlimited exposure to claims against the limited partnership; limited partners' exposure is limited to the value of their partnership interest.

family limited partnership (FLP) a limited partnership where all partnership interests, both general and limited, are earned by members of the same family.

Among the issues covered in this book:

- ✔ How adopting a step-by-step framework for financial decision making can help you avoid making emotional decisions.
- ✔ How to assemble a retirement plan that will allow you to sleep well at night.
- ✔ How recent tax law changes may affect when you should start taking Social Security distributions.
- ✔ A sensible and sustainable plan for making withdrawals from your retirement portfolio.
- ✔ How to avoid making mental mistakes that in the past may have hindered you from getting successful investment results.
- ✔ Why some index mutual funds should be avoided.
- ✔ Why no-load mutual funds are the safest and most cost-effective way to invest for most people with less than a $1 million portfolio.
- ✔ Criteria for selecting the best and safest no-load mutual funds.
- ✔ Criteria for researching and putting together a common stock portfolio.
- ✔ Determining your "money personality" and how it impacts your investment choices.
- ✔ Assessing the smartest way for you to make withdrawals from your retirement plan accounts.
- ✔ How to designate your individual retirement account (IRA) beneficiary.
- ✔ Deciding at what age you should file for Social Security benefits.
- ✔ Determining whether you need a trust and, if so, what type.
- ✔ Evaluating your long-term nursing care insurance needs.
- ✔ How you can find a qualified independent investment adviser.

These and many other questions and issues will be answered and explored in depth in the pages that follow.

Part One

Saving for Financial Independence

Chapter 1

Retirement Basics

WHAT DOES MONEY MEAN TO YOU?

When we work with new clients, we have to find out what money means to them. Many people have difficulty expressing their feelings about the subject of money, so we have developed both a series of money questions as well as a financial survey that helps us uncover people's true feelings about money. Answers to these questions will help you begin to explore the financial and emotional issues related to retirement.

What does money mean to you? For many people, it means security. A logical next question to ask is, why is security important to you? You may value financial security because it gives you the freedom to do the things that are most important to you and be with and take care of the people who are most important to you. Everyone is different, though, and some people value financial security because it gives them the opportunity to fund and focus on charitable endeavors or causes such as university scholarships. Others want to provide educations for their grandchildren. The key is finding why money motivates you and the end result that you hope to achieve from retirement and financial planning. With this end result in mind, you can be effective in developing your *financial plan* and in utilizing your professional advisers to help you achieve the best financial result.

financial plan a written blueprint for achieving goals while taking into account all issues and contingencies.

WHEN TO RETIRE

There is a saying in sports, "Never change a winning game plan." Similarly, if you are happy in your current circumstances, happy with your current job and lifestyle, then there is absolutely no need to consider retiring; in fact, many people work well into their 70s, 80s, and even 90s. We have a client in her 90s who still plays the piano in an orchestra. Americans are working longer and longer, led by 103-year old Milton Garland, who worked for 79 years for the Frick Company of Pennsylvania developing engineering ideas on refrigeration. His advice: "Worrying never solved anything."

Even if you are perfectly happy in your current job and plan on working forever, it is still to your advantage to have a financial game plan in case either your financial or health circumstances change. You want to make sure that you've put away enough money so that work becomes an option not a necessity.

The survey in Figure 1.1 will help you pinpoint some key financial issues and some of your key financial feelings so that you can plan more effectively.

Your answers to these survey questions should give you some framework for examining how you feel about retirement versus continuing to work. Everyone feels differently about retirement, and the subject of retirement is scary to many people. Because of this, many people procrastinate in focusing on their retirement planning and key retirement planning decisions. For example, one of the coauthors of this book and his wife had a hard time communicating about retirement issues. And they were only able to achieve a breakthrough when their son and financial adviser was able to help them work through some of the emotional issues related to retirement.

In 1989 Murray and Elinor Yolles were on what we like to call the perpetual three-year retirement plan (i.e., you talk about retirement but never do it). Murray had grown tired of the practice of law, his profession for 35 years, and Elinor was ready to retire from the school district. A key stumbling block was Murray's insecurity. Had they saved enough money to retire? Would the stock market continue to thrive during their retirement? Ron constantly reminded Murray and Elinor about their perpetual three-year retirement plan; however, they did not get off this retirement merry-go-round until 1995 when Ron was able to help them communicate more effectively about their fears pertaining to retirement. At this point Elinor was able to set a definite retirement date and Murray was able to retire from the practice of law to a new career as a financial adviser and author with Ron's investment management firm.

FIND YOUR RISK TOLERANCE

Determine your risk profile and investment objectives. The first step in the asset management process is to determine your investor profile. This profile will help define important factors such as your investment objectives, time horizon, and your attitudes toward investing.

This profile will help build the base of information needed for you to progress to the next step in the asset management process—the development of an appropriate asset allocation policy, which we will work on in Chapter 4.

To complete this profile, answer each question by circling the number that best matches your personal situation.

Your True Risk Tolerance Questionnaire

These questions will help you both realistically identify your risk tolerance and investment time horizon and choose an asset allocation between stock and bond funds that fits your needs and objectives. Use your immediate reaction to choose your answers.

A. **If the market declined 25 percent, you would . . .**
   1. Sell immediately and buy bank certificates of deposit.
   2. Sell half of my stock holdings and wait for the other half to break even before selling.
   3. Stock to my long-term plan and, if anything, buy more when the market is depressed.

B. **If you or your spouse had a medical emergency requiring a nursing-home stay costing $40,000 . . .**
   1. We would have to sell stocks to pay the nursing bills.
   2. We would take out a home equity loan to pay our nursing bills.
   3. We have sufficient cash reserves and/or a long-term nursing care insurance policy to cover this type of emergency.

C. **If you have a big tax bill at year-end . . .**
   1. We will sell shares to pay the bill.
   2. Our dividends are sufficient to pay a big tax bill and we are sure to reinvest the dividends we do not spend.
   3. We will reinvest all dividends and set aside sufficient cash for taxes.

(Continued)

FIGURE 1.1 Investor profile questionnaire.

D. **Regarding leaving money to your children . . .**

1. We loved, cared for, and educated our children. We want to enjoy our money while we are relatively young—our kids are on their own.
2. We'd like to leave a little something to our kids and grandkids to make their lives more enjoyable.
3. Fortunately, we have sufficient wealth that we have provided for our kids and the charities that are important to us in our estate plan.

E. **If a close friend with whom you play golf claims to have been averaging 18 percent in aggressive mutual funds and offers to help you invest, you . . .**

1. Probably would take my friend's advice and invest nearly all my money in the manner suggested.
2. Invest half my money in my friend's recommendations.
3. Stick with my investment plan that was returning only 9 percent, but was designed to meet my objectives.

F. **Which of the following investments would you prefer?**

1. An investment with a guaranteed 7 percent return.
2. An investment with an 80 percent chance of returning 10 percent and a 20 percent chance of returning zero.
3. An investment with an 80 percent chance of returning 20 percent and a 20 percent chance of *losing* 10 percent.

G. **You will need income from your investment portfolio . . .**

1. Immediately, because our existing sources of retirement income are insufficient.
2. Within three years as a supplement to our income from part-time work, Social Security, and/or pensions.
3. In three or more years when our portfolio is large enough that we will need to draw only part of the dividend income that the portfolio produces.

FIGURE 1.1 *Continued*

H. **Which of the following describes your feelings toward the stock market?**

1. The stock market is like Las Vegas; we've had friends or relatives lose all their money in the stock market.
2. The stock market is risky but does offer good potential returns for part of our money. But, we do not believe in putting all of our eggs in one basket.
3. The stock market is not gambling; rather, it allows investors ownership and participation in the growth of America's great companies, which is the core of capitalism. For example, buying a share of stock in McDonald's ties you to the success or failure of McDonald's.

I. **You would describe your investment knowledge and experience as follows . . .**

1. We have always put our money in the bank because of safety considerations.
2. We believe that there are better alternatives than bank certificates of deposit and we have faith that stocks, bonds, and mutual funds will produce better long-term returns.
3. We are willing to ride out market ups and downs because we have faith that stocks, stock mutual funds, and real estate investments will stay ahead of inflation in the long run.

J. **If you buy a stock or mutual fund that goes down in price . . .**

1. Always wait to get back to even before selling.
2. Normally sell because you should not throw good money after bad.
3. Review the fundamentals of the given stock or mutual fund, and if the fundamentals are sound we hold or add to our position, and if the fundamentals are no longer sound, then we would sell and find a better long-term holding.

(Continued)

FIGURE 1.1 *Continued*

K. **Within the next two years how much annual income or cash flow will you need from your investment portfolio to supplement your Social Security, pensions, and/or earned income?**

1. We will need to withdraw more than 8 percent annually from our investments, regardless of what these investments are earning.
2. We will need to withdraw 6 percent annually from our investments, an amount that we expect to be more than covered by the dividends that our investments produce.
3. We will withdraw less than 4 percent annually from our portfolio regardless of earnings.

L. **When do you intend to withdraw not only dividends from your portfolio, but also start to withdraw principal?**

1. We are already withdrawing principal from our portfolio because we either have no choice or have objectively developed a sustainable withdrawal plan.
2. Within 5 to 10 years.
3. We don't expect to need to touch our principal, at least not within the next 15 years.

Note: We encourage you to sign this form to reinforce the significance of this "investment plan/contract" you are about to make with yourself or your spouse. The act of committing your financial plan to writing and signing it increases the likelihood that you'll stick with the plan during tough times.

____________________	____________________	__________
Name of Investor	Signature of Investor	Date
____________________	____________________	__________
Name of Investor	Signature of Investor	Date
____________________		
Name of Adviser		

FIGURE 1.1 *Continued*

Risk Tolerance Questionnaire Score Sheet

This score sheet is provided as a tool to help determine which asset allocation portfolio may be best suited to meet your needs as an investor. We will refer to your portfolio type again in Chapter 4. This is based on your investment objectives, time horizon, and investment risk profile. In general, a lower point total indicates that you're closer to retirement. (Note that very wealthy people can have a high point total and still choose to retire).

Scoring Grid

Please record the number of your answer to each question in the appropriate space.

Question	Answer	Multiplier	Points
Example:	2	2	4
		Temperament Dimension	
A		1	
E		1	
F		1	
H		3	
I		1	
J		1	
	Temperament Total		
		Time Dimension	
B		1	
C		1	
D		1	
G		3	
K		3	
L		1	
	Time Horizon Total		

Scoring Chart

	Time Horizon	
Temperament	Short-Term (<20)	Long-Term (23–30)
Growth-oriented (17–24 points)	50% equity 50% fixed-income	70% equity 30% fixed-income
Conservative (16 or fewer points)	30% equity 70% fixed-income	50% equity 50% fixed-income

FIGURE 1.1 *Continued*

TEACHERS OFTEN MAKE THE HAPPIEST RETIREES

In our experience, teachers are often happier in retirement than people with several million dollars. Why? Teachers often have more peace of mind during retirement for the following reasons:

1. They have a clear retirement date. Normally, after 30 years of service in a school district, teachers are able to, and actually do, retire. People in other professions or businesses are often less certain as to when they will retire, and this uncertainty produces anxiety. Many people feel that they should retire at age 62 or 65 when Social Security starts; however, this is an antiquated social norm dating back to the 1930s when the Social Security Act was passed and the average life expectancy was only 68.
2. Teachers have a pension during retirement, which in conjunction with Social Security gives them approximately the same amount of income that they enjoyed during their career. People in other professions may have either no pensions or much less substantial pensions than teachers do. This lack of a definite retirement income produces a great deal of anxiety even for people with several million dollars because they are uncertain as to how much they can spend each year.
3. Teachers often have definite plans as to what they are going to do to keep active during retirement, as they develop leisure-time and outside activities during the summers that they have off from teaching.
4. Teachers are often friendly with other teachers who retire at approximately the same time, and this creates a sense of camaraderie in retirement. This group of fellow retirees helps teachers learn from each other about the nuances of retirement, which represents a brand-new stage in life. Comparing notes with friends or family members reduces anxiety. A retirement support network is often crucial to a happy retirement.
5. Teachers often have skills that are very transferable for consulting and other types of part-time work endeavors that nicely supplement other retirement activities.
6. Generous *403(b) plans* allow many young teachers to develop good saving and investing habits early in their careers.

One of our challenges, and an important goal of this book, is to provide nonteachers the same peace of mind and sense of fulfillment in retirement that many teachers have.

403(b) plan tax-deferred savings plan for public employees including educators, health care workers, and professionals.

In our experience, at least part of the answer to the question of when should you retire is a combination of two factors: career satisfaction and financial resources. First, are you happy with your career? If the answer is no, that's a good sign that either retirement or perhaps even an extended sabbatical between careers is called for. Also, consider part-time work as a bridge between full-time work and retirement. As people live longer, it will become more and more common to have several careers separated by sabbaticals. The second question is, do you have sufficient resources to either retire, semiretire, or take an extended sabbatical?

HOW MUCH DO YOU NEED?

The question of how much is enough is probably the most troubling question to most people who do not have a guaranteed pension. Many people are on the perpetual three-year retirement plan described earlier. One of the main things that separates humans from other species is our ability to deal with complex concepts, including the notion that nothing in life is certain.

Once you accept the notion that in all likelihood you will never be 100 percent certain that you have put away enough to retire, you will be better able to plan intelligently. Keep in mind that if you can achieve at least 95 percent certainty that you've planned effectively and you can evaluate a worst-case scenario for your retirement that is at least tolerable, then you are on the road to preparing for an enjoyable and fulfilling retirement accompanied by a great deal of peace of mind.

Large charitable endowments and foundations generally have a 5 percent annual spending rule, and this is a good starting point for your own financial planning. These endowments and foundations are required to pay out to their constituent charities 5 percent of their principals. Keep in mind that these endowments are designed to live in perpetuity, whereas you may feel comfortable not having your capital remain forever, but rather strategically spending some of your principal as you age. So with 5 percent spending as a starting point, you can determine that if you have saved $1 million, then perhaps your portfolio will comfortably produce $50,000 of annual income. This is merely a very preliminary starting point and we will go much more in depth into spending rules and what we call sustainable withdrawal rates in Chapters 5 and 6, which are devoted to investment and withdrawal strategies.

What can you do if you use our 5 percent test and find that you have a tremendous portfolio shortfall? Say that in our prior example you'd have saved $1 million but would need an annual spending rate of $80,000. In retirement planning you will find that there are only six variables that you can adjust to get the result that you want.

1. You can adjust your spending goal in retirement.
2. You can move back your retirement date so as to assure that you will have more capital. (Note that by moving back your retirement date you also have reduced your expected years in retirement, with the result that less money will be needed.)
3. You can explore innovative charitable gifting techniques and estate planning techniques that can boost your income during your lifetime.
4. You can find either higher yielding investments or, even better, investments with better *total return*.
5. You can work part time during retirement to supplement your other sources of income.
6. You can change your inflation assumptions.

total return dividends plus capital appreciation.

To help you evaluate your own retirement assumptions, we recommend you check out Financialengines.com, an innovative retirement planning site. The site, for a nominal charge, allows you to explore different retirement scenarios, and will also help evaluate the quality of your investment portfolio. The beauty of the Financialengines.com site is that it condenses your retirement planning into a single weather forecast to show you the probability of retiring successfully and comfortably. For example, if you program all of your data into the site and find that your weather forecast is 95 percent or 100 percent sunny, then you are well on your way to a completely comfortable and secure retirement. On the other hand, if your weather forecast comes out overcast or mostly cloudy, then in all likelihood there is less than a 50 percent probability of you being able to retire successfully and comfortably with the standard of living that you hope to achieve. The Financialengines.com site literally presents a weather forecast with a picture of either sun, clouds, or some combination of sun and clouds. The only other features of the Financialengines.com summary screen are the part of the screen where it tells you your probability of being able to retire successfully.

There are two big mistakes that we see many people make when doing their financial planning. First, they often dramatically overestimate the rate of return that they will be able to earn on their investments leading up to and during retirement. Second, they often underestimate their cost of living during retirement because they forget about how inflation changes prices.

We recently watched a 1985 videotape of a TV movie. On the tape there was a commercial advertising a Mazda for $6,200. The same type of car would sell for over $20,000 today. Many other items that you buy regularly (food, clothing, laundry detergent, transportation, etc.) are significantly more expensive today than 10 or 12 years ago, even with the relatively mild inflation we have had since the 1980s. With just 4 percent annual inflation, a box of cereal that costs $4 today will cost $8 in 18 years.

You're fooling yourself if you don't recognize and plan for inflation during your retirement. If you're living on $48,000 per year today, you may need as much as $96,000 a year if you retire in 18 years with just 4 percent inflation.

Rule of 72

The quick and easy Rule of 72 helps you determine how long it takes something to double in cost or value at a given rate of inflation or interest. You simply divide your inflation or interest rate into the number 72. At a 4 percent rate of inflation, the cost of our box of cereal will double from $4 to $8 in 18 years because 72 divided by 4 percent inflation equals 18 years. Similarly, if you have a $300,000 investment portfolio that earns 9 percent per year and you don't make any deposits or withdrawals, your portfolio will double in value to $600,000 in 8 years: 72 divided by 9 percent equals 8 years. The Rule of 72 can help focus your retirement thinking on rates of return, your portfolio's value, and inflationary costs.

ESTIMATE YOUR RETIREMENT COST OF LIVING

While planning your entire retirement spending needs is, at best, educated guesswork, you can accurately plan each year's expenses in an *annual review* with your investment and tax advisers. We have found this "annual checkup" approach to be more valuable, more flexible, and less costly than having an expensive leather-bound computerized financial plan. The challenge in an annual review is to estimate your spending needs both now and in the future. Those of you who are saving for retirement will find that these annual checkups will let you know if your retirement savings program is on track.

> **annual review** a financial checkup equivalent to an annual physical.

Many people find that their cost of living is lower in retirement, while others find that their retirement costs are higher. If a substantial portion of your annual spending was, or is, devoted to your children, including education costs, then you will probably find that your cost of living is much lower during retirement, particularly if you do not have and are not likely to have elderly parents to support. Additionally, if you anticipate trading down to a smaller house, condominium, or apartment during retirement, then your cost of living will be further reduced.

On the other hand, you could have a higher cost of living during retirement. If you choose to purchase a vacation home during retirement, your costs could skyrocket. Also, with more time on your hands during retirement for visiting your family and friends, your travel expenses can greatly increase.

YOUR PERSONAL INFLATION RATE

The best approach is for you accurately to figure your likely retirement cost of living and your *personal inflation rate*. The government's *consumer price index (CPI)* has little relevance to you because it describes price increases of a basket of goods that the average consumer purchases. However, there is no such thing as the average consumer. You should focus on determining your own costs and needs during retirement. Following that, the rest of this book will be devoted to providing you with both the tools needed to objectively determine whether your assumptions are realistic and what's required to implement the best and safest strategy to achieve your goals.

personal inflation rate defines annual price increases in items that *you* purchase.

consumer price index (CPI) describes price increases for goods and services that the average consumer purchases.

A starting point to determine your capital needs during retirement is to take a look at your current standard of living in today's dollars. While some people find it necessary to make a very detailed budget of their current standard of living, others find it more productive just to estimate their costs and get a general idea of their capital needs. The following method is appropriate for those who do not want to prepare a detailed budget.

Table 1.1 provides a quick and easy method for estimating your current standard of living. Using this work sheet, you can estimate what portion of your net after-tax income went to major savings and investment items. After these calculations, you can reasonably assume that you spent the remaining amount.

Take your adjusted gross income from your most recent tax return and subtract the total amount in taxes that you paid for the year. This is your after-tax net income, or what is more commonly called your *take-home pay*. Now, all that you have to do is subtract the amount of net deposits you made during the year to your savings and/or investment accounts, and the remaining figure that you are left with is a good approximation of your cost of living.

take-home pay the net amount of your paycheck after all taxes and deductions are withheld.

TABLE 1.1 Determining Your Cost of Living (COL)—The Easy Way

	Example	*Your COL*
Adjusted gross income	$72,000	
Federal income tax	(15,000)	
State income tax	(3,000)	
After-tax income	$54,000	
Investment deposits or withdrawals	(6,000)	
Savings deposits or withdrawals	(4,000)	
Your cost of living	$44,000	

Let's look at an example: Say that you had $72,000 of income during a given year and that you paid $18,000 in taxes. This would leave $54,000 as your net after-tax income (or take-home pay). Now let us say further that you and your spouse made contributions of $6,000 to 401(k) and retirement plan accounts. This would reduce your figure to $48,000. Assume further that your savings account balance at the start of the year was $20,000 and at the end of the year this account balance was $25,000. Of this increase, only $1,000 could be attributed to interest accrued on the savings account. Therefore, you know that you deposited $4,000 to your savings account during the year. This $4,000 saved further reduces your figure to $44,000. That is a good approximation of your cost of living (i.e., what you spent) for the year.

Perhaps part of your $44,000 standard of living includes gifts to children or grandchildren. There also may have been some noncash deductions such as donations of personal property to charity, your mortgage interest deduction, and/or renter's credits that you were allowed that reduced your income, but the $44,000 is a reasonable approximation of your cost of living.

The challenge is to take your current cost of living, the $44,000, and determine whether your needs during retirement will be similar. Perhaps they'll be more. Or, perhaps your needs will be less.

In our experience, most people have slightly lower spending needs during retirement than while they are working because, for example, they no longer have children to support. Your challenge during retirement is to determine if your cost of living will change and to determine what your personal inflation rate will be.

No one can predict what inflation will be in the future, but we do have a century of history that tells us that inflation has averaged about 3.7

percent yearly. If there is not better evidence available at the time of calculation, this 3.7 percent should be your default figure when estimating inflation. However, we find that retirement costs are not always subject to the same ravages of inflation as costs during your working years. For example, even during inflationary times, most people have a fixed mortgage that is a large part of their cost of living. Their mortgage payment does not change with inflation. (For those of you who pay rent on an apartment, typically your cost of living *will* increase with inflation.)

Food, clothing, transportation, and other costs may creep gradually higher; but, in our experience, these cost increases from normal inflation are often offset by certain obligations that you had during your working years that you no longer have to pay for during retirement. By the time you retire, in most cases your children will be independent and no longer an expense. However, occasionally and with increasing frequency, your parents or your in-laws could become an expense if they need support during their later years.

No matter how carefully you plan, unexpected expenses can always arise. However, detailed planning gives you the best chance of being prepared for expected and unexpected retirement expenses. These expenses are why it's also a good idea to keep at least six months' worth of living expenses in a money market account as your *emergency fund*.

emergency fund six months' worth of living expenses kept in a money market account to guard against the unexpected.

TAKING AN INVENTORY

What we are asking you to do at this phase of your retirement planning is take an inventory. Make an educated guess of what your costs are likely to be in retirement, but make sure to approach the problem from all angles: How is your health? Do you have adequate insurance to cover any medical emergencies that could throw you off your plan? How is your parents' health? Do they have adequate insurance, or might they be dependent on you? Have you saved enough for your children's college expenses? Is it possible that they will be moving back into the household, or at least need some continuing support after college?

Take a look at what type of expenses you'll have during retirement: Do you want to travel more? Will you buy a motor home, boat, or timeshare? Can you quantify an increase in expenses or at least make a reasonable guess?

In many ways, what we are doing with our clients, and what you should do when you make your retirement plan, is to take an inventory. This is similar to corporations preparing budgets—they are looking at sources and uses of cash flow. By making realistic projections, you will be able to make critical decisions and, most importantly, you'll acquire a sense of security, which is really what you are looking for.

No one wants to live beyond their means. Everyone wants to strike the proper balance between perhaps spending some capital during retirement years and not depleting one's nest egg. Only by taking a regular inventory the same way a corporation closely watches its cash flow and income can you be on top of your retirement plan. Similarly, only by taking an inventory can you tell if you are on track regarding saving for retirement. The following web sites have good financial calculators that help you forecast if you are saving enough for retirement:

Vanguard.com
Quicken.com
Strongfunds.com

Table 1.2 allows you to prepare a more detailed retirement budget and compare your cost of living to that of the median family in this country. Your costs may very well be less than these U.S. Department of Labor averages because you, as a retiree, do not have child care expenses.

By completing these retirement planning work sheets (Tables 1.1 and 1.2), you have taken an important first step in understanding and quantifying your needs during retirement. Once you can estimate your retirement spending needs, and in subsequent chapters gain an understanding of how to safely meet these needs, then you can begin to have confidence in your retirement planning and investment program.

Your level of comfort is necessary for your own enjoyment during retirement and also for the success of your retirement investment program. If you are comfortable with your plan, then you will stick to it even in bear markets, and sticking to this plan is critical for your long-term investment success.

Your stick-to-itiveness is critical, either as a do-it-yourselfer or as a client of an investment counseling firm. Despite the fact that the overall stock and bond markets have risen over the past 70 years, somehow individ-

TABLE 1.2 Your Cost of Living—Compared to the Average Family

Expenditure per year	*Average Budget*	*Percent*	*Your Budget*	*Percent*
Food	$ 6,737	13		
House/rent payment	12,093	22		
Furnishings	3,436	6		
Auto	11,422	21		
Clothing	2,871	5		
Personal care	440	1		
Medical	1,809	4		
Contributions	2,181	4		
Family consumption and child care	4,062	8		
Savings	2,251	4		
Social Security	6,633	12		
Total spending for a median family in 1996	$53,935	(100)		

Source: Bureau of Labor Statistics, U.S. Department of Labor.

ual investors have managed to do poorly. For example, stock investors have done over 10 percent worse than the overall market over the past 15 years.

STICK WITH A LONG-TERM PLAN

Table 1.3 shows how the markets have done, and Figure 1.2 shows how individual investors have done. A key to understanding why individuals tend to miss the boat by buying high and selling low comes from the study of the individual investor psychology and temperament. Most people when looking back on their own investment history can identify times when they clearly didn't act in their own best interests and often, in hindsight, they can explain why they acted in a self-destructive manner—namely, they failed to follow a long-term plan.

By examining your own and others' emotional investment mistakes, we hope to be able to prevent you from making these and other common errors. We hope that the insights we share with you on irrational emo-

TABLE 1.3 Stocks, Bonds, Treasury Bills, and Inflation (1926–1999)

Investment	*Annual Return*	*Standard Deviation*
S&P 500	11.3%	20.30%
Small-cap companies	11.9%	34.19%
Government bonds	5.1%	9.29%
Treasury bills	3.8%	3.30%
Consumer price index (CPI)	3.3%	4.50%

Source: Wiesenberger, Thomson Financial.

tional investment behavior will give you the wherewithal and the determination to stick with a long-term retirement plan and not to succumb to your temporary feelings of either euphoria or panic. Investment decisions must be made in an unemotional, objective fashion.

Family Financial Dialogue

The other thing that you have to examine is whether you expect to receive any sort of inheritance. For many people this is uncomfortable because we hope that our parents and loved ones will live forever; however, our parents in most cases want us to receive an inheritance either to make our lives somewhat easier or to make our children's lives easier. To a certain extent ignoring the possibility of receiving an inheritance defeats part of the purpose that our parents have in giving either us or our children the inheritance. One of the great joys that many parents could have is knowing that their children could retire or at least cut back on work, or take a sabbatical at an earlier age to enjoy all that this world has to offer, and

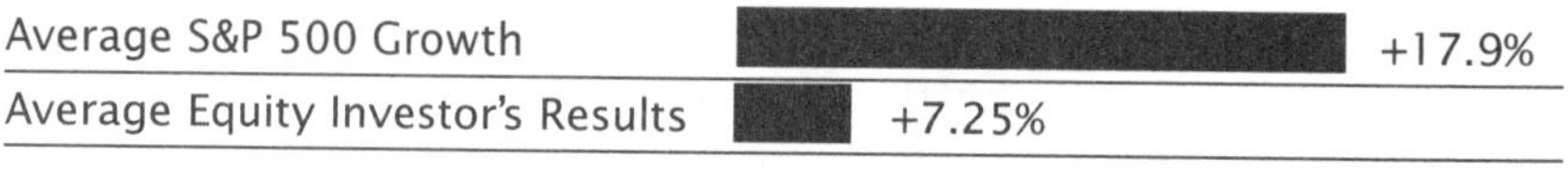

FIGURE 1.2 Sad but true: Markets rise, but investors miss the boat (1984–1998).
Source: Reprinted with permission from Dalbar, Inc.

perhaps even place more of an emphasis on enjoying and being with their children or grandchildren.

Many families have a hard time discussing money issues. Perhaps this book can act as a catalyst to help you discuss financial issues with your loved ones.

CASE STUDIES: A TALE OF TWO RETIREES—ONE WHO PLANNED FOR RETIREMENT AND ONE WHO DID NOT

The Case of Paul—An Early Retiree

Paul did not plan for his retirement. It was forced on him due to changes in the auto industry in the late 1980s. We have all known people like Paul—someone with a delightful personality who is loved by everyone, who appears happy on the surface but beneath the surface is probably unhappy and somewhat unfulfilled. Paul was a superb auto parts sales representative who had to sell his company when General Motors, Ford, and Chrysler started their Just-in-Time inventory requirements along with other changes.

Paul was used to living the good life in style and had to make dramatic adjustments since the buyout of his business provided him with only enough capital for an annual income of approximately $60,000. Paul should have been able to draft a plan to start a brand-new career or at least a part-time career. However, his ego prevented him from doing this because he feared that he would never be able to match the success and status that he had achieved as an auto parts representative. Paul retired in 1989 at the age of 37 and remains retired and somewhat unfulfilled today at the age of 47. He has dabbled in a few speculative ventures such as buying quarter horses, but nothing has panned out.

The Case of Carol—The Fulfilled Retiree

In contrast to Paul, Carol planned intelligently for her retirement after getting burned by an unscrupulous insurance agent when her husband died prematurely at the age of 48. The small inheritance that Carol's husband had left her was largely eaten up by hefty commissions on various insurance and annuity products that her insurance agent placed her in after her husband's untimely death. This bad experience served to motivate Carol to do her own research when it came time for her to plan her retirement in 1999 at the age of 55. She had a small pension from her librarian position; she was able to supplement this by starting a temporary help agency that provided law firms with legal secretaries. She also learned to invest her money much more effectively; this was in part due to joining an investment club that became a good learning experience.

Unlike Paul, Carol was able to master her emotions and become a successful investor. The next chapter will help you master your emotions and avoid costly mental mistakes.

Chapter 2

The Psychology of Retirement

BEHAVIORAL FINANCE—STUDYING THE PSYCHOLOGY OF INVESTORS

An understanding of investor psychology is important to you for two reasons: first, it helps you understand and avoid mental mistakes, and second, it helps you understand mistakes made by investment professionals and even mutual fund managers.

Behavioral finance helps us explain all of the irrational behavior on the part of both professionals and amateurs that we observe in the real world. By using scientific, academic methods this branch of financial economics avoids conjecture and hyperbole and instead presents facts to help investors understand investment reality and their own frequent mental mistakes.

There are four key psychological concepts that you should understand in order to become a better investor:

1. *Overconfidence.* Although the evidence overwhelmingly indicates that individuals are very bad investors (as shown by Figure 1.2), most investors believe that either they or family members or friends whom they rely on are excellent investors. This overconfidence can lead to severe investment mistakes. According to Professor Terrance Odean, investors are overconfident that they can distinguish between winners and losers, when

in fact his research found that the stocks that investors sell actually do better than the stocks that they buy.

2. *Heuristics.* In behavioral finance, heuristics are simple rules of thumb that represent widely held beliefs that upon further scrutiny are false. All of these simple rules of thumb involve investors engaging in behavior that is not necessarily the best way to achieve their objectives. One example of this is a study by Professor Richard Thaler in which he shows that participants in 401(k) plans most often merely divide their money equally among the choices offered in the plans with no regard for their objectives. For example, if a plan offered a stock fund, a bond fund, and a money market fund, then the participant would put one-third of the money in each fund instead of focusing on a particular objective, which, if the participant were a young person, would dictate putting more in the stock fund.

3. *Loss aversion.* Professor Odean has also found that investors have loss aversion and rarely sell their losing stocks because they hope that these stocks will get back to even (the price at which they were bought), even if these stocks represent companies that are failing in the marketplace. This behavior is irrational; in fact, it is often advantageous to sell losing stocks if these stocks are held in a taxable account, because you get a tax benefit in that you can write off the loss. In a similar vein, investors sell their winning stocks too early because they like to take profits. This is self-defeating in two ways: first, because these winning stocks often dominate their industry and have tremendous additional upside potential, and second, because by selling the investor has to pay tax.

4. *Fear.* This is the flip side of the overconfidence that leads investors to trade too often. Fear results in investor paralysis, which is a form of *market timing* that leads the investors out of the market when it is rising, and they often only reenter *after* the market has risen.

> **market timing** futilely trying to be in the stock market only when it is rising.

Our goal in this chapter is to help you avoid these and other mental mistakes that financial academics have identified. We hope that by avoiding such errors you will ultimately have a soundly written financial and investment plan that you will stick with. Sticking with a plan is what distinguishes successful, wealthy family-endowment type investors from individual investors. Other areas where overconfidence is evident in individual investors' behavior include buying stocks after the stocks have had lengthy run-ups, and overestimating, often by a factor of three, the likely returns that they will earn leading up to retirement, causing shortfalls.

IDENTIFYING YOUR MONEY PERSONALITY

For many of you, this is the most important section in the entire book. The single greatest cause of investment failures and losses that we have seen is self-destructive behavior, including greed in search of wild returns or fear resulting in excessive caution. In this chapter we will address the following four topics, among others:

1. Identify your money personality and how it might hurt your investment results.
2. Learn how to make your money personality work for you so that you will earn the best possible return and be able to sleep at night.
3. Do *lifeboat drills* so that you will know how to react when inevitable bear markets occur.
4. Discover your true tolerance for risk with our nine-question risk profile indicator, which will help you to structure a portfolio matching your temperament.

> **lifeboat drill** a rehearsal where you explore how you will react under a variety of adverse financial market conditions.

At one time or another, we all exhibit signs of fear and/or greed in our investment behavior. The challenge is to make objective decisions without allowing our human emotions to intrude. It's essential to leave fear and greed out of our financial decision making. To do this, you must learn to recognize the telltale signs of fear and greed manifesting themselves in your investment behavior and personality.

Behavioral finance is the scholarly term for the study of investing and individual investor behavior. It is a branch of financial economics, which is a social science. Both bear and bull markets and individuals' behavior in those markets are explained by financial economics. Individual results in those markets are subject to influence by the vagaries of human behavior. Often, not only do fear and greed end up negatively influencing our individual portfolio results, but they also can have an influence on the overall market—at least in the short run. This was vividly seen in the October 1997 "Gray Monday" 554-point decline in the Dow Jones Industrial Average as investors reacted to economic turmoil in Hong Kong, and it has been seen more recently in the wild speculation in Internet stocks and initial public offerings (IPOs).

Psychologists and behavioral scientists have helped us to understand how someone's emotions can lead to suboptimal investment results, portfolio designs, and behavior. Amos Tversky, PhD, of Stanford University and Meir Statman, PhD, of Santa Clara University have done innovative work on these topics in the field of behavioral finance.

In his pioneering research, Professor Tversky showed that individuals are actually more risk-averse than they should be when it comes to guaranteeing certain gain. Ironically, these investors are more willing to take risk when it comes to avoiding any nominal loss or when it comes to recouping a loss.

For instance, Professor Tversky has shown that individuals prefer a sure $240 gain to a 25 percent chance of a $1,000 gain, even though this one-in-four chance of a $1,000 gain may produce more profit in the long run. While this example may seem to be trivial, it merely serves as one instance where an individual's investment behavior may not be rational. Drawing on Professor Tversky's work as financial advisers, once we have identified all of the areas where individuals are likely to behave irrationally, then we can begin to help you avoid these mistakes.

Let's look at an example. Our friend Mitch worked for many years for the Burroughs Corporation, which later became Unisys Corporation. Mitch came to us in 1991 with a portfolio worth $540,000. Of this amount, $250,000 was in Unisys stock. Because he enjoyed his job and coworkers, Mitch had an emotional attachment to the Unisys stock, even though there were neither economic nor safety reasons to hold on to the stock. In fact, Mitch was taking 75 percent more risk (specific risk of 60 percent plus segment risk of 15 percent) in holding such a large position in this single stock than he would risk by holding a diversified portfolio (see "Typical Stock" in Figure 2.1). Unfortunately for Mitch, the Unisys stock stagnated, and he cheated himself out of significant returns from 1991 through 1997 when he finally sold the Unisys stock for $12 per share.

Mitch had kept hoping that Unisys's stock price would return to the $28 per share that he originally paid. Mitch was suffering from *mental accounting*. In this case, mental accounting meant that Mitch set his sell target for his stock holding in Unisys based on his original purchase price.

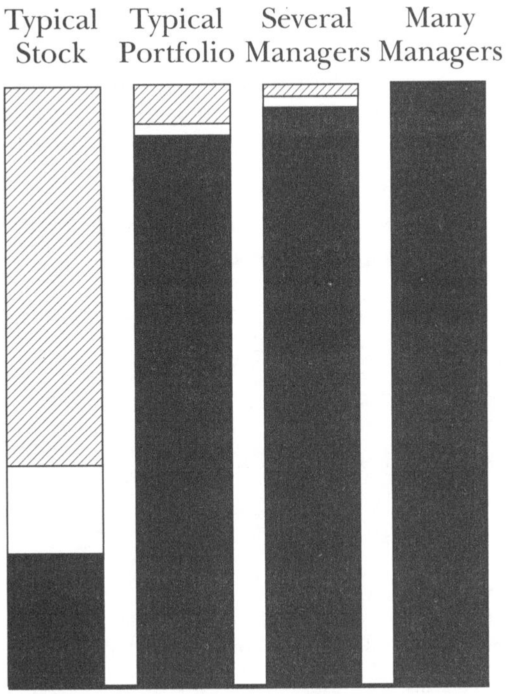

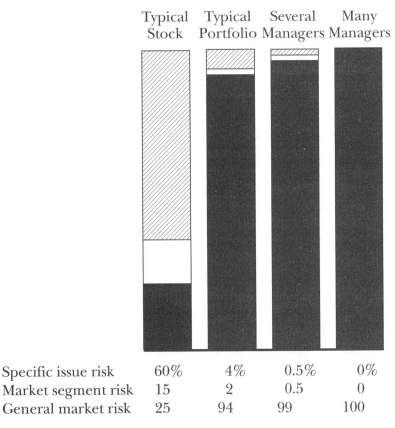

	Typical Stock	Typical Portfolio	Several Managers	Many Managers
Specific issue risk	60%	4%	0.5%	0%
Market segment risk	15	2	0.5	0
General market risk	25	94	99	100

FIGURE 2.1 What is your threshold for pain? How diversification reduces nonmarket risk.

Source: Reprinted with permission of The McGraw-Hill Companies from *Investment Policy—How to Win the Loser's Game*, 2d edition, by Charles Ellis. Copyright © 1993.

This is not rational. **A rational investor puts his or her capital to the best and safest use at all times with consideration given to the investor's required rate of return, tolerance for risk, and need for safety.** We like to say that money has no memory and the market does not remember the price at which you bought a given stock. It is much better for you to implement the proper portfolio today than to try to recoup old losses in an inferior investment.

mental accounting setting the sell target for a stock based on the original purchase price.

Figure 2.2 illustrates a break-even analysis showing how quickly a diversified portfolio can catch up to a single stock holding.

Mental accounting takes another form when a good portfolio of either no-load mutual funds or common stocks initially drops in value due to a decline in the overall market but then recovers as the market turns around. Too often investors will sell out when the market gets back to even and will sacrifice a perfectly good and properly diversified portfolio. ***Do not succumb to this tendency.***

Input Variables

Existing Position (i.e., stock, mutual fund)		cma
Current Market Value		$ 191,664
Cost Basis		$ 35,268
Tax Rate on Income & Short-Term Gains	(%)	39.60
Tax Rate on Long-Term Gains	(%)	20
Cost as Percent of Market Value	(%)	18.400951

Return Components

None ▼

Expected Pre-Tax Average Annual Return %	Existing *Position*	Tax *Managed*
Income	2.00	1.00
Short-Term Capital Gains	0	0
Long-Term Capital Gains	0	0
Unrealized Appreciation	5.00	10.00
Total Pre-Tax Return	7	11

Evaluate Reset

FIGURE 2.2 Breakeven analysis.

Breakeven Report

Years Sold	Terminal Value: Existing Position	Terminal Value: Tax Managed	Estate Value: Existing Position	Estate Value: Tax Managed
0	160,385	160,385	191,664	160,385
1	170,367	**174,184**	203,563	177,392
2	180,968	189,447	216,200	196,203
3	192,228	206,328	229,621	217,008
4	204,187	225,000	243,876	240,020
5	216,888	245,651	259,016	**265,471**
6	230,377	268,492	275,096	293,622
7	244,704	293,755	292,174	324,757
8	259,921	321,698	310,312	359,195
9	276,082	352,603	329,576	397,284
10	293,246	386,785	350,036	439,412
11	311,476	424,592	371,766	486,007
12	330,837	466,408	394,846	537,543
13	351,401	512,658	419,358	594,544
14	373,241	563,813	445,391	657,590
15	396,437	620,392	473,041	727,320
16	421,073	682,970	502,408	804,445
17	447,238	752,185	533,597	889,749
18	475,028	828,739	566,723	984,098
19	504,543	913,411	601,905	1,088,451
20	535,890	1,007,061	639,271	1,203,871
21	569,184	1,110,642	678,957	1,331,529
22	604,544	1,225,207	721,107	1,472,725
23	642,099	1,351,920	765,873	1,628,892
24	681,986	1,492,070	813,419	1,801,620
25	724,348	1,647,081	863,916	1,992,664
26	769,341	1,818,530	917,547	2,203,966
27	817,127	2,008,159	974,509	2,437,674
28	867,879	2,217,897	1,035,006	2,696,165
29	921,783	2,449,875	1,099,260	2,982,067
30	979,032	2,706,452	1,167,502	3,298,285

Note: Numbers in bold indicate the year in which the diversified tax-managed portfolio surpassed the single existing low-basis stock position in our example.
Source: Courtesy of Fama-French. Used with permission of DFA Securities Inc.

FIGURE 2.2 *Continued*

LIFEBOAT DRILLS

We use two techniques to help prevent investors from falling into mental accounting traps. One technique involves drafting a detailed portfolio policy statement (which we will discuss in Chapter 4). The second technique involves going through lifeboat drills to simulate how you will behave during predictable bear market conditions.

Table 2.1 shows how different types of portfolios are likely to behave during market downturns of various severities (see lowest annual return). Review your asset allocation and how your portfolio will likely behave during a downturn. Then use Figures 2.3 and 2.4 to test whether your portfolio fits into your comfort zone. You should do this so that you will not make unwise revisions to your solid long-term strategy based on short-term emotional pressures of a down market. We call this exercise a lifeboat drill.

Table 2.2 expands on the concepts illustrated in Figure 2.1. Here we show that all asset classes, and therefore all portfolios, become much less risky if held for the long term. If this table does not convince you to adopt a long-term investment discipline, then nothing will. *Please study it closely*.

REARVIEW MIRROR INVESTING

Another common problem that our firm sees all too frequently is what we call rearview mirror investing. This mind-set manifests itself in investors having too much confidence that the future will resemble the immediate past. Investors too often succumb to the temptation of believing that

TABLE 2.1 Optimal Portfolio Allocations (1969–1999)

	Conservative	*Moderate*	*Aggressive*
Equity	0%	60%	100%
Fixed income	100%	40%	0%
Compound return	7.9%	11.3%	13%
Annualized standard deviation	5.2%	10.4%	16.5%
Lowest annual return	−2.4%	−13.1%	−26%
Growth of $1	$10.56	$27.63	$43.96

Data Source: Yolles Investment Management.

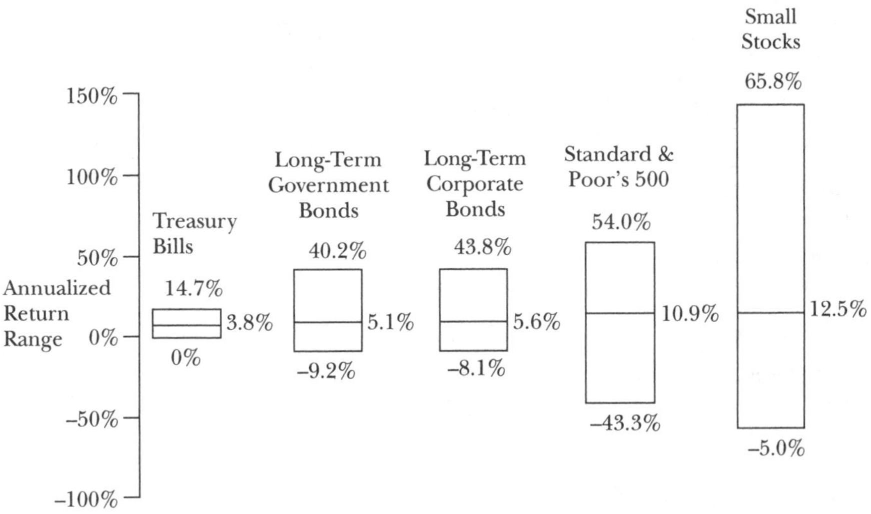

FIGURE 2.3 Risk/return trade-off in the short run, covering 70, one-year investment periods, 1929–1999.

Note: Each bar shows the range of compound average annual total returns for a different type of investment.

Source: Wiesenberger, Thomson Financial.

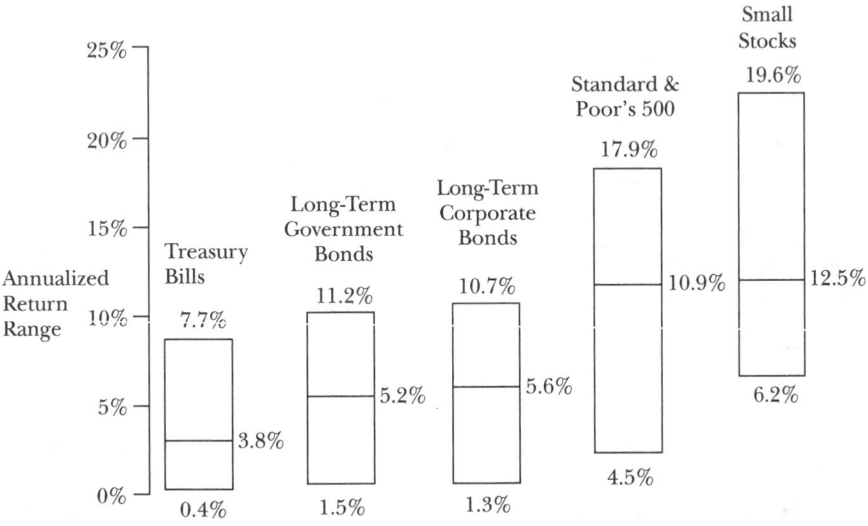

FIGURE 2.4 Risk/return trade-off in the long run, covering 52, 20-year investment periods, 1929–1999.

Note: Each bar shows the range of compound average annual total returns for a different type of investment.

Source: Wiesenberger, Thomson Financial.

TABLE 2.2 Range of Returns: Maximum and Minimum Values of Returns for 1-, 10-, and 20-Year Holding Periods

	Maximum Value		*Minimum Value*		*Times*
Series	*Return*[1]	*Year(s)*	*Return*[1]	*Year(s)*	*Positive*[2]
Annual Returns					
Large-company stocks S&P 500	53.99	1933	–43.34	1931	50
Small-company stocks	161.4	1933	–54.1	1937	44
Long-term corporate bonds	43.8	1982	–8.1	1969	52
Long-term government bonds	40.36	1982	–9.18	1967	48
U.S. Treasury bills	14.71	1981	–0.02	1938	69
10-Year Rolling Period Returns					
Large-company stocks	20.1	1949–58	–0.1	1930–39	59
Small-company stocks	29.4	1975–84	1.3	1965–74	60
Long-term corporate bonds	16.32	1982–91	0.98	1947–56	60
Long-term government bonds	15.56	1982–91	–0.07	1950–59	59
U.S. Treasury bills	9.17	1978–87	0.15	1933–42/ 1934–43	60
20-Year Rolling Period Returns					
Large-company stocks	16.86	1942–61	4.5	1930–49	50
Small-company stocks	22.7	1942–61	9.2	1969–88	50
Long-term corporate bonds	10.58	1976–95	1.34	1950–69	50
Long-term government bonds	10.45	1976–95	0.69	1950–69	50
U.S. Treasury bills	7.72	1972–91	0.42	1931–50	50

[1]Compound annual rates of return in percent.
[2]Out of 74 for annual, 60 for 10-year, and 50 for 20-year.
Source: Wiesenberger, Thomson Financial.

stocks or mutual funds that have done well over the past 5 or 10 years will continue to do well over the next 5 or 10 years.

There are many examples of investors losing money by following this rearview mirror approach. For example, during the 1970s the conventional wisdom was that hard assets such as gold, precious metals, energy, and real estate were the investment vehicles of choice. Unfortunately, during the 1980s financial assets such as stocks, bonds, and mutual funds prevailed. We say "unfortunately" because most investors waited until the beginning of the 1980s to go out and invest in the hard-asset type vehicles that had prospered during the 1970s.

In the late 1960s and early 1970s, the rearview mirror conventional wisdom dictated investing in mutual funds that held all or most of the "Nifty 50" stocks because they prospered tremendously. These stocks were termed one-decision stocks, because the only decision an investor had to make was to buy them.

Unfortunately, many of these stocks lost 80 percent, or even 90 percent, of their value during the 1973–1974 bear market. In fact, many of these stocks did not return to their 1972 levels until the 1990s. The Nifty 50 enthusiasm was a perfect example of both a stock mania or bubble, where stock prices were ridiculously inflated relative to the underlying economics of these 50 companies, and rearview mirror investing, where a profitable strategy during one time period (1969–1972) proved disastrous during a subsequent period (1973–1974).

Similarly, in the recent technology bull market, we've seen many popular Internet companies selling for outrageous prices even though the companies may never have earnings. The prevailing logic would seem to be that you cannot go wrong by investing in these Internet stocks. But, history has shown that you can pay too high a price for any stock. For this reason it is critical that each investor follow a diligent and rigorous analytical process to find reasonable values in his or her investments, or, even better, delegate this responsibility to professionals. Stories about stocks mean nothing! Psychologically, by following an informed process to find investments with reasonable prospects and prices, you can have confidence that these investments will profit in the long run.

YOUR RISK PROFILE

Figure 2.5 will help you understand how you will react under different market conditions. Over your lifetime you should expect a variety of market conditions, including bear markets every three or four years that may have severe magnitude and duration. Like the true Rorschach test that helps psychologists develop a personality profile even when the patient gives standard answers to direct questions, our "investment Rorschach" helps us dig deeper into a new client's canned answer of "I want 15 percent growth, but I'm conservative and don't want risk."

Table 2.3 shows the worst down markets over the past 70 years. If you know how often bear markets occur, you can get a better sense of the nature of capital and investment markets and the merits of long-term investing, as long as you don't get too upset over the inevitable temporary

Knowledge about your investment temperament can help you avoid unwise revisions to your well-thought-out retirement plan.

This quiz should help you identify your investment temperament. Please choose the best answer to the questions—go with your first instinct.

Finding Your Risk Tolerance

	Portfolio	*% In Stocks*	*% In Bonds*	*Worst Year*	*Best Year*	*Average Year*
1. In this table, which depicts actual investment data in the post–World War II era, choose the portfolio allocation between stocks and bonds that most closely matches your goals and temperament.	1	100	0	–26.5	52.9	13.5
	2	90	10	–23.4	48.1	12.7
	3	80	20	–20.3	43.5	11.8
	4	70	30	–17.2	39.0	11.0
	5	60	40	–14.1	34.4	10.1
	6	50	50	–11.1	31.8	9.3
	7	40	60	–8.0	32.8	8.4
	8	30	70	–6.1	34.7	7.8
	9	20	80	–5.8	35.6	6.7
	10	10	90	–5.0	36.9	5.9
	11	0	100	–9.2	40.4	5.0

2. On the golf course or at parties when others talk about their investing prowess . . .
   a. I listen closely because I don't want to miss out on a chance for big gains.
   b. I take everything with a grain of salt and always consider the source.
3. Which statement best describes your investment approach?
   a. My instincts about people and investment opportunities are very good; I trust these instincts.
   b. I'm methodical; I research every decision. *Consumer Reports* is my favorite publication.
   c. There is such a thing as information overload. I gather relevant information, decide, and then don't look back.
   d. Decisions are tough. I often procrastinate—you can never be too careful.

FIGURE 2.5 An investment Rorschach test: helping you find your investment temperament.

4. In this graph, which depicts risk and return characteristics of 11 different portfolios, choose the portfolio number that most closely balances your return objective with your gut feeling as to how much risk you can tolerate.

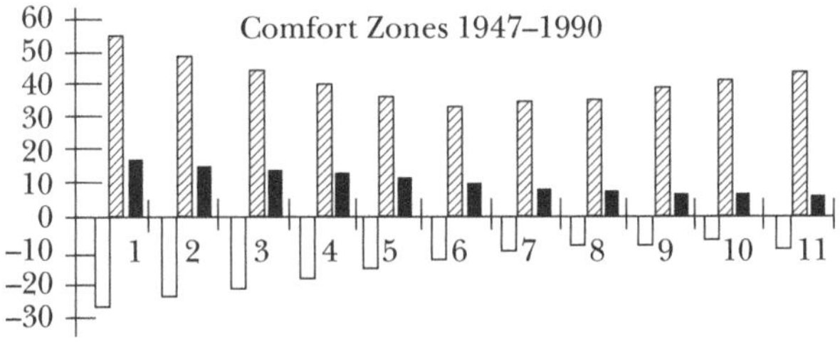

White bars show worst case, hatched bars show best case, and black bars show average scenarios. *Source:* Standard & Poor's.

5. Are you nervous about another stock market crash? If so, which of the following approaches to market risk feels best to you?
   a. A guaranteed 7 percent return would be sufficient to live on, and I'd take it.
   b. The best experts can consistently earn 20 percent per year; the challenge is to find them.
   c. The market always bounces back; I want to be aggressive and "buy on the dips."
   d. I'd like an expert to lay out an investment plan tailored to my needs; I don't know everything and believe in following the counsel of professionals in any field.
6. If most of the television commentators and our friends were convinced that rapid inflation had returned and that cash and precious metals investments would work best, you would . . .
   a. Buy gold and certificate of deposits (CDs)—this approach did well in the 1970s.
   b. Move some, but not all, of my portfolio into CDs and metals.
   c. Seek objective professional guidance.
   d. Stick to my existing long-term plan.
7. If these same friends and TV commentators felt that a depression or deep recession were about to occur and that government bonds were the only safe investment, you would . . .
   a. Buy government bonds.
   b. Move some, but not all, of my portfolio into government bonds.
   c. Seek objective professional guidance.
   d. Stick to my existing long-term plan.

(Continued)

FIGURE 2.5 *Continued*

8. In 1996, the stock market (S&P 500 Index) rose 37 percent. If your portfolio made only 15 percent, you would have been . . .
   a. Thrilled—that's all I need.
   b. Furious—I want to keep pace with the market.
   c. Disappointed—but I would stick with my long-term plan.
   d. Aware that only a percentage of my portfolio is in stocks or no-load stock mutual funds—I wouldn't expect my low-risk bonds and cash to keep up with the high-risk stock market.
9. During the furious bear market of 1987 (35 percent decline), the Saddam Hussein bear market of 1990 (20 percent decline), or the 11 percent market decline in October 1996, if your stock portfolio had declined nearly as much as the market at the time, you would have . . .
   a. Sold most of my holdings and bought safe CDs.
   b. Waited to get back to even and then sold everything.
   c. Added to my stock holdings by buying low.
   d. Done nothing, because I have only my long-term holdings in stocks or stock mutual funds and realize that stocks will fluctuate in the short run.

Answer Key

1. If you chose portfolio 1, 2, 3, or 4, score yourself 3 points; portfolio 5, 6, or 7, 2 points; portfolio 8, 9, 10, or 11, 1 point.
2. Choice (b) scores 2 points; choice (a), 0 points.
3. Choice (c) scores 3 points; choice (b), 2 points; choices (a) and (d), 1 point.
4. Same scoring as question 1.
5. Choice (d) scores 3 points; choices (a) and (c), 1 point; choice (b), 0 points.
6. Choices (c) and (d) score 3 points; choice (b), 1 point; choice (a), 0 points.
7. Choices (c) and (d) score 3 points; choice (b), 1 point; choice (a), 0 points.
8. Choice (d) scores 3 points; choice (c), 2 points; choice (a), 1 point; choice (b), 0 points.
9. Choice (d) scores 3 points; choice (c), 2 points; choice (b), 1 point; choice (a), 0 points.

FIGURE 2.5 *Continued*

If your score is . . .

17 to 26 points—You have the delegator or long-term investor temperament necessary to succeed.

10 to 16 points—You have an armchair quarterback temperament that can work during calm market conditions, but could break down under severe market stress.

Less than 10 points—Your emotions could hurt you during severe market conditions. Several times a year, you should practice the lifeboat drills described earlier in this chapter. Also, you should seek the counsel of a seasoned investment professional whom you respect.

FIGURE 2.5 *Continued*
Source: 1990 Standard & Poor's *Outlook*. Reprinted by permission of Standard & Poor's, a division of The McGraw-Hill Companies.

declines. It is also critical that you not alter your strategy based on emotional reactions when these inevitable normal declines occur. As you can see in Table 2.3, it usually does not take more than two or three years to bounce back from a bear market loss, although in some cases it did take as many as five or six years to bounce back.

After completing Figure 2.5 and carefully reviewing Table 2.3, you should walk yourself through a lifeboat drill. Look at different scenarios and the likely reaction of your portfolio during down market conditions; then test how you would react during those times. For example, if you have a $700,000 portfolio that declines to $600,000, will your intellect be able to outweigh your emotions? Will you stick with your long-term strategy, or will you abandon your well-diversified portfolio and retreat to cash, thereby eliminating the benefit of long-term investing?

In our experience, a thorough understanding of investment history can help you do the proper thing when bear markets occur—namely, *do nothing*. At Yolles Investment Management, we've developed an expression to describe how an investor should react to a bear market: "Don't just do something, sit there." In fact, if anything, bear markets are excellent times to add to your stock holdings. Remember: Buy low, sell high—always.

During a worst-case scenario, the returns you receive or losses you experience must fit within your tolerance for risk. This level of comfort will give you the best opportunity possible of realizing a solid rate of return by sticking with your long-term program. Figure 2.6 is a chart we use at Yolles

TABLE 2.3 Down Markets 1930–1999 (Annual Basis)

Year	*% Loss*	*Years to Make Up Loss*
1931	43.36	2
1937	35.02	6
1974	26.49	1
1930	24.89	5
1973	14.80	3
1941	11.60	1
1957	10.78	1
1966	10.06	1
1940	9.77	3
1962	8.75	1
1969	8.47	2
1946	8.08	2
1977	7.40	2

Data source: Yolles Investment Management.

Investment Management to help our clients understand the risk and return parameters of different portfolio approaches. While this chart is complicated, the *efficient market line* concept that it illustrates should make economic sense. Namely, if a portfolio contains more no-load stock funds and a smaller allocation to bond funds, the portfolio will be more risky than a portfolio that has less exposure to the stock market. However, the greater the stock fund allocation, the greater the likely "real" (after inflation) return.

efficient market line a series of points on a risk/reward graph which shows optimal portfolios for given levels of risk.

The graph shows 11 optimal portfolios for different levels of risk. As the word "optimal" implies, these 11 portfolio designs are ideal for different investors depending on their return requirements and their risk tolerance. There is an ideal portfolio for every investor. Our challenge is to help you find the ideal portfolio for you at different stages of your retirement.

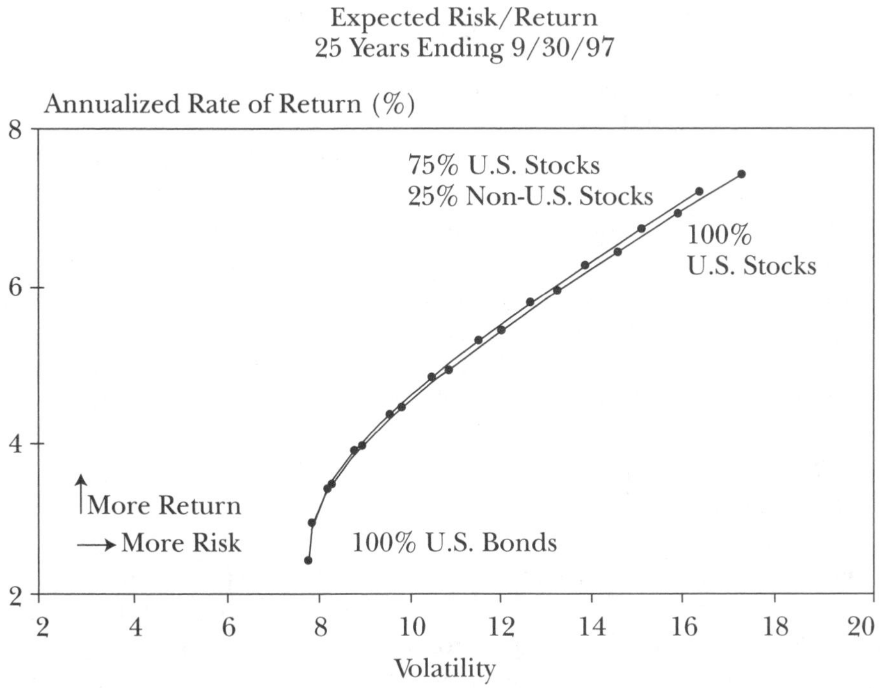

FIGURE 2.6 Efficient market line.
Source: Ennis, Knupp & Associates, Chicago, IL. Used with permission.

Also review Figure 2.6 to see various optimal portfolio allocations for different investors and the amount of risk present in each of these portfolios. It is worth taking the extra time necessary to understand the exact nature of these portfolios, even though it may be difficult to understand the features of these portfolios at first glance. Stay with us, and you'll have a successful retirement.

YOUR OWN PSYCHOLOGY WILL ALSO INFLUENCE WHEN YOU RETIRE AND WHERE YOU RETIRE TO

The only way that many of you who are not teachers or who do not have a hefty pension will find peace of mind is by using a book like this. The objective examples in this book will help you work through various retirement scenarios, including worst-case scenarios, and this should give you that feeling of confidence that teachers have.

Retirement often works best if you are able to take a trial run or even two trial runs. Many people retire and then are unhappy and choose to go back to either full- or part-time work but in a different specialty. These are issues that you will have to explore with yourself and your spouse. Many people find that retiring in stages works best: perhaps taking a part-time job in a different field prior to complete retirement.

The decision as to whether to move (typically to a warmer climate) after you have retired is also complex and requires a great deal of communication between yourself and your spouse. We recommend that if you plan on retiring to a warmer climate or a different locale that you take at least one trial run, even if this means that you must rent for an entire season rather than having equity ownership in a home or condominium. The following web sites can be very useful in determining where you might like to retire: www.retirement.com and www.retirementliving.com.

FOR WOMEN ONLY

Too often we see cases where women are not involved in their financial and retirement planning, and this causes many problems. Women frequently have a greater aptitude for money management in financial planning decision making than men. We want to take this opportunity to encourage and even implore all women, whether single, married, widowed, or divorced, to get involved with your financial planning. There are six reasons why women should get involved in financial decision making:

1. Life expectancy tables show that women often live up to seven years longer than men.
2. Evidence shows that women are often younger than their husbands, so when you combine this with their longer life expectancy they may live 10 or more years without their husbands.
3. We've seen many cases where women have to work after their husbands have passed away in order to survive; the earlier you plan for this, the better.
4. Getting involved in financial decision making alleviates part of the double-barreled stress that comes when a husband passes away; otherwise, the stress of the loss of one's husband is compounded by the stress of having to make financial decisions for the first time.
5. A study by Professor Terrance Odean has shown that women investors actually earn 1.2 percent more per year than men because they are more patient and trade less often.

6. Additional evidence shows that women are more successful investors than men because they are less likely to be overconfident and are more likely to know that they need professional help.

Research has found that women are less financially secure in retirement than men. Further research shows that 75 percent of the older people living in poverty are women—at least partly due to women earning lower incomes while trying to care for children and elderly parents. Other findings that should serve as a wake-up call for women to get more involved in their financial planning include:

- ✔ Single women have lower savings rates than single men.
- ✔ Women have higher medical expenses in old age.
- ✔ Women often are unable to stay with an employer long enough to become vested in the employer's retirement plan.
- ✔ Many women lack access to affordable health and long-term care insurance.

CONCLUSION

This chapter on your money personality is probably worth rereading due to its importance and the complexity of the material. Investment success has nothing to do with your IQ, career, or station in life and everything to do with knowing yourself and your own limitations, and getting the retirement planning help you need.

Chapter 3

Saving for Retirement: The Magic of Compound Interest

BABY BOOMERS—WE KNOW WHO YOU ARE

The baby boom generation has always been fiercely independent and bucked society's norms and conventional wisdom at every life stage they have encountered. Baby boomers will undoubtedly make similar major changes to conventional notions of retirement. This chapter will first define these unconventional notions of retirement held by baby boomers and then explore how you can achieve a comfortable retirement, and perhaps more importantly, achieve financial security even if your retirement is unconventional.

When baby boomers began buying their first houses in the 1970s, they created an explosion in housing prices. Similarly, when they started investing in the early 1980s, stock prices soared. Now, boomers, as well as some younger members of the World War II generation, are having a similar tidal-wave effect on the rules of retirement in the following 10 ways:

1. Studies by *AARP* show that retirement is no longer about golf and gardening but, rather, it's about returning to college; starting a new career; assuming a primary role in raising grandchildren; or expanding physical, mental, and emotional horizons in a variety of ways.

AARP formerly known as the American Association of Retired Persons, AARP is now an acronym that just represents a nonprofit group of vibrant people over 50.

2. Demographers estimate that by the year 2040, there will be several million people over the age of 100—enough to populate an entire metropolitan area. Retirement is becoming more than a short, final stage of life; in many cases, retirement can represent the *second half* of a person's life.
3. Medical innovations in biotechnology will extend our good years so that an 80-year-old in 2040 will live like a 55-year-old did in 1940.
4. Baby boomers are dramatically overestimating, by a factor of three, the returns that they will receive from the capital markets—which will cause severe shortfalls and stress. Individuals surveyed expected to earn over 20 percent per year in the stock market, while leading *strategic consultants* had the following annual estimates of stock returns: Callan Associates 9 percent, Ibbotson 8.9 percent, SEI 8 percent, and Morgan Stanley 6 percent.
5. Retirement itself is a misnomer as evidenced by the AARP organization, which now goes by only the AARP acronym (no longer "retired persons") and represents vibrant adults over the age of 50 who are anything but "retiring."
6. When Social Security legislation was passed in the 1930s, the average life expectancy was 58, so it was easy for the government to begin retirement benefits at age 65. Social Security will need to change to reflect longer life expectancies, and hopefully public sentiment will shift in this direction.
7. Retirement planners will have to take an entirely different approach to serve their clients' needs. On the financial front,

strategic consultants investment firms that provide state-of-the art investment designs typically for wealthy investors.

planners will need to open their clients' eyes to longer life spans. On the emotional front, planners will need to be trained to be more sensitive to the issues that their clients face as they reinvent their lives and careers. We are already seeing cases where investment managers work in partnership with *gerontologists* and psychologists.

8. Boomers want more involvement in their financial planning and the ability to track their progress. This is seen by the explosion of *self-directed investors*, proliferation of investors using the Internet, and rapid increase in the number of investment clubs.
9. Individual responsibility will replace government responsibility—as evidenced by surveys that show most people do not expect Social Security to be available when they retire.
10. Planners will learn to adjust for gender differences and also for differences in the way that people define their own age—not all 62-year-olds are alike.

gerontologist one who studies aging and all the ramifications of aging.

The single most important point about baby boomers is that because they have unconventional views about retirement they are also reluctant to save for retirement. This happens because baby boomers have always defined their lives by living in the present and saving for the long term seems to contradict this notion. Boomers can overcome this mental block by recognizing the tangible current and short-term benefits that come from sensible long-term retirement planning.

self-directed investors those who prefer to manage their own investments, in contrast to delegators.

HOW TO BECOME A MILLIONAIRE (AT LEAST IN SPIRIT)

Tax-deferred savings are the best way to accumulate money for retirement or financial independence. The beauty of tax-deferred savings is that they also provide very tangible current benefits. Let's look at an example of how a *401(k) plan* (also known as salary deferral defined-contribution plan) works.

tax-deferred income whose taxes can be postponed until a later date.

401(k) plan a defined contribution plan offered by a corporation to its employees, which allows employees to set aside tax-deferred income for retirement purposes.

Salary deferral means that part of your salary goes into your retirement plan. Let's assume that you have $50,000 in salary, you choose to contribute 8 percent of your salary to your 401(k) plan, and your employer has a 50 percent matching provision. Here is how this situation would work: On your $50,000 of income you can and will contribute $4,000, or 8 percent, and your employer will contribute another $2,000, which represents 50 percent of your contribution. Your $4,000 contribution reduces your taxable income from $50,000 down to $46,000. So if you are in the 28 percent marginal tax bracket you are saving $1,120 on your taxes.

Salary	$50,000
401(k) Contribution (8 percent)	4,000
Taxable Income	$46,000
Employer contribution ($4,000 times 50 percent)	$2,000
Tax savings ($4,000 times 28 percent)	$1,120
Total 401(k) Benefit ($4,000 plus $2,000 plus $1,120)	$7,120
Net cost of 401(k) contribution ($4,000 minus $1,120)	$2,880

If you are able to put $6,000 into a 401(k) or similar plan beginning at age 30 all the way up until age 60 and you earn 10 percent per year on the plan, you will have accumulated a total sum of $986,964. In addition, many 401(k) plans have features where you can take loans from your 401(k) plan to pay for things like your children's education. So there are some real current short-term benefits from 401(k) savings, and everybody should be motivated to save in this fashion—especially when your employer matches your contribution in some fashion. In the example we gave, the employer contribution gives you an instant 50 percent return ($2,000 divided by $4,000 equals 50 percent). We are not aware of any other guaranteed investment return of 50 percent or anything approaching 50 percent. The $1,120 tax savings that you would receive in our example makes the 401(k) even more attractive.

Another reason to start some form of savings plan is because savings is a good habit that can be very fulfilling. This sense of fulfillment gives many people great satisfaction. Conversely, the opposite of savings is consumption and we have found that consumption is often habit-forming. People get used to maintaining a certain lifestyle and it is difficult to give up this lifestyle. Problems can arise down the road from lack of savings. So start the savings plan early and the added benefit will be that you won't miss consumption that you never had. This will allow you to avoid at least part of the squeeze that many baby boomers feel (depicted in Figure 3.1).

Another way to think of and appreciate the short-term benefits of retirement savings is to recognize that saving money buys you freedom and financial independence, which are key values of baby boomers—and of all people, for that matter. The earlier you can start saving, the earlier you will feel at least a partial sense of financial independence. This will give you the freedom that many of us cherish, including the freedom to leave a very stressful corporate job for some career or other interest that is more

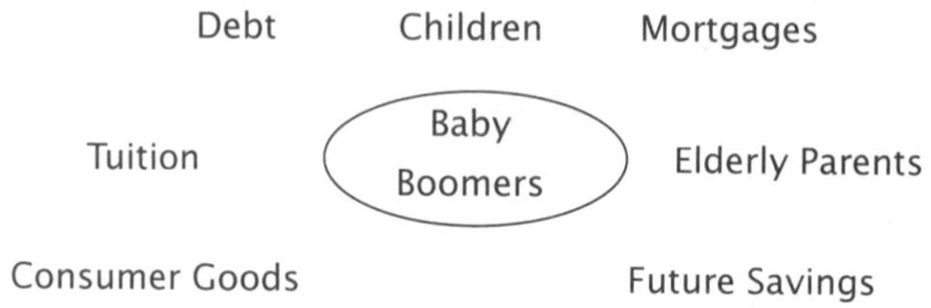

FIGURE 3.1 Overwhelming decisions.
Source: Yolles Investment Management.

fulfilling but less financially rewarding. This points out that the biggest issues facing baby boomers who are saving for retirement, and even people who have already retired, are emotional rather than financial issues. These emotional issues (as we mentioned in Chapter 2) must be resolved before you can embark on a sensible savings and retirement plan. Often this resolution can be found by coming up with a plan that is a healthy compromise between two alternatives.

For example, when it is difficult to make the decision to retire, particularly if you feel you have not saved quite enough money to retire, then an intermediate solution is to take a *preretirement sabbatical*. A sabbatical can be taken from work for one, two, or several years, and in essence you are able to recharge your batteries. There are many cases where people then return to work with a renewed sense of purpose and joy. If you have options, life is too short to stay in an unpleasant or dead-end job.

preretirement sabbatical taking a break from work for a period of time to embark on fulfilling activities, often followed by a healthy and enjoyable return to work at a later time.

HAVING A TARGET IMPROVES YOUR CHANCES OF SUCCESS

If you look back to any of the goals that you have accomplished, you will probably see that one key to accomplishing a goal is setting the goal in the first place. Another key, especially when the goal is long-term, is breaking down the goal into manageable chunks.

For example, anyone who has ever run a marathon knows that you have to start training many months in advance of the marathon, and you start training in two- and three-mile increments, eventually working your way up to 5-, 10-, 15-, and 20-mile training runs before you are finally ready to run the 26-mile marathon. If you want to lose weight, you don't take off 30 pounds immediately but rather take off a pound or two at a time over a period of several months.

In a different vein, athletes such as tennis players or golfers often comment on achieving their best performance when they can visualize the goal or visualize successful performance. They picture a successful result and then they achieve it.

This principle of having a goal and visualizing successfully achieving the goal works equally well in the world of finance. Additionally, breaking that financial goal down into manageable components will help you achieve the goal.

So how do you go about setting your retirement or financial independence goal? A good starting point is either to look at your current standard of living or to visualize and estimate your standard of living in retirement or in partial retirement. Once you can come up with a rough estimate of what you will need to retire (and we gave you some tools in Chapter 1 to help in this process), then you can start to analyze how much capital you will need to save to reach retirement or financial independence. Once you arrive at your retirement spending target, we suggest that you use what we call the *5 percent endowment spending rule* to determine how much you need to save. Here's how the 5 percent rule works: By law endowments must distribute 5 percent of their principal each year to various charities. Since endowments and foundations as a matter of law must live in perpetuity (forever), we can feel fairly secure that the normal 5 percent annual spending level that endowments use will be a safe level for individuals to spend on an annual basis if their portfolios are invested intelligently.

5 percent endowment spending rule by law an endowment must distribute 5 percent of its principal each year to various charities. This gives us a good estimate of a sustainable withdrawal rate for individual portfolios.

Let's say that you determine that you need $60,000 per year to live on if you want to be financially independent and/or retire. Let's further assume that you're too young to be receiving Social Security until many years in the future. Using our 5 percent endowment spending rule, you can see that you will need to save $1.2 million in order to be able to comfortably withdraw $60,000 per year from your portfolio. This $1.2 million figure then becomes your savings target. You can break your savings goal down into manageable chunks; for example, you can determine how much you will have to save and invest each week in order to arrive at your target.

So, if we take our earlier example where you would be putting $6,000 a year into your 401(k) and assume that you are able to earn 10 percent on that money, then we can calculate how much additional money you will have to put away outside of your 401(k) in order for you to reach your $1.2 million target. We find that if you want to retire in 20 years you have to put away $280.54 per month for 20 years; that will ultimately give you $1.2 million in combination with your 401(k). Please note that you may earn only 5 percent on your investments (or less), so you should also plan for this worst-case contingency.

Since financial economics is a social and not a hard science, it is best to plan for uncertainty and even bad results. If you can live with your worst-case assumptions, then you know that your planning is thorough.

Unfortunately, there is a tremendous amount of evidence that baby boomers are not saving nearly enough for retirement. This is partly a function of boomers having the attitude of living for today—they find it hard to put away money for the future. Also, boomers surveyed overestimate the returns they are likely to earn in the financial markets by a factor of three. That's right, many boomers are estimating that they will be earning more than 20 percent a year even though throughout recorded history returns greater than 10 or 12 percent a year have been very rare. You should not make the mistake of assuming that your rates of return will be high; it is better to prepare conservatively and be pleasantly surprised.

We are experts in finance rather than motivation, so you will have to find your own motivational secrets for getting started in your saving and investing program or in dramatically increasing your saving and investing program. We hope that the information we provide in this book will help you in this process and identify for you what you will have to do to achieve either financial independence or retirement. In our experience most people value the idea of being financially independent or being able to retire. Hopefully, this will serve as sufficient motivation to get you started on your savings plan.

LEARNED FINANCIAL HELPLESSNESS

Many people like to do some self-education before getting professional help with their financial and retirement planning. We are big believers in doing reading and getting background information before visiting your financial professionals in the same way that you would read about a serious illness before consulting a physician for a second opinion.

However, we want to encourage you to see financial professionals sooner rather than later, and we recognize that much financial information can be overwhelming and create information overload.

We hope that this book serves as a handy reference guide for you and dispels some of the fear or intimidation you might feel toward financial planning issues. Additionally, the following web sites can give you good, general information about financial planning: www.Vanguard.com, www.Investorama.com, www.onmoney.com, and www.better-investing.org.

If you are in a rut and having a hard time getting started with your financial planning, we encourage you to work in small steps. You have to start somewhere, and the easiest place to start is with the goal-setting exercises that we have discussed in this chapter. If you can determine both your goal and the small steps necessary, on a daily, weekly, and monthly basis, to achieve those goals, then you are well on your way to some successful financial planning.

Other ways to encourage you to stick with your financial planning include developing a support group or an investment club (check out www.better-investing.org). Additionally, you can use any of the following web sites to track your financial progress on a daily basis. Often this tracking becomes fun and further encourages you to get involved with your own investment planning: www.quicken.com, www.bloomberg.com, http://finance.yahoo.com, and www.bridge.com.

Chapter 4

Managing Your Portfolio

In our practice, investing is generally the area in which we see people make the most mistakes. There is still too much misinformation about investment strategy and planning. Too often we see investors grasping for so-called guaranteed investment vehicles or being seduced by various investment fads. Both of these traps almost always are detriments to maintaining a comfortable retirement in the long run.

DIVIDEND YIELD VERSUS CAPITAL APPRECIATION

When planning for retirement, most people add up their sources of capital including pensions and Social Security, and then have some idea of how much cash flow their financial portfolio will be required to produce to supplement these other sources. For example, if you felt that you needed $70,000 a year to live on and knew that Social Security would provide only $20,000 per year, then your portfolio would have to produce $50,000 per year. If the size of your portfolio was $500,000, then you could easily calculate that your portfolio would have to yield 10 percent annually to produce the required $50,000. This is a very normal case. Countless times every month, new clients come into our office and tell us that they need to achieve just a 10 percent annual yield from their portfolios. Sounds simple; however, never in the 200-year history of investment markets has any vehicle consistently produced close to a 10 percent yield.

You will recall from the previous chapters that stocks have been the best-returning asset class, averaging close to an 11 percent total return annually. Still, only 4 percent of this 11 percent has come from dividend yield, and the remaining 7 percent annually has come from capital appreciation. The annual returns from stocks and mutual funds are very unpredictable.

Table 4.1 shows a recent period in the investment markets and illustrates the high volatility of stock returns. The 27-year period shown covers the years 1973–1999. The 1970s were a miserable decade for financial assets and a good decade for hard assets such as precious metals, real estate, oil, and energy. In the 1980s and 1990s the opposite occurred: It was a wonderful time for financial assets such as stocks, bonds, and mutual funds. You can see from Table 4.1, stocks column, that while stock returns averaged 13.89 percent for the period, the returns were extremely variable from year to year with a low of –26 percent in 1974 and a high return of 37 percent in 1975. As a retiree making steady withdrawals for living expenses, you cannot tolerate this volatility, since you would deplete your capital during large down years.

Recall our previous discussions of sustainable portfolio withdrawal rates for retirees. In the next chapter, Table 5.1 is based on 100 years of data on reasonable returns from stocks, bonds, and cash equivalents such as certificates of deposit or Treasury bills. While many retirees would like to find an investment vehicle that would yield 10 percent, 12 percent, or 14 percent a year and from which they could make withdrawals, there are also many people who would like to find the Holy Grail.

If you don't familiarize yourself with various investment vehicles, then you are more likely to make a serious investment mistake when seeking higher yields. History is replete with examples of people investing hard-earned money in dubious investment vehicles that promise high yields but don't deliver. Many of these vehicles also cost people some or all of their principal. Unfortunately, there are plenty of unscrupulous investment salespeople out there who will seduce you with these too-good-to-be-true promises. Caveat emptor.

Some recent examples of "can't miss" investment opportunities that did miss—and missed in a big way—include real estate limited partnerships, oil and gas limited partnerships, junk bonds, various mortgage schemes, and on and on. We cannot emphasize enough the importance of understanding the capital markets and what is and is not possible on the return spectrum.

Two hundred years of historical data, and hopefully some common sense, show us that stock-type investments can return about 11 percent

TABLE 4.1 The Benefits of Diversification: Annual Returns, January 1973 to December 1999

	Stocks[1]	*Bonds*[2]	*60 Percent Stocks/ 40 Percent Bonds*	*Conservative Strategy*[3]	*Normal Strategy*[4]
1973	–14.67	4.61	–6.96	–3.35	–8.15
1974	–26.46	5.68	–13.60	–4.90	–11.70
1975	37.21	7.82	25.46	23.39	31.54
1976	23.85	12.88	19.46	18.42	22.49
1977	–7.18	1.40	–3.75	9.55	12.56
1978	6.57	3.49	5.34	13.31	16.94
1979	18.42	4.10	12.69	14.82	16.71
1980	32.41	3.90	21.00	18.55	21.99
1981	–4.91	9.44	.83	13.70	10.35
1982	21.41	29.10	24.49	21.26	20.52
1983	22.51	7.41	16.47	17.43	22.07
1984	6.27	14.03	9.37	10.21	9.68
1985	32.17	20.34	27.44	24.34	28.81
1986	18.47	15.13	17.13	19.39	22.80
1987	5.23	2.90	4.30	9.89	11.49
1988	16.81	6.09	12.52	14.38	18.11
1989	31.49	13.27	24.20	17.45	21.95
1990	–3.17	9.74	1.99	–.89	–5.30
1991	30.55	15.31	24.45	20.40	24.81
1992	7.67	7.20	7.48	8.76	9.98
1993	9.99	11.24	10.49	15.40	19.59
1994	1.31	–5.13	–1.27	–.04	.47
1995	37.43	16.11	28.90	15.52	18.05
1996	23.07	2.09	14.68	11.93	14.11
1997	33.37	8.38	23.37	9.77	11.27
1998	28.58	10.22	21.23	6.95	6.89
1999	21.03	–1.76	11.91	10.34	13.43
Annual Return	13.89%	8.48%	12.00%	12.18%	13.62%
Standard Deviation	16.71%	7.10%	11.37%	7.75%	10.62%

[1]S&P 500 Index.
[2]Lehman Bond Index.
[3]40 percent in a variety of domestic and international stocks; 60 percent in bonds.
[4]60 percent in a variety of domestic and international stocks; 40 percent in bonds.
Source: Dimensional Fund Advisors, Inc.

annually, bond-type investments can earn 6 percent or 7 percent annually, and cash-type investments can earn 4 percent annually over the long run. Stretching for returns beyond what has been possible will, in all likelihood, prove disastrous to your long-term retirement planning.

While investing is an essential part of capitalism and an essential part of what our economic system is founded on, greed and speculation are not healthy. When you invest in a share of stock or the shares of a mutual fund that invests in numerous stocks, you are becoming an owner in the corporations from which you are buying stocks. As an owner, you will share in the success or failure of those corporations.

History has shown us that, over time in developed countries, corporations do fairly well for their stockholders and produce excellent returns far superior to returns provided by instruments such as certificates of deposit, Treasury bills, or bonds. Here we emphasize that *in the long run* stocks produced these types of returns. *In the short run*, stocks can be very volatile and can, and often will, lose you money.

If you will look at Table 4.1 showing the benefits of diversification and review the stock column, you will see that in 5 of the 27 years shown, stocks lost money. What conclusion can you draw from this example? Mainly that if you need an immediate return of all your capital in a short period of time, such as a one-, two-, or three-year horizon, then your money does not belong in stock funds. On the other hand, if you have a fairly long time horizon and in the meantime and you do not need a return of your principal, but may require only some dividend income, then stocks are likely, though not guaranteed, to produce superior returns. Like any recipe where both the ingredients and their proportions are critical, *asset allocation* describes how investable dollars are divided between the three major asset categories: stocks, bonds, and cash. Research shows that asset allocation determines 90 percentof any investor's results.

> **asset allocation** how investment dollars are divided between the three major asset categories: stocks, bonds, and cash.

YOUR RISK TOLERANCE

Please look back to the "Investor Profile Questionnaire" (Figure 1.1) score sheet complete with your answers to these questions and your scoring. This score sheet should have identified your recommended portfolio;

Table 4.2 shows how your recommended portfolio should be broken down between stocks and bonds.

Please note that you should not feel obligated to implement the recommended portfolio based on the results of your questionnaire: particularly if you do not feel comfortable with the downside risk (indicated in the rightmost column of Table 4.2) that corresponds with your recom-

TABLE 4.2 Asset Allocation

Model Objectives	*Allocations*[1] *Bonds*	*Allocations*[1] *Stocks*	*Annualized Return*[2]	*Best Year*	*Worst Year*
Conservative income Minimal downside risk	70%	30%	7.8%	34.7%	–6.1%
Income with growth Long-term growth of the income stream	60%	40%	8.4%	32.8%	–8.0%
Balanced portfolio Long-term growth of capital and some income stream	50%	50%	9.3%	31.8%	–11.1%
Balanced growth Primary goal of capital appreciation Stability of principal and level of income of little importance	40%	60%	10.1%	34.4%	–14.1%
Long-term growth Capital appreciation with high volatility Investment time horizon of 15+ years	30%	70%	11.0%	39.0%	–17.2%
Aggressive growth 20+ year time horizon	20%	80%	11.8%	43.5%	–20.3%
All stocks Very aggressive	0%	100%	13.5%	52.9%	–26.5%

Disclaimer: Annualized returns are not a guarantee of future performance. Figures are based on historical returns. To be used only as a guide for statistical expectation.

[1]Allocations may vary ± 5–7%.

[2]Based on information for 1947 to 1990, which we feel best represents market conditions.

mended portfolio. For example, even if your answers to the questionnaire indicated that your profile was long-term growth, meaning that you should have 70 percent in stocks and 30 percent in bonds, you should not implement this asset mix if you feel uncomfortable with the –17.2 percent volatility on the downside shown in Table 4.2. The most important feature of investing is having a portfolio tailored to your needs and your comfort level. If you find that you are staying awake at night because of too much risk in your portfolio, then your portfolio is not appropriate even if experts and various books indicate that that level of risk is appropriate for you. We like to tell our clients that we have not done our job properly even if we earn them excellent returns over a 10-year period if in the meantime they've developed an ulcer and could not sleep at night.

Once you have determined the amount of assets that you should have in stocks and in bonds, it is time to establish your optimal portfolio.

We strongly recommend that you take what we call an institutional approach to establishing your best portfolio. The reason for this is that *institutional investors*, such as wealthy family offices or endowment and pension funds, are much more successful than individual investors. Recall Figure 1.5, which showed that individual investors have done 10 percent worse than the overall stock market in recent years.

institutional investors corporations, pensions, endowments, and wealthy families.

We run our firm like a family office in that we focus on accessing the best talent and the best information for our clients in the same way that an orchestra conductor would try to access the "first chairs" of the music world to assemble a world-class orchestra. The approach used by institutional investors has evolved greatly over the past 50 years.

PROFESSIONAL INVESTMENT ADVICE HAS GONE THROUGH THREE STAGES

Stage 1—The All-Star Team (1952–1990)

Endowments and pensions led the way by using the leading money management firms or funds in the three major investment areas:

- ✔ Domestic stocks.
- ✔ International stocks.
- ✔ Bonds.

Stage 2—All-Star Team plus Domestic Index Funds (1991–1998)

Endowments, pensions, and wealthy family offices were among the first to recognize that money managers buying blue-chip U.S. stocks were rarely able to beat the S&P 500 Index in the long run, so they changed the model to include domestic index funds along with all-star managers in the fixed income and international stock specialties.

Stage 3—All-Star Team plus Quantitative Funds with an Industry-Neutral Approach, plus a Small Amount of Venture Capital (1998–)

All-star managers should be used in the following areas:

- ✔ International stocks.
- ✔ Bonds.
- ✔ Venture capital funds (only for aggressive accounts).

Using all-star managers means finding the best money management talent in the three areas mentioned in a similar fashion to what the U.S. Olympic committee did when it assembled the Dream Team of basketball including Michael Jordan, Larry Bird, and Magic Johnson. Sophisticated software tools have helped us identify the following all-star money managers:

International Stock Managers

- ✔ Mark Yockey, CFA, of Artisan International.
- ✔ Chris Browne of Tweedy Browne Global.

Bond Managers

- ✔ Bill Gross, CFA, of PIMCO.
- ✔ Joe Gabriel of Gabriel Hueglin (municipal bonds).

Venture Capital

- ✔ Champion Ventures, which combines leading venture capital firms including Accel Partners, Benchmark Capital, Sequoia Capital, and Redpoint Ventures.

- ✔ Managers Capital "Post Venture" Fund, managed by Joseph McNay of Essex Capital and Kevin Riley, CFA, of Roxbury Capital.

Domestic Stocks

- ✔ Jim Weiss, CFA, at J. P. Morgan.
- ✔ Emerson Tuttle, CFA, at SSGA (State Street Global).
- ✔ Wayne Wicker, CFA, of PIMCO Capital.

We recommend quantitative or structured stock selections and quantitative fund managers because they provide all the benefits of index funds while avoiding the risk that index funds take by concentrating their portfolios in the 50 biggest stocks in the index.

We recommend industry-neutral portfolios, which, as the term suggests, have broad representation in all industries in proportion to the market capitalization of each industry group relative to the total stock market as represented by the *Russell 3000* or *Wilshire 5000* total stock market indexes. Largest industry groups include technology and telecommunications and Internet services (labeled "services" on Morningstar reports). This industry-neutral approach should provide the most stable returns. Leading industry groups in the Russell 3000 Index as of October 1999 were:

Technology	30%
Telecommunications	9%
Health care	12%
Financials	17%
Industrials	11%
Consumer and Retail	14%

Russell 3000 a broad index, covering over 3,000 common stocks. This gives an accurate idea of how the stock market is performing.

Wilshire 5000 an index of approximately the 5,000 largest U.S. companies.

DETERMINE YOUR OPTIMAL PORTFOLIO

Assembling an optimal portfolio is a very complex process, and includes mathematical formulas containing items such as *correlation coefficients* and *standard deviations*. For our purposes here, and really for any investor, the real value to you comes in having an understanding of different optimal investment alternatives. Many trained Chartered Financial Analysts (CFAs) and other investment professionals will be more than willing to help you review optimal investment alternatives.

> **correlation coefficient** a measure that shows the relationship between two asset classes.

> **standard deviation** a statistical measure of volatility.

You should think of the process of assembling an optimal portfolio as similar to implementing a recipe. For example, when baking a cake, you need the proper proportions of flour, sugar, baking powder, and eggs, or your cake will neither be the correct consistency nor rise properly. Similarly, when assembling a portfolio you need the proper amounts of stock, bond, cash-equivalent, international, and convertible-bond funds or your portfolio will not perform properly. If you do not have an optimal, or ideal, portfolio design, then you are cheating yourself by taking too much risk and/or receiving too little return. An optimal portfolio design ensures that you will get the maximum return for the amount of risk that you are willing to take. Conversely, for the expected return that you wish to achieve, you will take no more risk than is necessary.

To carry our analogy one step further, just as you may want to add more sugar to your cake recipe, you may be tempted to concentrate your money in one hot mutual fund. You should resist this temptation, because too much sugar or too much of one fund could make you sick and cause either tooth or portfolio decay.

While the mathematical calculations of things like correlation coefficients and covariances are very complex when establishing optimal portfolio designs, the rationale behind optimal portfolios and the rationale behind diversification should be intuitively obvious. Different asset classes behave differently, so by holding various asset groups such as domestic and foreign stock, bond, convertible, cash, and resource funds, you are diversifying and spreading your risk. Figure 4.1 shows the risk and return characteristics of different optimal portfolios of U.S. stocks and bonds, and Figure 4.2 shows how portfolios can be made better and safer by adding international (non-U.S.) funds.

Between the United States and other countries, we have over 100 years of investment market data to use in studying how different asset classes complement each other. These relationships make economic sense.

For example, in reviewing market history, we see that when U.S. stock and bond markets are doing poorly the U.S. dollar is also doing poorly. Not surprisingly, we often, but not always, see hard currencies in the low-inflation countries such as Switzerland, Germany, and Japan do well when the U.S. dollar is doing poorly. Given this piece of historical data, it should not be surprising that a portfolio that includes both U.S. stocks and international bond funds, including bonds from Switzerland, Germany, Japan, and other foreign countries, should give a smoother, less volatile return than a less diversified portfolio that contains only U.S.

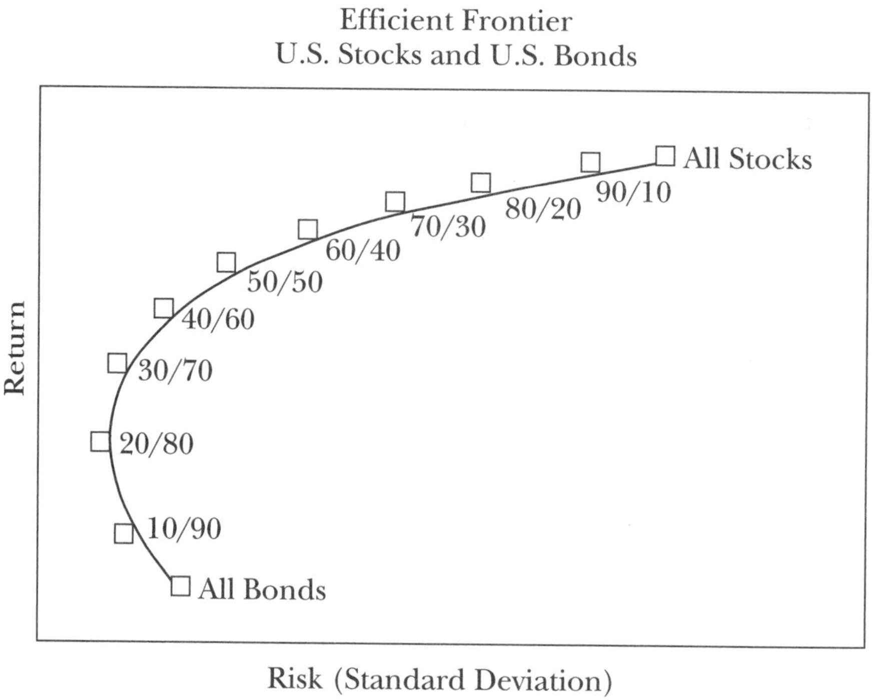

FIGURE 4.1 Optimal portfolio (domestic holdings).
Source: Ennis, Knupp & Associates, Chicago, IL. Used with permission.

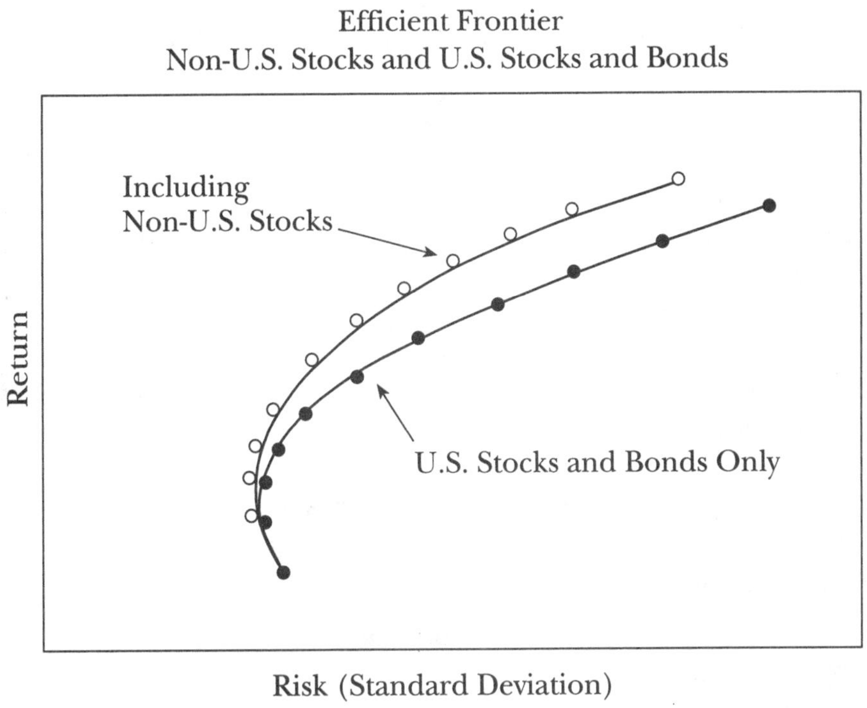

FIGURE 4.2 Optimal portfolio including international holdings.
Source: Ennis, Knupp & Associates, Chicago, IL. Used with permission.

stocks. In essence, the international bonds and U.S. stocks complement each other since they perform well at different times. This is the very essence of diversification. Figure 4.2 illustrates this phenomenon.

In Table 4.3 we show a sample optimal portfolio for a moderate-risk investor. We define a moderate-risk investor as someone who has a 12- to 16-year time horizon before he or she would consider withdrawing dividends. In addition, the investor should be able to tolerate a 15 percent dip in principal value during a bear market, while not allowing nerves to force a premature sale. Please note that this is what we would call the technical definition of the moderate-risk investor.

A moderate-risk investor could also describe the temperament of someone who has a much longer time horizon but is unwilling to take a great deal of risk. As you can see from Table 4.3 our moderate-risk investor has approximately 50 percent of the assets in stock mutual funds and 50 percent in fixed-income funds for an optimal portfolio allocation. Based on historical data, we would expect that this optimal portfolio would return 9.25 percent compounded annually and have a standard deviation of 9.5 percent.

TABLE 4.3 Optimal Portfolio for the Moderate-Risk Investor

Fund	*Allocation*
Domestic Stock Funds	
Large Cap	
PIMCO Capital Appreciation	14%
J. P. Morgan Disciplined Equity	11%
Small Cap	
DFA 6–10	5%
Tweedy, Browne American	5%
International Stock Funds	
Artisan International	10%
Tweedy, Browne Global	5%
Fixed-Income Funds	
DFA Global Bond	15%
PIMCO Foreign (international bond)	10%
PIMCO Real Return	10%
PIMCO Total Return (domestic high-quality bond)	15%

Parameters

Return Target	*Risk Tolerance*	*Risk and Return Ranges*
9.25%	−10% to −15% in a bear market	Normally (70% of the time) −0.25% to 18.75% Rarely (25% of the time) −9.75% to 28.25% Very rarely (5% of the time) <−9.75% or > 28.25%

Note for long-term investors: If you hold this portfolio for at least 10 years, your expected return is still 9.25%, but your range of returns should narrow to from 3% to 15.5%.

Source: Yolles Investment Management.

A standard deviation of 9.5 percent on a 9.25 percent expected return means that in a normal year the returns on the moderate-risk portfolio would average 9.25 percent and fall within 9.5 percent above or below that 9.25 percent average. So, in a typical year, the return would range from –0.25 percent to 18.75 percent. (This is found by taking 9.25 percent and either adding or subtracting 9.5 percent.) For the statistically inclined, normal years mean 7 out of 10 years. However, in the other 3 out of 10 years, history has shown that abnormal results are likely to occur on either the plus side or the minus side. Therefore, in 3 out of every 10 years, returns may be worse than –0.25 percent or better than 18.75 percent.

If you define yourself as a moderate-risk investor, then you have to feel comfortable with these parameters and rest assured that you will not alter your long-term strategy during market downturns, or, for that matter, during outstanding market advances. Most often, either greed during those unusual advances or fear during those unusual declines throws investors off track and spoils their long-term plans.

Table 4.4, illustrates some examples of a few model portfolios and model portfolio guidelines that we use for investors with different levels of risk. When we work with top strategic investment consultants, their guidelines for portfolio allocations are very similar to the guidelines shown in this table.

Table 4.5 shows a recommended asset allocation for the growth-oriented investor. We define the growth-oriented investor as someone with a time horizon in excess of 16 years. This 16-year time horizon should allow the growth investor to go through at least four market cy-

TABLE 4.4 Optimal Portfolio for Different Risk Levels

	Conservative	*Balanced-Growth*	*All-Stock*
Aggressive stocks or stock mutual funds	0%	5%	15%
Blue chip stocks or stock funds	20%	30%	40%
Small stocks of funds	4%	10%	15%
Foreign stocks or mutual funds	6%	15%	30%
Bonds	60%	35%	0%
Money market funds	10%	5%	0%

Source: Yolles Investment Management.

TABLE 4.5 Optimal Portfolio for the Growth-Oriented Investor

Fund	*Allocation*
Domestic Stock Funds	
Large Cap	
Individual stocks: Intel, Cisco, IBM, Wal-Mart, Wells Fargo, etc.	10%
Manager's Capital	4%
PIMCO Capital Appreciation	12%
State Street Global (SSGA) Growth and Income	12%
Small Cap	
DFA 6–10	6%
Tweedy, Browne American	5%
International Stock Funds	
Artisan International	14%
Tweedy, Browne Global	7%
Fixed-Income Funds	
DFA Global Bond	9%
PIMCO Foreign	6%
PIMCO Real Return	6%
PIMCO Total Return	9%

Parameters

Return Target	*Risk Tolerance*	*Risk and Return Ranges*
11%	–20% to –25% in a bear market	Normally (70% of the time) –1.9% to 23.9%
		Rarely (25% of the time) –14.8% to 36.8%
		Very rarely (5% of the time) <–14.8% or >36.8%

Note for long-term investors: If you hold this portfolio for at least 10 years, your expected return is still 11%, but your range of returns should narrow to from 1% to 21%.

Source: Yolles Investment Management.

cles. A normal four-year market cycle will include both a bull and a bear market. The past 100 years of investment history show us that bear markets recur once every three or four years, hence our calculation of at least four market cycles over a 16-year period. The long-term growth investor will not be withdrawing any dividends from the portfolio but, rather, will reinvest these dividends. This investor is looking strictly for long-term growth and is willing to tolerate a large amount of volatility.

We would expect the growth portfolio in the long run to average 11 percent compounded annually and have the standard deviation of approximately 12.9 percent. This means that in a normal year the portfolio's return would range between –1.9 percent (11 percent minus 12.9 percent) on the low side and 23.9 percent (11 percent minus 12.9 percent) on the high side. This range should cover normal market behavior that will likely occur in 7 out of every 10 years; and as mentioned earlier, 3 out of every 10 years should be expected to be unusual and have returns either below –1.9 percent or above 23.9 percent.

Growth investors should have long-term faith that their portfolios, which are heavily weighted toward individual stocks and stock funds, will perform better than any alternative, although with a larger amount of volatility than more conservative portfolios. The growth investor should have faith that the historical relationship of stocks providing superior returns to bonds or cash equivalents will hold up in the future and that stocks in corporate America will do better than certificate of deposit (CD) and bond alternatives. Please note that individual stocks plus stock mutual funds make sense for growth investors who can take risk, while more conservative investors should stick to stock mutual funds for their stock market exposure.

Our growth allocation has 70 percent of the portfolio in stocks or stock funds and 30 percent of the portfolio in fixed-income funds. The stock fund allocation includes 21 percent allocated to international funds, 38 percent to large cap stocks and funds, and 11 percent to small cap stock funds. The 30 percent allocation to fixed-income funds is divided about equally among international bond funds, high-yield bond funds, and high-quality domestic bond funds, which include government and high-grade corporate bonds.

Please note that some investors are in a position to have even more of their assets allocated to equity funds. This group could include very wealthy investors and families with little need for any dividend income during their lifetime, with the likelihood that they will be passing all of their mutual fund and stock holdings to their children, who will receive a stepped-up basis (estate taxes are discussed in detail in Chapter 10). This would also include investors who have significant fixed-income holdings, which they cannot control through their retirement, and are looking to balance those fixed-income holdings with significant equity holdings. If this or some other reason dictates that you have more than 70 percent of your portfolio in stocks, you should merely reduce the fixed-income proportions shown for our growth investor accordingly and divide the money among the stock categories shown in Table 4.5, including international, in the same proportions that we have used.

Table 4.6 shows the model portfolio for a conservative investor. You

TABLE 4.6 Optimal Portfolio for the Conservative Investor

Fund	*Allocation*
Domestic Stock Funds	
Large Cap	
J. P. Morgan Disciplined Equity	8%
Vanguard Growth and Income	9%
Small Cap	
Tweedy, Browne American	7%
International Stock Funds	
Tweedy, Browne Global	8%
Fixed-Income Funds	
DFA Global Bond	22%
PIMCO Foreign	12%
PIMCO Real Return	12%
PIMCO Total Return	22%

Parameters

Return Target	*Risk Tolerance*	*Risk and Return Ranges*
8.5%	–6% to –12% in a bear market	Normally (70% of the time) 1.5% to 15.5%
		Rarely (25% of the time) –5.5% to +22.5%
		Very rarely (5% of the time) <–5.5% or >22.5%

Note for long-term investors: If you hold this portfolio for at least 10 years, your expected return is still 8.5%, but your range of returns should narrow to from 4.5% to 12.5%.

Source: Yolles Investment Management.

can see that the expected return for the conservative portfolio is 8.5 percent and, since the range of returns is 1.5 percent to 15.5 percent, that the standard deviation is 7 percent. This means that in a normal year the returns for our conservative investor will fall between 1.5 percent (8.5 percent minus 7 percent) and 15.5 percent (8.5 percent plus 7 percent). As mentioned earlier, this normal range of returns should be achieved in 7 out of every 10 years, with 3 out of every 10 years producing unusual returns either less than 1.5 percent or more than 15.5 percent.

You can see that the allocation for our conservative investor focuses very heavily on fixed-income funds, with 68 percent of the portfolio allocated to fixed-income funds and only 32 percent to stock funds.

We hope that this broad framework of asset allocation guidelines for different types of investors is useful to you. For most of you, this asset allocation outline will prove to be the perfect starting point for shaping your retirement portfolio and creating a proper asset allocation. In one sense, the asset allocations that we have provided should be fairly intuitive. More aggressive investors have larger allocations to equity funds and more conservative investors have larger allocations to fixed-income funds.

The portfolio designs we have shown have assumed that a given investor has a tax-deferred portfolio such as an individual retirement account (IRA) or profit sharing account, and we have consciously not used tax-free municipal bonds in any of our optimal allocations. If you are a taxable investor or you have a taxable portfolio, then merely substitute 80 percent of the asset allocation shown for domestic high-quality fixed-income funds with municipal funds. As an example, in Table 4.7, we show an allocation for a taxable moderate-risk investor.

Usually, you should put most of your fixed-income holdings in tax-deferred retirement accounts. However, muni bond yields are so attractive today that they should take precedence for the fixed-income portfolio allocation of high-bracket investors.

TAX-FREE MUNICIPAL BONDS VERSUS STOCK FUNDS

Too often, investors who need income during retirement devote too much of their money to municipal bonds. This is another example where the conventional wisdom is often dead wrong. Investors who purchase municipal bonds almost entirely are ignoring diversification. They are subjecting themselves to an extremely high risk of not keeping up with inflation and they are, in all likelihood, cheating the next generation—namely their heirs. Accountants who encourage their clients to concentrate on tax-free investments put the cart before the horse in focusing

TABLE 4.7 Taxable Moderate-Risk Portfolio

Fund	*Allocation*
Domestic Stock Funds	
Large Cap	
J. P. Morgan Disciplined Tax-Aware	11%
PIMCO Capital Appreciation	14%
Small Cap	
DFA 6–10	5%
Tweedy, Browne American	5%
International Stock Funds	
Artisan International	10%
Tweedy, Browne Global	5%
Fixed-Income Funds	
Individual Muni Bonds	40%
PIMCO Real Return	10%

Source: Yolles Investment Management.

strictly on the tax issue. They should focus on the investment merits of a properly diversified portfolio and the inflation protection that this diversified portfolio will provide.

The evidence is overwhelming that a broadly diversified portfolio works much better, even for income-oriented investors in any tax bracket. Table 4.8 shows the effects of a municipal bond portfolio versus the effects of a more broadly diversified portfolio for investors. Note that the broadly diversified Vanguard Balanced Fund also takes a tax-efficient low turnover approach to investing.

Too often, brokers, bankers, and certified public accountants (CPAs) oversell munis by saying a 5.5 percent muni is equivalent to a 9 percent stock fund. This is a grossly incorrect and misleading comparison. The correct comparison moves in the other direction by showing that a 87

TABLE 4.8 Return 1981–1996

Fund	*Pretax*	*Posttax*
Vanguard Balanced	12.7%	11.1%
Vanguard Municipal	6.4%	6.1%

percent tax-efficient, balanced fund averages 12.7 percent and produces a 11.1 percent after-tax return (12.7 percent × 87 percent) compared to the 6.1 percent municipal.

Conclusion

It is clear that the broadly diversified investor wins on all fronts. The investor wins with safety, diversification, and, ultimately, superior cash flow. It's a slam dunk. No contest. In Table 4.8, the Vanguard Balanced Fund produced an 11.1 percent after-tax return compared to a 6.1 percent for the Vanguard Municipal Fund.

HOW TO CHOOSE SPECIFIC STOCKS AND MUTUAL FUNDS

We've now talked about how to determine your optimal portfolio, and we've even shown you some examples of optimal portfolios for different risk levels. Your next question, and the next area that we'd like to explore, is how to determine which stocks, mutual funds, and bonds you should invest in in order to execute your best strategy. We recommend the approach described earlier that is taken by institutional investors. A shorthand way we've described this approach is the "all-star team plus quantitative approach."

Many investors we see know that they need diversification in their portfolios but don't know how to go about selecting a good portfolio of no-load mutual funds. This is another area where conventional wisdom often does a great disservice to investors.

Much of the conventional wisdom recommends selecting your mutual funds based on a financial magazine's top 50 performers list. This rearview mirror approach is probably the worst way to invest in mutual funds. Generally, the funds that have done particularly well last year, or over the past couple of years, are not likely to do well in the future. Table 4.9 shows how dismally the top funds have performed in subsequent years. Table 4.10 shows that only one of the top funds of recent decades retained that status the next decade.

We see well-meaning investors attempting to diversify a mutual fund portfolio who often end up buying funds that are substantially similar. For example, in August 1997 we received a call from a woman who was attempting to diversify her small IRA portfolio in which she held two mutual funds. The two funds that she held, Twentieth Century Ultra and Seligman Communications, were virtually the same; they both focused almost entirely on

TABLE 4.9 Where Did They Rank in the Years That Followed?

	1982	*1983*	*1984*	*1985*	*1986*	*1987*	*1988*	*1989*
Oppenheimer Target	1	136	606	216	779	1,160	25	768
Loomis Sayles Capital	2	318	529	22	75	71	1,386	788
New England Growth Fund	3	418	506	90	228	59	1,368	594
United Services Gold Shares	4	563	639	767	47	26	1,463	2
Strategic Investments	5	573	645	768	74	40	1,464	3
IDS Progressive	6	265	465	164	725	562	199	1,304
Fidelity Sel. Technology	7	3	602	740	931	1,123	1,402	847
Putnam Vista	8	329	554	250	188	307	480	414
Mass Financial Emerging Growth	9	50	514	360	549	1,099	477	412
Fidelity Precious Metals	10	599	632	769	55	17	1,461	175
Oppenheimer Regency		1	624	159	785	541	712	618
Java Growth		2	Fund may not exist					
Fidelity Sel. Technology		3	602	740	931	1,123	1,402	847
Alliance Technology		4	601	341	596	55	1,378	1,528
First Inv. Discovery		5	643	684	939	1,167	374	—
Strong Investment		6	175	582	265	755	846	1,281
Lindner Dividend		7	34	635	160	944	104	1,211
Royce Value Fund		8	382	287	821	694	110	894
Legg Mason Value Trust		9	84	155	745	1,036	83	679
Strong Total Return		10	159	376	176	237	435	1,585
Prudential-Bache Util.			1	117	59	1,066	132	95
Vanguard High Yield Stock			2	207	138	971	76	1,582
Copley Fund			3	387	271	1,057	225	795
SLH Amer. Telecomm			4	122	95	654	341	10
Franklin Utilities			5	462	108	994	678	408
Energy & Utility Shares			6	No trace of fund				
Fidelity Sel. Utilities			7	157	104	1,083	381	67
Fidelity Qualified Dvd.			8	368	154	952	790	704
Windsor Fund			9	268	169	623	52	941
Sequoia Fund			10	274	508	197	713	317
Fidelity Overseas				1	7	60	931	848
Fidelity OTC				2	636	592	128	234
New England Zenith Capital Growth				3	1	4	1,434	221
PaineWebber Atlas				4	44	333	219	678

TABLE 4.9 *Continued*

	1982	*1983*	*1984*	*1985*	*1986*	*1987*	*1988*	*1989*
Putnam Intl. Equities				5	48	165	867	474
Alliance International				6	33	988	23	257
BT International				7	14	749	400	767
Hemisphere Fund				8		Does not exist		
Fidelity Sel. Health				9	136	780	881	42
GAM International				10	26	103	376	582
New England Zenith Cap. Growth					1	4	1,434	221
Merrill Lynch Pacific					2	87	38	870
Nomura Pacific Basin					3	20	387	574
Tyndall-Newport Far East					4	527	542	1,296
Financial Post-Pacific					5	138	119	680
GT Pacific Growth Fund					6	465	118	20
Fidelity Overseas					7	60	931	848
BBX International					8	435	666	1,020
T. Rowe Price Int'l.					9	176	305	508
GT Japan Growth					10	6	161	4
Oppenheimer Ninety-Ten						1	1,418	1,548
DFA Japan Small Company						2	27	73
Oppenheimer Gld & SP Min.						3	919	127
New England Zenith Cap. Growth						4	1,434	221
IDS Precious Metals						5	1,447	806
GT Japan Growth						6	161	4
DFA United Kingdom Sm. Co.						7	847	1,662
Franklin Gold Fund						8	1,438	46
Van Eck Gold/Resources						9	1,459	739
Colonial Adv. Str. Gold						10	1,440	1,108
Kaufmann Fund							1	22
Integrated Eq. Agg. Growth						2	544	
Parnassus Fund							3	1,583
Columbia Special							4	183
Calvert Ariel Growth							5	446
Gabelli Growth							6	60
Fidelity Sel. Retail							7	258
Fidelity Sel. Trans.							8	296
Harbor Intern. Fund							9	98

TABLE 4.10 Top 15 Funds (Load and No-Load) for Different 10-Year Periods

Rank 1968–1977	Rank 1978–1987	Rank 1988–1997
1. Templeton Growth	1. Fidelity Magellan	1. Fidelity Sel.: Home Finance
2. Mutual Shares	2. Loomis Sayles Capital Dev.	2. Kaufmann Fund
3. Amer. Insur. & Indust.	3. Twentieth Century Growth	3. Fidelity Sel.: Electronics
4. International Investors	4. International Investors	4. Fidelity Sel.: Regional Bank
5. Financial Ind. Inc.	5. Merrill Lynch Pacific	5. J. Hancock Regional Bank/B
6. Paramount Mutual	6. Twentieth Century Select	6. Seligman Commun. & Info./A
7. Security Investment	7. New England Growth	7. INVESCO Strat.: Financl Svc.
8. Kemper Total Return	8. Weingarten Equity	8. T. Rowe Price Science & Tech
9. OTC Fund	9. Franklin Gold	9. INVESCO Strat.: Technology
10. Founders Special	10. Phoenix Stock	10. Fidelity Adv. Eq. Grth./Inst.
11. Pioneer	11. Phoenix Growth	11. INVESCO Strat.: Health Sci.
12. Windsor	12. Lindner	12. Fidelity Sel.: Health Care
13. Decatur Income	13. Amer. Capital Pace	13. Vista: Growth & Income/A
14. Investors Selective	14. Quasar Associates	14. AIM: Aggressive Growth
15. Eaton & Howard Incm.	15. AMEV Growth	15. Spectra Fund

technology stocks. Ironically, the woman felt that she needed to purchase a third fund to achieve better diversification, and the fund she was considering was the T. Rowe Price Science and Technology Fund, which would have merely duplicated her two existing holdings.

Assembling a well-diversified portfolio is very similar to assembling an all-star baseball team. On an all-star baseball team, you want the best players at different positions, including pitchers, catchers, infielders, outfielders, and hitters—each with a different specialty. Similarly, in a properly diversified portfolio, you want the best experts in different areas. Many factors go into choosing a well-managed mutual fund. (See Table 4.11) We will describe in detail what factors to look for.

Figure 4.3 shows the 104 mutual funds that meet most of our tests.

We have used screens or tests to create what we call our short list of the highest-quality mutual funds on a risk-adjusted basis that have succeeded in the real world. We will highlight one fund from this list and give our rationale for choosing this fund—The PIMCO Capital Appreciation Fund.

It's worth reminding you that the Securities and Exchange Commission (SEC) requires the magic words "past performance does not guarantee *future* performance" after all mutual fund performance advertising for a good reason, and you should do some of your own research in conjunction with your qualified adviser.

HOW ONE MUTUAL FUND PUTS TOGETHER A QUANTITATIVE STOCK PORTFOLIO

Most of the financial press covers mutual fund investing as if it were a horse race or a beauty contest. They look for short-term top performers. We try to dig deeper, much deeper, in the same fashion that analysts dig deeper when buying common stocks.

I believe that investors should look for mutual funds that apply sound investment principles. Look for funds that use a thorough approach to the way that they buy and sell stocks and in the way that they assemble a diversified portfolio of stocks with representation in all or most industry groups. We call this an industry-neutral portfolio. Here is what you should look for:

- ✔ Does the fund invest in growing companies that can sustain their growth?
- ✔ Does the fund advocate buying these companies at prices that make sense?
- ✔ Does the fund have written buy and sell criteria that are unemotional?
- ✔ Does the fund diversify by investing in a variety of industries?
- ✔ Does the fund have a reasonable expense ratio and low turnover?
- ✔ Does the fund and/or the fund's manager have a good track record?

TABLE 4.11 Quantitative and Qualitative Factors for Choosing a Good No-Load Mutual Fund

Quantitative Factors	*Qualitative Factors*
1. Look for a manager with a solid track record in both good and bad market conditions either in private accounts or in a public mutual fund.	1. Look for a manager who owns part of the management company so there is little chance that the manager will leave to go to another mutual fund organization.
2. Look for a fund that has produced superior risk-adjusted returns relative to its fund peers.	2. Look for a single manager as opposed to management by committee.
3. The manager and/or fund must have a track record covering at least one significant bear market.	3. Look for an eclectic manager who puts a little different spin on the ball than the Wall Street herd. In the investment profession, you have to be a maverick.
4. The no-load fund being examined should have an expense ratio below the average expense ratio for similar funds.	4. Look for a manager who "eats one's own cooking" by having a significant financial stake in his or her own mutual fund.
5. Portfolio turnover should be less than 50 percent, which means that the fund should hold its average stock for at least two years.	5. Look for a manager and research team with superior academic and professional credentials including the Chartered Financial Analyst designation (CFA), master's degrees or PhDs in finance or business administration from top-notch universities, as well as significant experience at first-rate investment or research organizations.
6. The manager who established the track record for the fund, or for the private accounts in question, should be managing the no-load fund at the time of review.	6. Your manager should have a written discipline for when he or she sells stocks.
7. The manager should buy stocks selling at a 20 percent discount on a price-to-book-value basis relative to the price-to-book-value ratio of the Standard & Poor's 500 Index.	
8. The manager should buy stocks with price-to-earnings ratios that are at least at a 10 percent discount to the price-to-earnings ratio of the S&P 500 Index.	

TABLE 4.11 *Continued*

Special Factors for Bond Funds

1. For domestic bond funds, look for an expense ratio of less than 0.5 percent.
2. Look for a domestic bond manager who has unconventional expertise for adding value in an area outside of garden-variety government bonds.
3. Look for a bond manager with the flexibility and expertise to move between different segments of the bond market as values present themselves.
4. Look for significant assets under management in excess of several billion dollars, because advantages in bond investing accrue with the largest firms, including economies of scale.

One fund that meets all of these criteria is the PIMCO Capital Appreciation Fund (800-927-4648), which is managed by Cadence Capital Management of Boston. The vital statistics of the fund are as follows:

Price-earnings ratio (P/E)	30.3
One-year earnings growth	31.2%
Five-year earnings growth	21.4%
Average market cap	$76 billion

The fund's 10 largest stock holdings:

1. Cisco
2. GE
3. Wal-Mart
4. Oracle
5. Home Depot
6. Royal Dutch
7. Immunex
8. Motorola
9. Applied Materials
10. Teradyne

Primary Rank: ▲ Fund Name
Secondary Rank:

Fund Name	Expense Ratio	3 Yr Earn Gr	P/E Ratio	P/B Ratio	Mstar Risk 3 Yr	Sharpe Ratio	Mstar Avg Rating	Annual Return 1999
1 AARP U.S. Stock Index	0.50	17.6	32.9	8.6	0.90	0.94	4.0	22.01
2 Aetna Index Plus Large Cap A	0.95	19.4	35.7	10.2	0.90	1.00	4.0	24.28
3 Aetna Index Plus Large Cap I	0.70	19.4	35.7	10.2	0.89	1.02	4.0	24.51
4 Alliance Growth Adv	0.88	20.0	35.8	6.8	0.97	0.91	4.0	25.96
5 Alliance Utility Income Adv	1.20	20.2	17.4	4.1	0.56	1.31	4.4	18.41
6 Ark Blue Chip Equity A	1.07	23.3	35.6	9.4	0.85	1.06	4.0	26.15
7 Ark Blue Chip Equity Instl	0.91	23.3	35.6	9.4	0.85	1.07	4.5	26.26
8 Ark Mid-Cap Equity Instl	1.06	21.6	36.4	9.5	1.05	0.92	4.0	23.70
9 Artisan International Intl	1.38	-	42.0	8.6	0.71	1.11	5.0	81.29
10 Barclays Glbl Inv LP 2030	0.95	16.7	35.1	8.9	0.73	0.93	3.8	15.77
11 BlackRock Index Equity Instl	0.18	16.6	34.5	8.7	0.92	0.90	4.4	20.62
12 BT Instl Equity 500 Index	0.10	19.7	33.9	9.2	0.92	0.91	4.8	20.75
13 BT Investment Equity 500 Idx	0.25	19.7	33.9	9.2	0.92	0.90	4.8	20.59
14 California Invmt S&P 500 Idx	0.20	20.3	35.3	9.9	0.92	0.91	4.4	21.02
15 Capital World Growth & Inc	0.78	-	33.3	5.4	0.52	0.91	4.8	27.30
16 DFA U.S. Large Company	0.15	20.4	35.4	9.8	0.92	0.91	4.0	20.81
17 Dreyfus Basic S&P 500 Stock	0.20	20.2	35.4	9.8	0.93	0.90	5.0	20.62
18 Dreyfus Premier Balanced R	1.00	24.9	32.3	9.0	0.48	1.03	4.0	7.55
19 EAI Select Managers Equity	1.15	21.2	33.6	8.6	0.87	1.06	4.0	30.91
20 Enterprise Small Co Value Y	1.30	6.9	22.8	3.5	0.59	0.93	3.9	16.60
21 Excelsior Equity Instl	0.70	18.5	38.8	10.5	0.89	1.02	4.1	31.98
22 Excelsior Value Equity	1.05	21.0	21.9	8.5	0.96	0.93	4.1	34.43
23 Excelsior Value Equity Instl	0.70	21.0	21.9	8.5	0.95	0.95	4.2	34.77
24 Federated Equity-Income F	1.36	15.7	27.9	7.3	0.72	0.91	4.0	17.21
25 Fidelity Adv Grth & Inc A	1.11	21.3	37.8	10.1	0.83	1.09	4.0	25.19
26 Fidelity Adv Grth & Inc Inst	0.75	21.3	37.8	10.1	0.83	1.11	4.0	25.64
27 Fidelity Adv Grth & Inc T	1.30	21.3	37.8	10.1	0.84	1.08	4.0	24.95
28 Fidelity Blue Chip Growth	0.70	21.2	35.5	9.8	0.86	1.08	4.9	24.26
29 Fidelity Freedom 2010	0.08	18.1	29.2	8.5	0.59	1.13	4.0	19.04
30 Fidelity Freedom 2020	0.08	18.1	31.1	8.4	0.70	1.11	4.0	25.31
31 Fidelity Freedom 2030	0.08	18.0	31.6	8.4	0.77	1.08	4.0	28.50
32 Fidelity Magellan	0.60	22.3	35.0	8.9	0.87	1.01	4.7	24.05
33 Fidelity Real Est Hi-Inc	0.89	-	14.1	1.1	0.23	0.96	4.3	7.76
34 Fidelity Spartan 500 Idex	0.19	19.2	33.0	8.8	0.93	0.90	3.9	20.65
35 Fidelity Spartan U.S. Eq Idx	0.18	18.4	32.7	8.4	0.92	0.90	3.8	20.66
36 Fidelity Utilities	0.83	30.9	30.9	6.3	0.54	1.46	3.9	26.75
37 Fifth Third Quality Grth A	1.21	23.9	38.5	10.3	0.79	1.02	3.8	23.55
38 First Funds Growth & Inc I	0.83	14.1	27.4	5.9	0.73	1.02	4.9	22.35
39 First Funds Growth & Inc II	1.14	14.1	27.4	5.9	0.74	1.00	4.6	22.04
40 Fundamental Investors	0.63	9.5	33.7	7.7	0.71	1.00	3.8	24.58
41 Gabelli Asset	1.36	13.7	30.9	4.7	0.69	1.08	4.3	28.49
42 GE Premier Growth Equity A	1.12	18.9	36.1	9.5	0.83	1.18	4.7	35.75
43 GE Premier Growth Equity Y	0.88	18.9	36.1	9.5	0.83	1.18	4.7	36.09

MORNINGSTAR Principia™ Pro for Mutual Funds

FIGURE 4.3 High-quality mutual funds.

Source: Reprinted with permission from Morningstar, Inc.

Primary Rank: ▲ Fund Name
Secondary Rank:

Fund Name	Expense Ratio	3 Yr Earn Gr	P/E Ratio	P/B Ratio	Mstar Risk 3 Yr	Sharpe Ratio	Mstar Avg Rating	Annual Return 1999
44 GMO Tobacco Free Core III	0.48	16.5	31.3	8.3	0.87	0.96	4.8	21.25
45 GMO U.S. Core II	0.55	16.1	30.8	8.2	0.87	0.91	4.3	18.55
46 GMO U.S. Core III	0.48	16.1	30.8	8.2	0.87	0.91	4.4	18.60
47 Guardian Park Avenue A	0.78	26.2	36.1	9.6	0.84	1.14	4.1	30.25
48 Hartford Advisers Y	0.90	18.9	35.9	8.9	0.57	1.04	3.9	12.63
49 Hartford Stock A	1.44	19.3	35.9	9.0	0.84	1.02	4.3	22.32
50 Hartford Stock Y	0.96	19.3	35.9	9.0	0.78	1.11	4.6	22.91
51 Invesco Leisure	1.41	19.2	31.3	6.3	0.72	1.36	4.4	65.59
52 Investment Comp of America	0.55	15.2	32.8	7.9	0.75	0.91	4.0	16.56
53 JP Morgan Inst Disc Eqty	0.45	14.4	28.1	6.9	0.93	0.90	3.5	18.32
54 JP Morgan Tax-Aware U.S. Eq	0.85	18.9	37.1	10.1	0.86	0.98	4.0	18.31
55 Kayne Anderson Intl Rising	1.38	17.7	35.0	9.0	0.55	0.91	4.2	31.06
56 Legg Mason Value Nav	0.73	33.7	32.5	10.4	1.07	0.91	5.0	27.99
57 Lord Abbett Intl A	1.31	-	30.1	7.0	0.63	1.00	4.0	27.26
58 MainStay Inst Asset Inst Svc	1.05	18.8	32.9	8.7	0.58	1.03	4.0	11.53
59 MainStay Inst Indx Eq Inst	0.30	18.8	32.9	8.7	0.92	0.90	4.0	20.83
60 MainStay MAP-Equity I	0.70	19.3	28.1	6.2	0.64	1.05	3.9	12.18
61 Managers Captl Appreciation	1.29	28.8	51.2	18.6	1.12	1.19	4.0	103.02
62 Masters' Select Intl	1.55	-	38.7	8.1	-	-	-	75.01
63 Merrill Lynch Fundmntl GrthA	0.87	20.9	33.2	8.9	0.79	1.35	4.4	36.31
64 Merrill Lynch Fundmntl GrthD	1.11	20.9	33.2	8.9	0.79	1.34	4.0	35.99
65 Merrill Lynch Global Value A	0.90	8.9	29.1	4.1	0.58	0.93	4.0	10.44
66 Merrill Lynch Global Value D	1.15	8.9	29.1	4.1	0.58	0.92	4.0	10.23
67 MFS Massachusetts Inv Grth I	0.49	28.0	37.9	8.9	0.76	1.47	5.0	39.38
68 Nations Equity-Index Prim A	0.35	18.7	32.9	8.6	0.92	0.90	4.9	20.66
69 One Group Equity Index I	0.35	20.2	35.2	9.8	0.92	0.90	4.1	20.54
70 PaineWebber Tactical Alloc Y	0.67	18.7	32.9	8.6	0.87	0.95	4.6	18.82
71 PIMCO Capital Apprec Inst	0.71	16.2	39.8	11.4	0.94	0.96	4.0	22.30
72 Prudential Europe Growth A	1.43	-	39.0	8.8	0.60	0.99	4.5	27.27
73 Prudential Europe Growth Z	1.18	-	39.0	8.8	0.59	1.00	4.5	27.55
74 Prudential Global Growth Z	1.07	14.6	40.0	8.5	0.71	0.96	4.0	48.96
75 Prudential Stock Index Z	0.40	18.7	33.0	8.6	0.92	0.90	4.6	20.50
76 Putnam Europe Growth A	1.23	-	24.8	4.2	0.65	0.91	4.2	23.15
77 Putnam Investors M	1.39	29.7	37.1	9.5	0.97	1.00	4.4	29.58
78 Putnam Investors Y	0.64	29.7	37.1	9.5	0.96	1.03	4.0	30.47
79 Republic International Eqty	1.09	-	35.5	4.7	0.68	1.02	4.3	71.01
80 Schwab 1000 Inv	0.46	21.1	35.0	10.0	0.91	0.92	4.0	21.00
81 SEI Index S&P 500 Index E	0.25	20.3	35.4	9.8	0.92	0.90	3.9	20.82
82 SSgA Growth & Income	1.03	19.0	36.2	10.1	0.90	1.04	4.5	20.87
83 SSgA S&P 500 Index	0.17	19.3	35.4	9.8	0.92	0.90	4.8	20.89
84 T. Rowe Price Blue Chip Grth	0.91	24.0	37.9	10.5	0.86	0.94	5.0	20.00
85 T. Rowe Price European Stock	1.05	-	34.2	6.9	0.57	0.95	3.8	19.70

MORNINGSTAR Principia™ Pro for Mutual Funds

FIGURE 4.3 *Continued*

Primary Rank: ▲ Fund Name
Secondary Rank:

	Fund Name	Expense Ratio	3 Yr Earn Gr	P/E Ratio	P/B Ratio	Mstar Risk 3 Yr	Sharpe Ratio	Mstar Avg Rating	Annual Return 1999
86	Transamerica Prem Index Inv	0.25	18.5	32.7	8.7	0.93	0.90	4.7	20.65
87	UMB Scout WorldWide	0.86	-	33.7	7.4	0.46	1.09	4.8	31.43
88	United Income A	0.89	17.0	31.6	8.4	0.70	1.04	3.9	16.41
89	United Income Y	0.71	17.0	31.6	8.4	0.71	1.05	4.0	16.68
90	USAA S&P 500 Index	0.18	17.8	30.4	8.0	0.91	0.91	4.5	20.67
91	Vanguard Asset Allocation	0.49	20.3	35.3	9.8	0.55	1.05	4.0	5.22
92	Vanguard European Stock Idx	0.29	-	30.0	6.2	0.63	0.93	4.1	16.66
93	Vanguard Health Care	0.36	5.1	32.9	8.5	0.62	1.23	4.8	7.04
94	Vanguard Instl Index	0.06	18.7	33.0	8.6	0.92	0.91	4.1	21.17
95	Vanguard Tax-Mgd Gr&Inc	0.19	20.4	35.4	9.8	0.92	0.91	4.9	21.12
96	Vanguard Tot Stk Mkt Idx	0.20	20.8	34.5	10.3	0.91	0.95	4.0	23.81
97	Victory Growth	1.35	20.4	37.7	10.5	0.93	0.94	4.2	17.90
98	Vintage Balanced	1.28	18.1	31.6	7.6	0.56	1.00	3.9	11.66
99	Waddell & Reed Total Ret Y	1.15	17.4	32.0	8.6	0.68	0.94	3.8	13.00
100	WEBS Index France	1.18	-	39.1	3.6	0.74	0.96	4.8	27.15
101	Weitz Partners Value	1.25	17.5	19.4	2.2	0.65	1.13	4.5	22.02
102	Weitz Value	1.26	17.3	19.6	2.2	0.65	1.09	4.2	20.97
103	Wells Fargo Index I	0.25	20.3	35.4	9.8	0.92	0.90	4.9	20.59
104	Wilmington Large Cap Core I	0.80	21.5	36.3	10.4	0.82	0.99	3.9	22.41

MORNINGSTAR Principia™ Pro for Mutual Funds

FIGURE 4.3 *Continued*

Similar statistics for the S&P 500 Index are as follows:

P/E	27
One-year earnings growth	21%
Five-year earnings growth	17%
Average market cap	$143 billion

Foundations of the Cadence Approach

Cadence Capital Management follows a stock selection process that looks for leading companies in a variety of industries. This is summarized in Cadence's core investment principle, "We believe in investing in growing, profitable companies at prices that make sense." Specific aims are:

- ✔ Improved fundamentals lead to improving stock prices.
- ✔ Avoiding excessive valuations lessens downside risk.
- ✔ Objective buy and sell criteria avoid costly emotional decisions.

Figure 4.4 is a diagram that in a visual fashion summarizes all of the elements of the Cadence approach. For example, Cadence looks for company management that is sustaining and growing revenue, profit margin, and balance sheet trends. Cadence also believes in applying buy/sell decisions consistently across all portfolios. Finding mutual funds that follow sound principles is not easy, but if you follow a sensible and thorough research process, then you will be happy with your results.

YOUR QUANTITATIVE PORTFOLIO FOR THE LONG TERM

By taking the type of quantitative industry-neutral approach that we suggest, you should earn consistent, dependable returns. You may not hit too many home runs, but you will not strike out often, either. This refers to the bulk of most investors' portfolios; we do suggest that it is appropriate for younger and more aggressive investors to allocate perhaps 10 percent or even 20 percent of their portfolios for more aggressive investment vehicles. But again, the lion's share of anyone's serious money should be invested for consistent and dependable returns.

We feel that this is a very appropriate choice of words for all investors. We rarely, if ever, meet investors who are looking to hit home

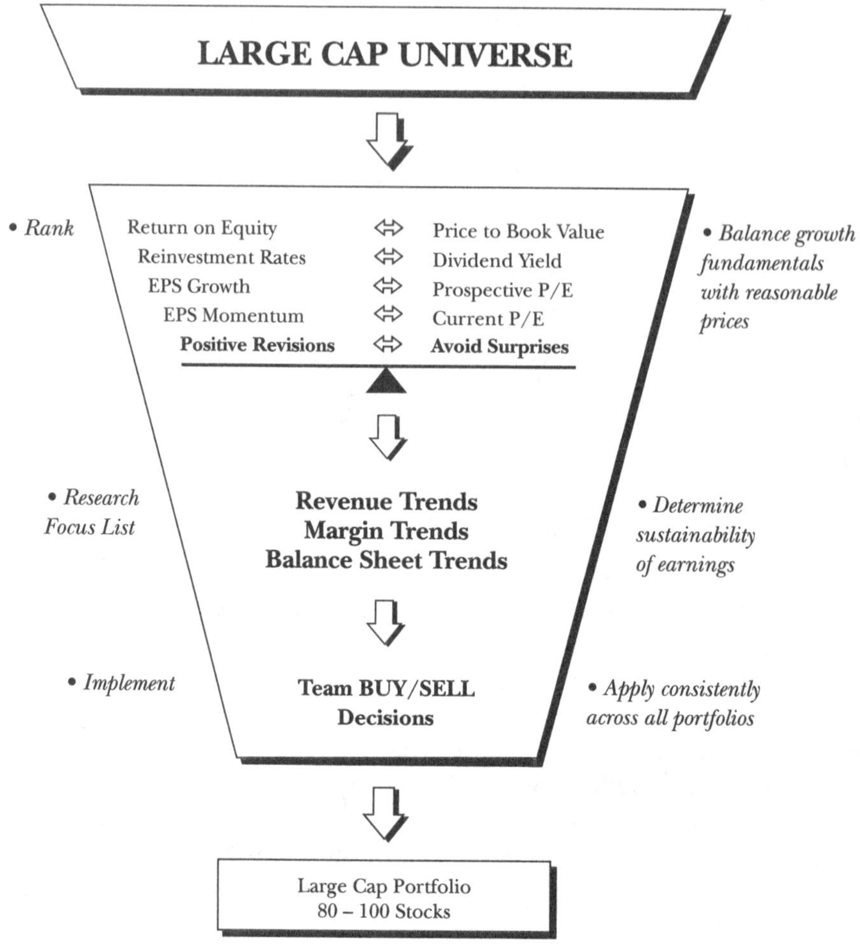

FIGURE 4.4 Cadence investment process.

runs with all of their capital. Rather, we find that most people recognize that they will save a significant amount of capital over their lifetimes, and they are looking for investment advice on preserving and safely growing this capital. They are not looking for spectacular profits, but rather for reliability.

In Figure 4.5, we put all these pieces together and show a sample model portfolio for the moderate-growth investor.

Avoiding risky funds that may have had a period of spectacular performance is often a larger challenge for investors than choosing sensible, consistently well performing funds. As humans, we are all susceptible to

Portfolio Snapshot Report: Client Summary | Page 1 of 1 | Data Updated Through: 02-29-2000

Balanced Model (50/50)

Benchmark: Russ 3000

Portfolio Value
$ 1,000,000.00

Analysis

Composition %

	Portfolio	Bmark
Cash	5.23	0.00
US Stocks	33.65	99.90
Non-US Stocks	16.25	0.10
Bonds	38.11	0.00
Other	6.78	0.00

Current Investment Style

Style

Value	Blend	Growth	
23	23	25	Large Size
29			Medium
			Small

Fixed-Income Investment Style %

Maturity

Short	Interm	Long	
61	27		High Quality
12			Medium
			Low

Sector Weightings

% of Stocks	Portfolio	Bmark
Utilities	0.80	3.30
Energy	3.81	4.20
Financials	18.85	17.40
Industrial Cyclicals	11.50	10.70
Consumer Durables	2.92	2.60
Consumer Staples	7.31	7.20
Services	22.25	17.20
Retail	4.72	6.10
Health	8.14	12.00
Technology	19.82	19.30
Not Available	0.00	0.00

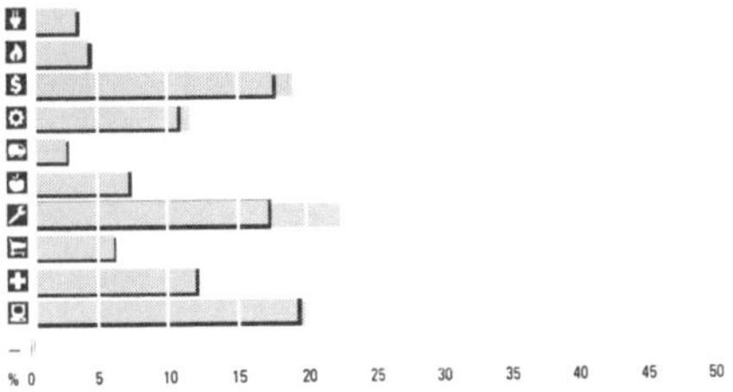

Regional Exposure

% of Assets	Portfolio	Bmark
U.S. & Canada	28.65	99.90
Europe	17.37	0.10
Japan	3.77	0.00
Latin America	0.75	0.00
Pacific Rim	1.84	0.00
Other	1.47	0.00
Not Available	0.53	0.00

Performance

Trailing Returns [1]

Returns Through 02-29-2000	3 Mo	1 Yr	3 Yr	5 Yr	10 Yr
Pre-Tax Portfolio Return	6.72	19.31	16.83	17.84	14.01
+/- Benchmark Return	3.56	1.76	-5.15	-6.77	-3.99

Best/Worst Time Periods [1]

	3 Months	Return%	1 Year	Return%	3 Years	Return%
Best	05-97/07-97	11.43	08-96/07-97	26.89	04-95/03-98	19.88
Worst	06-98/08-98	-5.88	02-94/01-95	-3.40	01-92/12-94	7.10

Morningstar Statistics [2]

	3 Yr	5 Yr	10 Yr		
Mstar Return	0.72	0.74	0.71	Est Portfolio Rating	★★★★
Mstar Risk	0.42	0.38	0.37	Rating Class	Domestic Stock

Investment Activity Graph [1]

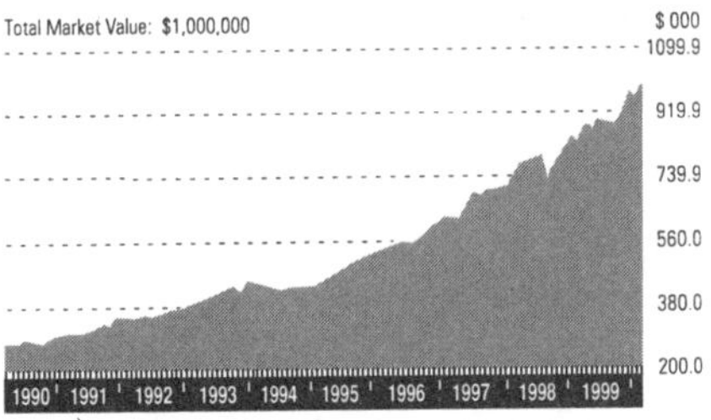

Holdings

Top 5 holdings out of 10	Type	Holding Value $	% Assets
DFA Global Fixed-Income	MF	170000.00	17.00
PIMCO Total Return Instl	MF	170000.00	17.00
JP Morgan Inst Disc Eqty	MF	120000.00	12.00
PIMCO Capital Apprec Inst	MF	120000.00	12.00
Artisan International Intl	MF	90000.00	9.00

Next 5 holdings out of 10	Type	Holding Value $	% Assets
Tweedy, Browne American Val	MF	80000.00	8.00
PIMCO Real Return Bond Instl	MF	80000.00	8.00
Tweedy, Browne Global Value	MF	80000.00	8.00
Hotchkis & Wiley Low Dur	MF	50000.00	5.00
Managers Captl Appreciation	MF	40000.00	4.00

[1] Portfolio and benchmark returns are calculated by asset-weighting the monthly returns of the underlying holdings and thus reflect the pretax results an investor would have achieved by rebalancing the portfolio on a monthly basis. These same returns are used to calculate all returns-based statistics. Returns for individual holdings are trailing total returns.

[2] This star rating is not an official rating. It is estimated by comparing portfolio returns that are not adjusted for transaction costs to load-adjusted open-end mutual-fund returns. Portfolios are compared against one of three rating classes: domestic stock, international stock, or taxable bond. Municipal-bond fund returns are not adjusted to a tax-equivalent basis.

MORNINGSTAR® Principia® Pro

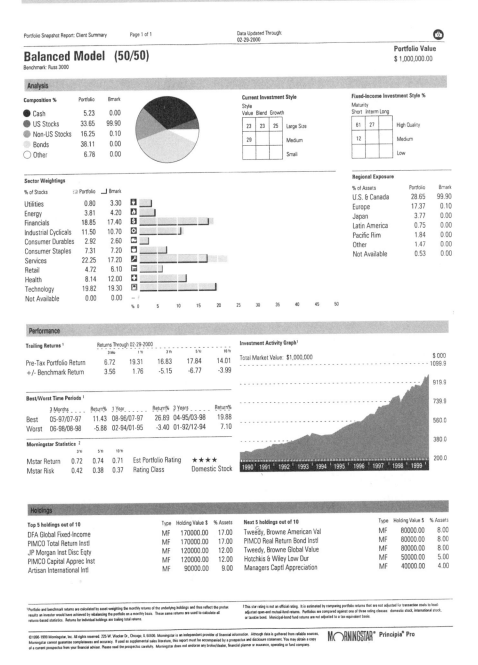

FIGURE 4.5 Balanced model portfolio developer report.

Source: Reprinted with permission from Morningstar, Inc.

being seduced by the promise of extraordinarily high returns. If you keep in mind our tests or what professionals call screens for dependable funds, you will be able to steer clear of these ephemeral hot performers. They are like the meteorites that shine brightly for a brief period and then burn out. Certainly during your retirement you cannot afford to have investments that burn out; rather, you need consistent performers that will endure over many market cycles. Table 4.12 shows a number of these

TABLE 4.12 Hot-Performing Funds: "Where Are They Now?" Go-Go Funds of the 1960s—Mutual Fund Performance 1970–1974

Name	*Value of $10,000*	*Percent Change 1970–1974*
Eaton and Howard Growth	$4,949	–50.5
Enterprise	4,714	–52.9
Fidelity Trend	5,887	–41.1
Growth Fund of America	4,990	–50.1
Hartwell Growth	4,694	–53.1
Manhattan	2,888	–71.1
Mates Investment	1,961	–80.4
Mathers	5,895	–41.1
Midamerica Mutual	5,063	–49.4
Nicholas Fund	5,634	–43.7
Pennsylvania Mutual	1,312	–86.9
Pilgrim Fund	5,299	–47.0
Price New Horizons	5,890	–41.1
Scudder Stevens Common Stock	6,048	–39.5
Selected American Shares	6,024	–39.8
State Farm Growth	5,899	–41.0
20th Century Growth	6,353	–36.5
Value Line Fund	4,930	–50.7
Vanguard	2,224	–77.8
Average for All Funds	$5,641	–43.6
DJIA Price Change	7,694	–23.1
S&P 500 Price Change	7,445	–25.5

Source: Standard & Poor's and *Growth Stock Outlook*. Reprinted by permission of Standard & Poor's, a division of The McGraw-Hill Companies.

hot-performing funds from the 1960s that burned out, never to be heard from again. Many of today's hot Internet funds and stocks could similarly flame out in a bear market.

Once your portfolio is established and you have implemented the asset allocation that fits both your temperament as well as your investment and income needs, you should plan on holding all of your no-load funds for the long run. Only an extraordinary event should prompt you to sell one of your funds. The following are some of the instances in which you should sell:

1. A change of managers occurs where the new manager is inexperienced.
2. A fund either raises its expense ratio or initiates an onerous 12b-1 fee program.
3. A fund superior to a fund you own becomes available for the first time on a no-load basis.
4. A change in your personal circumstances requires a greater allocation to equity funds or fixed-income funds.
5. A fund consistently underperforms in its peer group for an extended period of time with no reasonable explanation.
6. A fund becomes too large and unwieldy to execute its management style effectively.

Mutual Fund Fees

Since no one works for free in the investment industry, your challenge is to avoid excessive costs.

- ✔ All mutual funds charge an annual management fee of approximately 0.5 percent for bond funds, 1 percent for domestic stock funds, and 1.4 percent for international stock funds.
- ✔ Avoid any fund that charges either a front- or back-end load. These are used to pay the stockbroker, financial planner, or insurance agent who sells a given fund. You are better off buying no-load funds either directly or through a discount brokerage firm like Charles Schwab and Company.
- ✔ A 12b-1 is an extra fee of approximately 0.25 percent charged by some funds for distribution and marketing. In general, avoid a fund with a 12b-1 fee unless that fund's overall expense ratio is low.

REBALANCING, REVIEWING, AND MONITORING YOUR PORTFOLIO

Thus far we have discussed several elements of the portfolio management process. We have explained the critical need for you to focus on your objectives. Ask yourself what you're trying to accomplish with your portfolio. Do you need a consistent monthly income? Are you funding charitable obligations? Are you supporting your children or an elderly parent? Are you living off a pension and planning on passing this money on to your heirs?

We also have examined issues relating to your personal risk tolerance. The timing of your retirement will influence both the amount of risk you can take and the amount of your portfolio that you can afford to have allocated to equity funds. These funds should produce a higher return but are more volatile.

We've also shown that risk tolerance is a function of your temperament. You may be able financially to take significant risk but, if you're not comfortable doing so, you can give up several points on the return side for more stability. It's worth repeating that the investment markets can be dangerous, and you need to know your comfort tolerance.

We have discussed how to establish your proper asset allocation, your optimal portfolio design, and the specifics of selecting no-load funds. Now it is time for us to move on to the process of managing your portfolio on an ongoing basis and reviewing your individual holdings and personal circumstances that might require a change in your portfolio.

In consultation with your investment adviser, you should have a written investment policy statement that specifies the objectives for your portfolio and the review process. (A sample investment policy is shown in Figure 4.6). This policy statement should set out your broad asset allocation guidelines. At least quarterly or semiannually, you should review your portfolio with your adviser to make sure that your portfolio has stayed within these guidelines.

For example, there will be periods when either the domestic equity funds or the international equity funds in your portfolio dramatically increase in value. The equity funds would then represent a larger portion of your entire portfolio than your initial allocation dictated. All things being equal, you may want to consider what is called rebalancing your portfolio at this time by reducing some of your holdings in these appreciated funds and adding to segments of your portfolio that have not appreciated. To a certain extent this is counterintuitive; however, history shows us that this discipline will in fact force you to buy low and sell high. Normally, you do not want to rebalance too often because this activity may create a taxable

Portfolio Policies for Mr. & Mrs. John Q. Smith
March 2000

Objectives

Return Requirements: Growth to stay ahead of inflation. At retirement, a *growing* cash flow to maintain the Smiths' purchasing power.

Risk Tolerance: Average relative to other investors.

Constraints

Time Horizon: At least a 30-year joint life expectancy.

Liquidity: Only for emergencies and $200,000 per year for the Smiths to live on in today's dollars.

Regulations: IRA withdrawal rules.

Taxes: Retirement accounts are tax-deferred.

Unique Needs: Mr. Smith wants to keep between $300,000 and $1 million in his outside brokerage account for speculative purposes.

Strategy and Asset Allocation

An allocation that emphasizes growth investments and broad portfolio diversification will best meet the Smiths' objectives. The portfolio should have 38 to 48 percent in domestic equities; 18 to 22 percent in international funds; 20 to 28 percent in domestic bond funds; 6 to 10 percent in international bonds; and 3 to 7 percent in short-term bond funds. This mix hedges inflation and deflation risk.

A long-term investment policy is critical to prevent unwise revisions based on short-term pressures. A broad portfolio can best provide diversification, low cost, professional management, and liquidity.

FIGURE 4.6 Moderate policy.

event. Only when your portfolio gets significantly out of balance—by, say, 10 percent—should you rebalance.

LESSONS FROM INVESTMENT HISTORY

To invest successfully over your lifetime, you must be a student of investment history. The philosopher George Santayana counseled that "those who cannot remember the past are condemned to repeat it." Similarly, investors who do not study financial market history are condemned to repeat the mistakes that other investors have made.

Investment history teaches us three things:

1. The twin demons of fear and greed have cost people fortunes over the centuries.
2. If something appears too good to be true, it is.
3. Over the past 200 years, *in the long run*, relative and nominal investment returns from stocks, bonds, and cash equivalents have been remarkably stable and remarkably predictable.

History is replete with examples of either fear and/or greed leading investors astray. We will start with examples of greed because they're more dramatic.

In his 1841 classic, *Extraordinary Popular Delusions and The Madness of Crowds*, Charles Mackay identified many investment bubbles where people allowed greed to lead them to pay ridiculous prices for certain types of investments. Needless to say, like the story about the emperor with no clothes, these investments turned out to be "barely" worth anything at all.

We will recount a few of these bubbles by way of illustration, so that you can see the warning signs of investment types and investment attitudes to avoid. In Holland in the early 1600s there was a tulip bulb mania, with Dutch citizens paying ridiculously inflated prices for particularly colorful tulip bulbs, all because speculators whipped up a frenzy among tulip buyers. In the end, this tulip mania subsided and tulip bulbs that at one point sold for double the price of a house ultimately sold for the equivalent of the price of a glass of water.

A recent mania in the United States was the "Nifty 50" stock bubble in the 1960s and early 1970s. At that time, investors bid up the price of the 50 most popular blue chip stocks in the United States to ridiculous levels. Some of these stocks were bid up to 50, 100, or even 150 times their annual earnings. The average stock sells for about 14 times earnings, and history has shown that it is rarely a good idea to pay more than 20 times earnings for a given stock.

The final bubble we will look at occurred in Japan in the 1980s, when Japan was called "Japan, Inc.," and its markets were thought to be invincible. Suffice it to say that today both common stocks and real estate in Japan are selling for less than half the price that similar assets sold for 10 years ago. No investment is invincible.

These three situations show that greed has led investors to try to earn unrealistic returns. We're seeing similar features in the current Internet stock mania. Now let's look at the opposite circumstances, where investors have been overly fearful and exercised excessive caution.

Perhaps the most painful example of investor overcaution occurred in the post–World War II era, when many invested almost exclusively in government and corporate bonds. This strategy, in many cases, was an overreaction to the losses from the Crash of 1929 and the Great Depression and the conventional wisdom at the time that common stock investments were excessively risky. Unfortunately, as shown in Figure 4.7, the 1944 government bond investor had lost 90 percent of the bonds' purchasing power 26 years later because of rapidly increasing inflation in the 1950s and 1960s.

In our practice, we witnessed similar symptoms of overcaution in the mid-1980s and again after the market crash of 1987. Some investors limited themselves to fixed-income vehicles like certificates of deposit, which had very low returns that did not keep up with inflation on an after-tax basis. More importantly, they cheated themselves out of the only investment that historically has outpaced inflation—namely, sensible common stock or stock fund investments.

COMMON INVESTMENT MISTAKES TO AVOID

If we analyze all of the mistakes we've seen investors make over the years, these errors can be grouped into three general categories:

1. Allowing emotions to overrule intellect.
2. Getting caught up in an investment fad.
3. Not getting professional, objective advice.

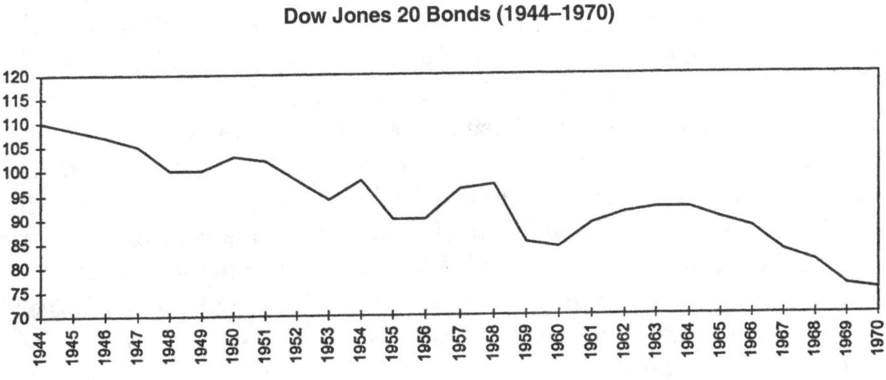

FIGURE 4.7 Bond returns from 1944 to 1970.

As an example, in our era much of the conventional wisdom dictates that *index funds* are the investment vehicle of choice. A stock or bond index merely tracks and measures the value and performance of a given group of stocks or bonds. For example, the popular Standard & Poor's 500 Index tracks the performance of the 500 largest companies in the United States. These are blue chip companies like Merck, Johnson & Johnson, Microsoft, General Electric, and General Motors. Similarly, the Dow Jones Industrial Average tracks the performance of 30 large industrial companies, and the Lehman Government Bond Index tracks the performance of government bonds. An index fund replicates the performance and specific holdings of an index.

index fund tracks and measures the value and performance of a given group of stocks and/or bonds.

Unfortunately, the people who are now getting caught up in the index fad are much more likely to get burned than the people who invested in index funds 15 years ago when such funds were at bargain prices before they reached fad status. Large-cap index funds did particularly well from 1982 through 1997. However, funds based on the Standard & Poor's 500 and Dow Jones Industrial Average did poorly from 1966 to 1982, when both of these popular indexes did not appreciate at all. The bulk of mutual funds did substantially better than these indexes during that 16-year flat period, as did the majority of private money managers.

Similarly, many who invested in real estate limited partnerships in the late 1980s lost a great deal of money. These partnerships were popular during the late 1970s and early 1980s when hard assets such as real estate did well and there were plentiful tax benefits. However, the 1986 Tax Reform Act eliminated many benefits from these partnerships and signaled the beginning of a long bear market in real estate.

Rather than trying to anticipate each and every investment fad (this timing is commonly referred to as "the loser's game"), investors are much better off drafting and sticking to a sensible long-term investment policy. Earlier in this chapter we provided a format for drafting your own investment policy and setting out a plan of action for achieving your goals. Reviewing this policy can remind you of your objectives during times when your emotions may lead you astray because of short-term concerns that cause greed and/or fear.

ASSEMBLING YOUR OWN STOCK PORTFOLIO

If you decide to invest in some individual common stocks to supplement your mutual fund holdings, you should keep in mind the industry-neutral approach followed by many institutional investors. Institutional investors succeed where individuals fail by making sure that they at least have broad representation in many industry groups. The industry breakdown for the Russell 3000 Index was shown earlier in this chapter. Table 4.13, which was developed from Morningstar data by Craig Israelsen, PhD, shows that a diversified portfolio such as a mutual fund is less likely to have losses than a few individual stock picks.

Once you have begun your research as to which stocks to include in your portfolio, you should take several factors into account: Always ask the question when examining a stock, "Do I know something about this stock that Wall Street does not know?" If the answer to this question is no, then you have to consider that you may be playing a game that you cannot win. If you apply a number of consistent and logical criteria to selecting a portfolio of stocks that are not widely followed on Wall Street, you may have more success in the long run. Here are a few criteria to keep in mind:

- ✔ Look for companies that are the dominant competitor in their industries.
- ✔ Look for companies that should be able to sustain growth in their sales and earnings over the next 5 to 10 years.
- ✔ Look for well-managed companies that are improving their profit margins on a consistent basis.

TABLE 4.13 Stocks Are Riskier Than a Diversified Portfolio like a Mutual Fund (12/31/99)

	1 Year	*3 Years*	*5 Years*	*10 Years*
Percentage of individual stocks with losses	54%	46%	31%	22%
Percentage of stock mutual funds with losses	13%	2.5%	0.4%	0.4%

Data source: Morningstar, Inc.

There are three web sites that can give you good financial information on a number of stocks:

1. www.morningstar.com provides comprehensive data on most stocks.
2. www.investorama.com is the broadest clearinghouse of all information about stock research.
3. www.better-investing.org, the web site for the National Association of Investors Corporation (NAIC), provides good information on both stock investing and how to start an investment club.

For many of you, starting an investment club might be the best way to learn about stock investing. This has the additional advantage of allowing you to pool money with your family and friends to buy more stocks and achieve better diversification quicker. We believe that most people can learn better in groups that help reinforce and clarify the learning process.

The best place to start is by contacting the National Association of Investors Corporation (NAIC) at 711 West Thirteen Mile Road, Madison Heights, Michigan 48071; 248-583-6242; www.better-investing.org.

While investing in common stocks is gratifying and provides a good learning experience, until you develop a high degree of confidence in your own stock picking you should probably initially focus on no-load mutual funds, which allow you to access the best talent in the world to make your stock and bond selections. Also, even if some of your initial stock choices are profitable, do not make the mistake of being overconfident in your own stock picking ability. Honesty is important, and it's very likely that these initial successes may have been a function of either luck or a bull market period. Do not leave investing to emotion or hot tips from relatives. And do not overestimate your own ability.

Part Two

Life Stage Financial Strategies

Chapter 5

Investing Is Different Once You're Retired: Withdrawing Income from Your Portfolio

In this chapter, you will learn:

- ✔ A sensible and sustainable way safely to begin withdrawing your dividends, and even some principal, from your portfolio.
- ✔ How your withdrawal rates should change during the three stages of retirement.
- ✔ How open communication with both your spouse and professional advisers is the best approach to meet your joint investment goals and sleep at night.
- ✔ How working with economic and market facts will produce better results than emotional investment decision making.

Often, the most important source of cash flow or income during retirement will come from your capital, or what we like to call your investment portfolio. Did you hear the one about the chicken farmer and the egg farmer? This useful analogy comes to us from James Garland, CFA, of The Jeffrey Company, a prominent investment counseling firm. We encourage our retiree clients to act like egg farmers instead of chicken farmers. Chicken farmers are really speculating on the price of their chickens. They raise chickens and frequently sell them in the open market every week hoping, or speculating, that the price of those chickens will go up. This behavior is similar to that of investors who are buying and selling stocks or mutual funds frequently (what we would call trading), speculating that the price of those stocks or funds will go up on a daily or weekly basis.

BE LIKE AN EGG FARMER OR A LANDLORD

At our firm, we much prefer the mentality of the egg farmer. The egg farmers nurture their chickens to consistently and regularly produce eggs, which the farmers' families either consume or sell in the market. They plan on living off those eggs for the course of their lifetimes. This is similar to investors who live off their dividends or cash flow from their mutual funds, common stocks, or bonds without having too much concern for short-term fluctuations in the price of those mutual funds, common stocks, or bonds. Likewise, the egg farmer is not concerned with short-term fluctuations in the price of chickens as long as the egg production is consistent.

Another analogy we use with our clients is to encourage them to act like landlords instead of land speculators. The land speculator buys and sells property hoping the price of the property will go up for a profit when sold. The landlord owns high-quality property for the long run, and is concerned with the monthly income from the rental property and the fact that over time the rent goes up to outpace the rate of inflation. Don't act like a land speculator or a chicken farmer.

While we are examining using your capital or your investment portfolio as a source of cash flow during retirement, it is critical that we emphasize that there are other crucial aspects of your financial planning, such as medical or family emergencies that could deplete your capital base. It is absolutely essential that you have adequate health insurance, disability insurance, and long-term care insurance.

You can have the perfect investment portfolio set up to produce a nice level of cash flow, but if you are not protected against medical or other emergencies, then all of your diligent and intelligent investment planning is worthless. Protection from catastrophe or emergency is critical. Chapters 8 and 10 deal with insurance and health issues in detail.

In Chapter 6 we will look at your nonportfolio retirement sources of cash flow including work, wages, Social Security, and pensions. We will now explore what is probably your primary source of cash flow during retirement: your investment portfolio, or what we call your capital base. We will also look at how much sustainable cash flow your capital base will produce.

YOUR CAPITAL: THE PRIMARY SOURCE OF INCOME—MAKING IT LAST DURING RETIREMENT

Take a careful look at the size of your capital base that you will be able to use during retirement. Younger people should estimate how much they will need to save to accumulate a sufficient capital base. This is your so-called nest egg, which will fund the bulk of your retirement expenses. Nearly all clients who come into our office for advice concerning retirement planning face the same dilemma: how to enjoy their money effectively without depleting their capital too soon.

Most people have a hard time wrestling with this issue, and often do not spend as much or enjoy themselves as much as they could during retirement. We often see people leaving larger estates to their children and their heirs than they would anticipate.

Since the investment markets are unpredictable, there is no surefire formula for dictating the size of the withdrawals you will comfortably be able to make from your portfolio during retirement. However, later in this chapter we will show you how much you can be withdrawing prudently each year from a broadly diversified retirement portfolio. At this point, however, we merely want to identify your capital base or sources of capital that you have working for you during retirement. In addition, we'll present some parameters that will give you an idea of what to expect as a minimum to withdraw from your capital without depleting your capital too soon.

Using Figure 5.1, you should take an inventory of your sources of retirement capital, including items in your portfolio, IRA, Keogh, pension and retirement plan, personal trust, and custodial accounts. In addition, as previously mentioned, you should consider other investments for your inventory such as real property, land contracts, and income-producing property, as well as hidden capital in your home that can be unlocked with a mortgage. As a rule of thumb we have provided Table 5.1, which gives you an idea of how much you can be withdrawing from your capital during different stages of your retirement.

Later, we explain in detail how to derive these sustainable portfolio withdrawal rates for retirees. By way of disclaimer, let us say that every investment environment is different; flexibility is required to be successful. Here we are giving broad guidelines that we believe will prove useful during the current environment.

Assets	*In Your Name or Trust*	*In Your Spouse's Name or Trust*	*In Joint Names*
Your home (fair market value)	$______	$______	$______
Other real estate	______	______	______
Bank accounts	______	______	______
Other savings accounts	______	______	______
Stocks, bonds, and mutual funds	______	______	______
Life insurance (face value)	______	______	______
Business partnership interests	______	______	______
Retirement plan accounts:			
IRA	______	______	______
Keogh	______	______	______
SEP	______	______	______
Other—such as 401(k) or profit-sharing plans)	______	______	______
Personal property (replacement value of jewelry, autos, household furnishings, etc.)	______	______	______
Annuities, trusts, or other assets	______	______	______
Collectibles (market value of fine art, precious metals, etc.)	______	______	______
Total assets	$______	$______	$______
Liabilities			
Mortgages	$______	$______	$______
Life insurance loans	______	______	______
Other loans or debts			
....	______	______	______
Total liabilities	$______	$______	$______
Net estate (assets less liabilities)	$______	$______	$______

FIGURE 5.1 Asset inventory.

THREE STAGES OF RETIREMENT

We also look at past historical periods to show how our guidelines would have held up under different conditions—periods of economic growth, economic recession, or economic inflation. As Table 5.1 shows, during what we call the early retirement years (ages 55 to 70), we feel that a 5 percent withdrawal rate is prudent and sustainable. During the midretirement years, ages 70 to 80, we feel that a 6 percent portfolio withdrawal rate is prudent and sustainable. During the later retirement years, ages 80 and over, we feel that an 8 percent or greater withdrawal rate can be sustainable, given your personal circumstances.

Table 5.1 suggests guidelines for withdrawing money from your investment portfolio. From ages 55 to 70, your portfolio must at least keep up with inflation and taxes. If your portfolio's total return (appreciation plus yield) is 10 percent, then you should withdraw only 5 percent annually (see Table 5.1). After paying taxes, you will still see your portfolio grow fast enough to keep pace with inflation. For example, if you retire or semiretire at age 55 with a portfolio worth $500,000, then you can withdraw $2,083 per month and still see your portfolio grow in 10 years to $728,683 if you earn 10 percent annually (8 percent after taxes).

Later, we will review different retirement scenarios and work through

TABLE 5.1 Sustainable Portfolio Withdrawal Rates for Retirees

	Ages 55–69	*Ages 70–79*	*Ages 80 and Up*
Primary objective	Save for retirement	Some income but also growth	A steady or growing income
Time horizon	30+ years	20+ years	10+ years
Projected return from a diversified portfolio	10%	9%	8%
Tax effect	(2%)	(2%)	(2%)
Inflation effect	(3%)	(3%)	(3%)
Real return	5%	4%	3%
Age adjustment	—	2%	5%
Sustainable portfolio withdrawal rate	5%	6%	8%

Source: Yolles Investment Management.

some case studies. But, as a starting point, these sustainable withdrawal rates are broad guidelines. If, for example, you and your spouse are both 63 years old, have a $600,000 capital base to retire on, and are receiving $18,000 a year from Social Security as your only other source of retirement income, then, using our guidelines, a 5 percent withdrawal on a $600,000 portfolio would provide $30,000 of additional retirement income to supplement your Social Security. This means that you could live comfortably on a $48,000 income ($30,000 plus $18,000) during your retirement. Now we explain how you should recalibrate your annual portfolio withdrawal rate every five years and how you can recalibrate your portfolio withdrawal as you both age.

In our example, if you need substantially less than $48,000 a year to live, then you have no worries whatsoever, and your portfolio can comfortably sustain your standard of living. If you need close to $48,000 a year, then you will have to watch your capital closely and reevaluate your situation annually with the help of a competent financial adviser.

The following case studies may help illuminate different retirement issues that you are facing or retirement strategies that you are considering.

Case Study—Scott and Suzanne

Our first case study involves Scott and Suzanne. Scott worked as an attorney for 40 years. His law practice literally dried up, partly because eight years ago he thought that he could retire, so he stopped practicing law for two years. But then he realized that he needed more capital to fund his retirement. However, his return to the practice of law has not been very lucrative at all.

Scott and Suzanne always enjoyed a rather high standard of living. Scott has become very concerned about whether their capital will last during their retirement; Suzanne is interested in enjoying retirement and continuing their lavish lifestyle, even hoping that they can buy a winter retirement home in Phoenix. Scott has developed insomnia, worrying about whether their lifestyle will be possible during retirement. In addition, most of Scott and Suzanne's close friends are financially better off than they are and are enjoying a very comfortable retirement lifestyle. For Scott and Suzanne, emotional issues and pressures have been mounting, making it difficult to be comfortable participating in activities, vacation, travel, dining, and cultural events that they have always enjoyed with their friends, but now question whether they can afford.

In December of 1994, Scott and Suzanne came to Yolles Investment Management, Inc., with these and other issues. Here's a look at how we helped the couple gain a feeling of control, organization, comfort, and safety in their financial lives.

In 1994, Scott turned 66 and Suzanne was 63. They had accumulated a portfolio including IRA accounts of $584,000. They were receiving $1,000 per month, which would continue through 1999, on a land contract from a piece of real estate that Scott had invested in. Their Social Security provided $16,700 a year. They owned their own home free and clear of mortgage debt and estimated that their home was worth $200,000, with very little appreciation potential. Scott was in very good health. Suzanne was also in good health although she did have diabetes. Their investment portfolio consisted entirely of cash and domestic common stocks and bonds that Scott had either selected himself or bought with the help of various brokers over the years. The portfolio was a hodgepodge, with little appropriate diversification or coordination between Scott's holdings and different industry groups.

Since the bulk of Scott and Suzanne's portfolio was in retirement accounts, we were able to immediately help them restructure their portfolio into a broadly diversified portfolio of no-load mutual funds. Not only were we able to substantially reduce the risk in Scott and Suzanne's portfolio as measured by standard deviation (which we were able to cut in half), but we were also able to improve the expected return through broader diversification including international funds. Even their portfolio's dividend return improved by $1,057 per month:

Scott and Suzanne's Monthly Distributions, 1994

Before	*After*
Stocks and bonds: $2,165 per month	Mutual fund portfolio: $3,222 per month

Case Study—Alan and Faye versus Bert and Iris

Another case study involves the tale of two retired couples, Alan and Faye and their counterparts Bert and Iris. By 1985, each family had accumulated $200,000 for retirement. Alan dominated his household and, against Faye's better judgment, insisted that all of their retirement funds be put in certificates of deposit, which at that time were yielding 8 percent.

In contrast, Bert and Iris sought and received professional investment counsel from an adviser who advocated broadly diversifying their portfolio. It should be noted that both couples were 65 years old in 1985, in good health, and had just retired. In the late 1980s and into the early and mid-1990s, Alan and Faye continued to roll over their CDs, and as inflation declined, the rate of interest on their CDs also declined sharply. Rates reached a trough in 1990 when the couple received only

4.5 percent on their CDs and they had to start dipping into their principal. (See Table 5.2.)

Bert and Iris, with their broadly diversified portfolio, thrived and were able to increase the amounts of their withdrawals while the value of their principal grew smartly over time. From 1985 to 1998, the difference in their standards of living and quality of life during their retirement has been nothing short of startling. Bert and Iris' broadly diversified portfolio has averaged 13 percent a year and has grown in size to more than $600,000 over the 13-year period. They have made a grand total of $270,000 in withdrawals from their portfolio over that 13-year period and have felt comfortable enough to make gifts to their grandchildren and also to two grown children who entered low-paying professions.

Alan and Faye have been forced to tap into their principal. Their portfolio size has declined steadily to about $117,000. If it wasn't for their son-in-law, who is a successful film director, the prospects for a disastrous retirement and complete depletion of their capital by the time they are in their early eighties would be a very real threat.

TABLE 5.2 Alan and Faye versus Bert and Iris

	Alan and Faye		*Bert and Iris*	
	Principal	*Withdrawals*	*Principal*	*Withdrawals*
1985	$200,000.00		$200,000.00	
1986	216,000.00		226,000.00	
1987	233,280.00		255,380.00	
1988	251,942.40		288,579.40	
1989	272,097.79		326,094.72	
1990	253,981.70	29,000.00	368,487.04	
1991	236,140.97	28,000.00	416,390.35	
1992	217,586.61	28,000.00	470,521.10	
1993	198,290.08	28,000.00	462,788.84	68,900.00
1994	178,221.68	28,000.00	522,951.39	
1995	157,350.55	28,000.00	509,835.07	81,100.00
1996	135,644.57	28,000.00	576,113.63	
1997	113,070.35	28,000.00	531,008.40	120,000.00
1998	117,593.16		600,039.49	
Totals	$117,593.16	$225,000.00	$600,039.49	$270,000.00

INVESTING DURING RETIREMENT—AN OVERVIEW

This section will provide a general overview of investment concepts, attitudes, and planning; we will answer the following eight questions:

1. What type of investment portfolio can produce a growing cash flow that stays ahead of inflation?
2. Are aggressive funds good investments for retirees?
3. What is low-dispersion investing and why is this such a critical investment concept?
4. What is a reasonable and sustainable annual portfolio withdrawal rate for a retiree?
5. Are certificates of deposit (CDs) the safest way to invest during retirement?
6. If you have had good success with aggressive mutual funds or stocks, then why should you change to a lower-volatility approach during retirement?
7. Why should you have a thorough financial checkup every year, and what should this checkup entail?
8. How much should you give to your children and grandchildren during retirement?

As mentioned earlier, we counsel our clients and all retirement investors to act more like landlords than land speculators. The beauty of the successful landlord is that he or she receives a steady cash flow every month, and generally that cash flow increases at more than the rate of inflation. In fact, many savvy parents and grandparents have started investing in real estate in college towns for their children or grandchildren. Their kids have a place to live, and the parents can collect rent from other students once their kids graduate and vacate the property.

INVEST TO BEAT INFLATION

We encourage retiree investors to adopt a similar attitude with their no-load stock mutual funds or high-quality common stock holdings, because stocks and stock mutual funds, along with real estate, are the only investments to beat inflation in the long run. Your attitude should be that, as long as your dividends are secure and gradually increasing over time, fluctuations in your principal are normal and expected. As long as the quality of your investments is high, fluctuations should not cause you undue worry. Since you are not a speculator and you're not dipping into your principal, you should not be concerned with short-term fluctuations in your portfolio value but, rather, with the consistency of your cash flow or dividend stream.

Retired investors most often fail by succumbing to either fear or greed. If you succumb to fear, you are likely to put too much of your portfolio in bonds or bond funds and barely keep up with inflation. If you succumb to greed, you will speculate on earning excess returns and unwittingly put your principal at risk. We want to present evidence that will encourage you to be a long-term investor, rather than give in to greed by speculating on one extreme, or fear by just buying bonds on the other extreme (we call these extremes lending or saving your money instead of investing). Too often retirees focus too much on income and miss out on the growth that stocks provide.

Let's take this opportunity to summarize the investment world.

There are three things that you can do with your money: speculate, save, or invest. Speculation is for gamblers, and we refuse to devote more than one sentence of this book to the topic. Savers put their money in bank certificates of deposit or Treasury bills, both of which barely keep up with inflation; this is an inadequate approach for all but the wealthiest retirees. This book focuses on the third alternative: investing. Investing is not gambling but rather ownership. When you buy a share of stock in McDonald's, you are an owner, and your success or failure will be tied to the economic success or failure of McDonald's.

In the long run, the stock price of McDonald's, and any company, moves in direct proportion to the financial success of the company. As Figure 5.2 illustrates, the stock price of McDonald's over the past 33 years has moved in unison with the company's underlying earnings and dividends.

Figure 5.2 shows that while the earnings growth of McDonald's has been remarkably stable, its stock price, in the short run, has been much more volatile in reaction to world, economic, and market events. But in the long run, stock price and company earnings always move in unison. This economic fact should make sense to you; if not, please reread the last few paragraphs—the concept is that critical.

Investing is not gambling. It's the essence of capitalism: Investors provide the liquidity for corporations like McDonald's to grow and hire more people and improve productivity. Everyone benefits. Investing—in stocks, mutual funds, or real estate—is the best way to stay ahead of inflation in the long run *if you can stick with your investment program*. The question then becomes, how can you stick with your program?

As mentioned earlier, adopting an attitude like a long-term landlord is paramount to becoming a successful investor. Stick with high-quality mutual funds or stocks through market ups and downs, just like land-

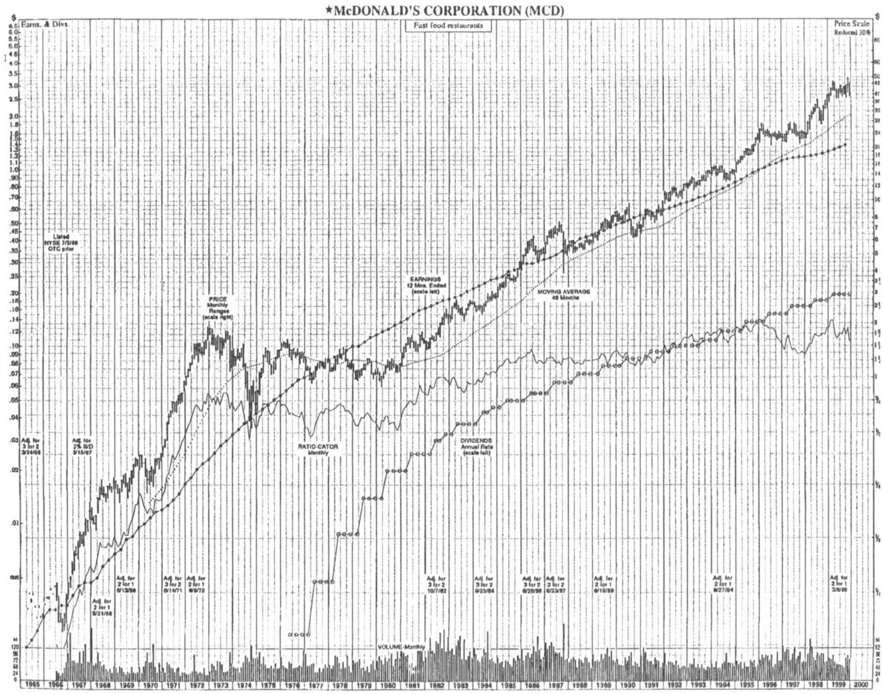

FIGURE 5.2 McDonald's stock analysis.
Source: Chart courtesy of Securities Research Company, 400 Talcott Avenue, Watertown, MA 02472.

lords hold on to properties through the real estate market's ups and downs. And, as shown by history, you will be rewarded.

There is a saying that "knowledge is power" (Francis Bacon, 1597). A study of the stock market from 1926 to 1999 should provide you with this necessary faith in the superior long-term characteristics of high-quality stock and mutual fund investments to ride out market ups and downs. The next section clearly illustrates that you can earn the superior long-term stock market returns by adopting a reasonably safe balanced approach.

AGGRESSIVE INVESTING CAN BE HAZARDOUS TO YOUR WEALTH

No matter how wealthy they are, retirees and preretirees are perpetually worried about whether their money will last.

At Yolles Investment Management, Inc., we have developed a study of sustainable withdrawal rates for retirees. Our professionals found that most retirees are concerned with how much they can withdraw from their portfolios without depleting their principal. They generally rely on an IRA rollover account and their personal savings to supplement their Social Security during retirement. Some are fortunate enough to have lifetime pensions through their employers. Our clients will often say, "We just need $80,000 a year from our investments to supplement our annual $18,000 from Social Security. Then we can maintain our living standard, including taxes." This experience led us to research different types of retirement portfolios and to develop guidelines for retirees.

Most investment professionals agree that the old conventional wisdom of retirees focusing on fixed-income instruments and certificates of deposit has been dispelled. There's now overwhelming research evidence that fixed-income-only portfolios don't work because of two factors: inflation and the fact that people are living longer and spending up to 30 years in retirement or semiretirement.

With this in mind, the question then becomes what type of balanced portfolio works best for retirees. As Table 5.3 shows, a volatile portfolio like a *Standard & Poor's 500 Index fund* will not accommodate a large withdrawal rate. An index fund replicates the performance of a given group of stocks and/or bonds. In this case, 500 of the largest industrial companies in the United States, including General Electric, General Motors, Microsoft, Intel, IBM, and Citicorp, are represented. It is a myth that S&P Index funds are conservative. Any index will have as little or as much volatility as the stocks or bonds in the index. Although blue chip stocks make up the S&P 500 Index, in many cases these stocks fluctuate more than other mutual funds.

Standard & Poor's 500 Index fund an index fund that contains 500 of the largest industrial companies in the United States.

Even though returns on the S&P 500 Index fund averaged about 10.8 percent annually between 1965 and 1996, the Index fund would have accommodated only a 7 percent annual withdrawal rate. Table 5.3 shows that a 7.2 percent withdrawal rate would have depleted this S&P 500 Index portfolio by 1994. Large down years in 1966, 1974, and 1977 were particularly detrimental to the S&P Index portfolio relative to a more stable balanced portfolio. We use the S&P 500 Index as an example of a volatile portfolio,

TABLE 5.3 Retirement Withdrawal Program: Growth of a $100,000 Investment

Year	*Annual Withdrawals*	*S&P 500 Index Portfolio*	*Balanced Portfolio*[1]
1965	$0	$100,000	$100,000
1966	7,200	82,965	89,154
1967	7,200	95,126	106,348
1968	7,200	97,854	124,883
1969	7,200	82,700	101,515
1970	7,200	77,830	89,487
1971	7,200	81,331	100,086
1972	7,200	88,853	104,806
1973	7,200	69,026	82,042
1974	7,200	44,500	61,801
1975	7,200	53,410	72,127
1976	7,200	58,338	84,217
1977	7,200	46,832	82,047
1978	7,200	42,378	82,458
1979	7,200	42,374	93,205
1980	7,200	47,610	110,476
1981	7,200	38,141	104,480
1982	7,200	37,616	121,621
1983	7,200	38,488	144,439
1984	7,200	33,153	134,542
1985	7,200	35,416	168,177
1986	7,200	34,562	190,848
1987	7,200	29,943	188,314
1988	7,200	27,219	213,475
1989	7,200	27,801	255,227
1990	7,200	19,608	224,101
1991	7,200	17,576	292,273
1992	7,200	11,286	309,809
1993	7,200	4,914	364,980
1994	7,200	0[2]	352,856
1995	7,200	—	437,420
1996	5,400	—	514,293
Totals	$221,400	$0	$514,293
Average index return		10.77%	10.78%

[1]Lipper Averages as follows: Equity Income, 17%; Fixed Income, 30%; Global, 17%; High Yield, 25%; Small Company, 11%.
[2]Portfolio depleted by September 30, 1994.
Source: Wiesenberger, Thomson Financial.

but keep in mind there are many investments that are substantially more volatile than the S&P and would prove our point dramatically.

Table 5.3 shows that a balanced or blended portfolio worked out much better for retirees, even though this balanced portfolio also averaged 10.8 percent return between 1965 and 1996. The greater stability in volatile years such as 1966, 1974, and 1977 allowed this blended portfolio to easily accommodate a 7.2 percent withdrawal rate and, in fact, grow from $100,000 to $514,293 by 1996. In fact, the blended portfolio would have accommodated an 8.8 percent withdrawal rate.

The technical term *dispersion* describes the stability or lack of stability in a given portfolio. Dispersion is the degree of scatter of returns around a given average return. For example, in Table 5.3, both the S&P 500 Index and the balanced portfolio averaged approximately 10.8 percent; however, the balanced portfolio had a lower dispersion, with a best return of 34 percent and a worst return of –16 percent, while the S&P 500's range was 37 percent to –26 percent. All but the wealthiest retirees should take a low-dispersion investment approach.

> **dispersion** degree to which a return in any single year is likely to vary from the average annual return.

THE STORY OF BILL AND LIBBY

The volatile nature of the S&P portfolio, coupled with negative returns in the 1966, 1974, and 1977—the early years for a 1965 retiree—led the professionals at Yolles Investment Management, Inc., to develop the hypothetical story of Bill and his "backward" sister Libby to illustrate the random nature of a volatile retirement approach. Table 5.4 shows that Bill's retirement fund was wiped out due to poor returns in the early years, while "backward" Libby's portfolio, which earned identical returns but in reverse order, thrived because bad returns didn't occur until the late years.

A Volatile Retirement Portfolio Leaves Too Much to Chance

The identical rates of return, but in a different order, can make the difference between a comfortable retirement and a completely depleted retirement portfolio. Table 5.4 shows that if a retiree's portfolio is faced with large losses during the early years of retirement (Bill's portfolio), the port-

TABLE 5.4 Bill and Libby: $100,000 Retirement Portfolio with a 7.2 Percent Annual Withdrawal

Year	*Bill's Return*[1]	*Bill's Portfolio*	*Same $ Annual Withdrawal*	*Libby's Portfolio*	*Libby's Return*[1]
0	—	$100,000	$0	$100,000	—
1	30%	126,000	7,200	140,000	40%
2	−10	107,000	7,200	136,000	3
3	−33	71,000	7,200	145,000	11
4	14	73,000	7,200	159,000	14
5	−5	63,000	7,200	178,000	16
6	−14	48,000	7,200	199,000	15
7	23	52,000	7,200	228,000	17
8	11	50,000	7,200	320,000	37
9	4	45,000	7,200	300,000	−4
10	6	40,000	7,200	330,000	12
11	14	39,000	7,200	372,000	14
12	12	36,000	7,200	388,000	6
13	−4	27,000	7,200	396,000	4
14	37	31,000	7,200	434,000	11
15	17	28,000	7,200	538,000	23
16	15	25,000	7,200	460,000	−14
17	16	22,000	7,200	431,000	−5
18	14	18,000	7,200	487,000	14
19	11	12,000	7,200	342,000	−33
20	3	5,000	7,200	303,000	−10
21	40	0	7,200	399,077	30
Summary	8.22%	$0	$151,200	$399,077	8.22%

[1]Annual return without withdrawals.

Source: Yolles Investment Management.

folio will never recover. We often use this illustration to provide the conclusion that a balanced approach to retirement, which eliminates large fluctuations, is probably best.

DIVERSIFY YOUR PORTFOLIO FOR STABILITY

As you can see from the prior examples, a broadly diversified portfolio that has a great deal of stability and little dispersion is a much sounder approach for retirees than an aggressive S&P 500 Index or other high-dispersion strategy.

A broadly diversified portfolio is also a much sounder approach than a fixed-income-only strategy. Recall the earlier information about how bonds and cash investments are clearly inferior to equity investments and broadly diversified portfolios that include international investments.

Your broadly diversified investment strategy should be part of your well-coordinated financial plan. The best way to make sure that all parts of your financial life are properly balanced is to go through an annual review checkup with your independent financial adviser. Steps for your financial checkup are highlighted next.

YOUR FINANCIAL REVIEW CHECKUP

Like your yearly physical with your doctor, your annual review with your financial adviser should make sure that all aspects of your financial life are functioning in an effective and complementary fashion. At least all of the following should be checked:

- ✔ *Cash flow.* Are your monthly and annual spending needs being met?
- ✔ *Inflation protection.* Do you have enough growth investments to cover future inflationary increases in your cost of living?
- ✔ *Overall diversification.* Have you minimized your dispersion of returns to secure the stable cash flow that you need?
- ✔ *Your comfort level.* Do you understand all aspects of your retirement plan?
- ✔ *Tax and estate plan.* Have you had an efficient plan created?
- ✔ *Insurance protection.* Do you have enough insurance to protect you in case of needed extensive medical care or a long-term nursing home stay?

RETIREMENT INVESTING CASE STUDIES

Irene, the 77-Year-Old Retiree

Irene came to us in 1990 with $400,000 entirely in Treasury bills and certificates of deposit. At that time, Treasury bills were yielding approximately 5.5 percent and Irene was not spending all of the interest her portfolio produced because she was extremely frugal. Our professionals analyzed her portfolio and took a careful look at her current and future cash flow needs. We also took a detailed look at all of her finances in order to make sure that her affairs were arranged to accomplish her financial objectives, including making provisions for her two children and her grandchild.

We found several glaring weaknesses in Irene's overall financial strategy, including a severe lack of inflation protection. As illustrated in Table 5.5, we were able to assemble and manage a broadly diversified portfolio of no-load mutual funds that fit within Irene's tolerance for risk. The table shows, over time, how diversification significantly improved her cash flow from dividends, particularly as her principal grew. Education became a key part in helping her understand the features and nature of each investment market. Any investor owes it to herself or himself to know what is and isn't possible for a given set of objectives. We've found that these illustrations and graphs are excellent communication tools to help any investor understand what to expect under different market conditions. Once we were able to help Irene understand the benefit of conservative diversified no-load investing, she felt comfortable implementing the investment program.

With any investment program, you will gain more confidence over time as you see how your portfolio behaves in both good and bad market conditions. We feel it is crucial for you, ideally in conjunction with your seasoned independent adviser, to review alternative investment programs and scenarios in both present and past market conditions. We will cover this in detail in the next chapter.

As shown in Table 5.5, through September 1997, Irene's portfolio had grown to $626,672 and her annual yield is $42,300. Alternatively, the annual yield from her T-bill–CD portfolio would have been $21,191 and her portfolio would have been worth only $427,065. Over time, as this illustration shows, the equity and fixed-income markets work to outpace inflation.

Any investor must have a long-term horizon outlook and be willing to weather market ups and downs. Irene was fortunate that her investment horizon encompassed wonderful years for the markets. But the validity of a broadly diversified strategy has also been tested and proven successful during adverse market conditions.

There were other elements of her financial picture that also needed immediate attention. We referred Irene to a competent tax attorney who was able to create some trusts and update her will. Irene wanted to accomplish three objectives: To make provisions for her asset distributions to her two grown sons, such as restricting how the assets would be passed to her younger son, who was less responsible and having marital difficulties. Having long-term care insurance to prevent her assets from being depleted if at some point she required extended nursing-home care or at-home care. (We referred her to both an independent fee-for-service insurance consultant

TABLE 5.5 Case Study: Irene—An Investment Makeover

	Before (T-bill–CD Only)		*After (Diversified)*	
Year	*Principal*	*Annual Withdrawal*	*Principal*	*Annual Withdrawal*
1990	$400,000	$14,712	$400,000	$14,712
1991	408,906	14,712	429,282	14,712
1992	408,541	14,712	436,009	14,712
1993	406,299	14,712	478,696	14,712
1994	409,363	14,712	458,131	14,712
1995	417,959	14,712	512,556	14,712
1996	424,331	14,712	563,492	14,712
1997	427,065	14,712	626,672	14,712
Current annual yield	$21,191		$42,300	
Dividend yield	4.95%		6.75%	

and AARP to investigate low-cost alternatives in the long-term care area.) To provide money to Irene's only granddaughter, Elaine, at appropriate ages to fund Elaine's college education a separate trust was drafted.

The Nervous Dentist: Applying Investment Therapy

A successful dentist was referred to us in November 1987 immediately after seeing his portfolio shrink from $1.2 million to $800,000 in the market crash of October 1987. He was 55 years old and in good health (at least before the crash of 1987). Worried about his investments, he was seriously considering putting all of his money in certificates of deposit and Treasury bills for the rest of his life. But he knew that the interest from these would not support his standard of living. Although not extravagant, he felt he would require $120,000 per year. We estimated that the dentist needed to accumulate $2 million in order to supplement the money he would receive from Social Security at retirement. If he averaged 10 percent a year (the historical return on an equity portfolio), he would have accumulated the necessary $2 million within nine years, by age 64.

Fortunately, the tail winds provided by the great bull market of the 1980s allowed our dentist—even with a conservative portfolio allocation of 55 percent in stock funds and 45 percent in bond funds—to average 14 percent a year and reach his retirement goal by age 62.

Any experienced investment adviser has to be a bit of an investment therapist in order to help clients feel reasonably comfortable with the capital markets so that they can enjoy the long-term returns that the markets provide. This is often much easier in hindsight than during the real-world events when market declines can be terrifying, even to ordinarily calm people. We were able to help our dentist through market ups and downs and provide enough stability and information so that he was able to stick with his long-term strategy and not react emotionally to normal market volatility.

In fact, the performance of the dentist's portfolio was so successful that we had to help him get appropriate tax counsel regarding potential excise and estate taxes if his overall portfolio, and more specifically his retirement plan portfolio, grew too large at too early an age. These tax issues are detailed in Chapter 10. Suffice to say that our dentist was thrilled to have these solvable tax problems in exchange for the real danger of having an underfunded retirement that he faced after the market crash of 1987 and, more importantly, because of his own fears of investments of any type.

The Spendthrift Pediatrician and His Frugal Wife: Finding a Comfortable Middle Ground

In the movie *Hello Dolly,* Barbra Streisand stars as Dolly Levi, an eccentric, lovable woman with expensive taste. By movie's end, she has successfully bewildered, courted, and ultimately married Horace Vandergelder, played by Walter Matthau. Vandergelder is an extremely frugal man who, by the end of the film, is coaxed by Dolly into spreading his money around "like manure."

A similar husband-and-wife team came into our office in 1990, but this time the roles were reversed. At age 70, a pediatrician was much more a spendthrift than his 57-year-old wife, who was concerned about making their money last and enjoying their ultimate retirement. The wife worked with her husband in his medical practice.

The husband wanted to make gifts to his children and grandchildren while he was still young enough to enjoy seeing them using these gifts. The wife's desire was to make sure that she and her husband would have a secure retirement. We presented them with illustrations and detailed spread sheets that tracked different investment scenarios in both favorable (Table 5.6) and unfavorable (Table 5.7) investment climates. Through this education and changes we made to the couple's portfolio, we were able to help the couple find a happy middle ground.

Ultimately, a strategy was agreed upon whereby no more than 1 percent of their \$800,000 portfolio (\$8,000) would be used for gifts during any calendar year. When the husband reached age 75 this gifting percentage would be increased to 1.5 percent. At 80, it would be 2 percent. Tables 5.6 and 5.7 show how the husband and wife's gifting pattern would work at various ages with two different return assumptions.

TABLE 5.6 A Gift Program for "Dolly and Horace" (9 Percent Annual Return)

Year	*Portfolio Value*	*Annual Withdrawal*	*Gifts*	*Year-Ending Value*	*Horace's Age*
1997	$ 800,000	$40,000	$ 8,000	$ 825,015	70
1998	825,015	40,000	8,000	852,376	71
1999	852,376	40,000	8,000	882,305	72
2000	882,305	40,000	8,000	915,041	73
2001	915,041	40,000	8,000	950,848	74
2002	950,848	40,000	8,000	977,506	75
2003	977,506	45,000	14,263	1,006,665	76
2004	1,066,665	45,000	14,263	1,038,559	77
2005	1,038,559	45,000	14,263	1,073,445	78
2006	1,073,445	45,000	14,263	1,111,604	79
2007	1,111,604	49,768	22,232	1,140,835	80

Note: This table is designed as an illustration of the gifting principle; in the real world, this couple would probably make larger gifts to reduce their taxable estate.

TABLE 5.7 A Gift Program for "Dolly and Horace" (3 percent Annual Return)

Year	*Portfolio Value*	*Annual Withdrawal*	*Gifts*	*Year-Ending Value*	*Horace's Age*
1997	$800,000	$40,000	$8,000	$775,667	70
1998	775,667	40,000	8,000	750,594	71
1999	750,594	40,000	8,000	724,759	72
2000	724,759	40,000	8,000	698,138	73
2001	698,138	40,000	8,000	670,707	74
2002	670,707	40,000	8,000	642,442	75
2003	642,442	40,000	8,000	613,317	76
2004	613,317	40,000	8,000	583,306	77
2005	583,306	40,000	8,000	552,382	78
2006	552,382	40,000	8,000	520,518	79
2007	520,518	40,000	8,000	487,684	80

Note: This example is shown as a contrast to Table 5.6. In real life, if the portfolio averages only 3 percent annually, then adjustments downward would be made to the annual withdrawal and gifting rate.

Chapter 6

When Can You Afford to Retire? The Focus on Withdrawal Planning

This chapter begins with an overview of withdrawal planning starting with the stage that your saving and investing program is at now and determining reasonable goals that take into account all your resources. We then summarize withdrawal planning from an investor's qualified retirement plan accounts. Finally, we review withdrawal options under Social Security retirement income benefit programs. (Other programs administered by the Social Security Administration that deal with health care concerns—a critical area in the planning of most retirees—are covered in Chapter 8.)

WITHDRAWAL PLANNING

Withdrawal planning is a lot like dieting. If you need to diet, you want to find the ideal diet for you, lose the weight, and live your new life as a thinner person. In planning for withdrawals during retirement, you want to determine how much you will need, secure the ideal amount, and live your new life as a financially secure retiree. But in both cases it's not that simple. Frequent monitoring and reassessing are necessary.

The comparison to dieting doesn't stop there. A magazine or newspaper article describes losing weight by reducing carbohydrate intake or increasing the intake of particular foods or utilizing certain food supplements. Financial publications contain articles with charts and tables describing how to determine how much is needed to retire, and this information can appear on web sites. Whether dieting or retiring, either the charts and tables don't emphasize the limitations or, even if they do, the impatient reader brushes them aside because it's human nature to want to get on with it.

Case Study—Tom and Sandy

Tom and Sandy are in their late fifties and need $100,000 a year to live on at year 2000 prices. They will receive $30,000 per year in combined Social Security and pension benefits, leaving $70,000 per year to be provided by their investment portfolio. Since their portfolio totals $660,000, $70,000 would be about 10.6 percent of this sum (10.6 is the factor given in Table 6.1 for 30 years of withdrawals from a portfolio with an annual return of 10 percent). Since an average annual return of 10.7 percent per year for common stocks was achieved during the 1926 to 1996 period, their position would seem secure. This is not so, though, because of the volatility. As Table 5.3 showed, for the 1965 to 1996 period, a $100,000 portfolio with an average annual return of 10.77 percent achieved by matching the S&P 500 Index's performance for that period could not survive an annual withdrawal rate of even 7.2 percent of $100,000 ($7,200

TABLE 6.1 Withdrawal Rates: Amounts That Could Be Withdrawn If Annual Returns Never Fluctuated

DO NOT USE[1] DO NOT USE DO NOT USE

Number of Years for Portfolio to Last	*Annual Return* 6%	7%	8%	9%	10%	11%
10	13.4%	14.0%	14.8%	15.5%	16.2%	16.9%
15	10.2	10.9	11.6	12.3	12.7	13.8
20	8.6	9.3	10.0	10.9	11.7	12.6
25	7.7	8.4	9.3	10.1	11.0	11.8
30	7.2	8.0	8.8	9.5	10.6	11.5

[1]"For illustrative purposes only" is not enough to protect the reader from relying on this type of table to his or her detriment.

per year) because of the volatility of the S&P 500 Index—that is, *steep ups and downs in short-term performance can undermine a withdrawal program, even if the annual average of performance is substantially higher than the withdrawal rate.*

In another table (not reproduced here) Tom and Sandy could look for the average withdrawal rate for 30 years of retirement with a portfolio of 50 percent stocks and 50 percent bonds. With a "50–50" portfolio if average returns are achieved, then 5.9 percent can be withdrawn the first year, or $59,000 on a million-dollar portfolio. Should they trust this approach more than Table 6.1? No, because volatility can undermine this approach as well. Tom and Sandy may assume with these tables that 100 percent certainty is involved in using "average" returns. But it may be 51 percent certainty—if that! Do not put yourself in a position to fail if historical average rates of return are not achieved consistently.

Even valid analytical programs forecasting retirement withdrawal rates that take the rate of certainty (probability) into account should be adjusted and reapplied annually. If returns are even less than a percentage point a year below the historical averages and you or your spouse live several years longer than anticipated, withdrawal rates could be substantially overstated and you or your spouse could run out of funds.

While Tom and Sandy are looking at tables and checking withdrawal rates, they are determining if they have saved enough. As this chapter is being written in August 2000, economists are again warning that Americans like Tom and Sandy are not saving enough. How severe a problem is this nationally? An economist for the Brookings Institution stated recently that the average American worker is behind in his or her savings by about one-half of a year's earnings, and workers in their early sixties, are about two years behind. For most U.S. workers, these figures indicate that this is a manageable problem. Working two years longer before retiring or working part-time for a period to make up the difference are reasonable bailout strategies to the extent that increased saving is not possible.

Funding Your Retirement

A chart to determine where you are at in funding your retirement is Figure 6.1.

"Cash inflow" includes more than income. Those who have rental property are aware that you can have a cash inflow even if your accountant says that you have a loss (sometimes called a paper loss). Example: Jim has three rental properties in Ann Arbor, a college town. At the end of the year he had collected $10,000 more in rent than he had paid out in costs for repairs, maintenance, and property taxes. His accountant said

Source	$ Amount
Pensions	
Social Security	
Work or consulting fees	
Real estate and land contracts	
Other	

FIGURE 6.1 Expected sources of retirement cash inflow other than your investment portfolio.

that since he could depreciate the cost of the properties (not including the cost of the underlying land) over the estimated useful lives of the properties, he had an $11,000 *depreciation* deduction for the year. Subtracting this deduction from the $10,000 Jim had netted results in a $1,000 loss by accounting and tax standards. Still, Jim had the additional $10,000 in his bank account.

depreciation the deduction allowed annually for federal income tax purposes as a reasonable allowance for the exhaustion and wear and tear of property held for the production of income. Rules as to reasonableness and other qualifying requirements are prescribed by laws, rulings, and regulations.

In this chapter, we are evaluating what is a sustainable withdrawal rate for someone who is contemplating retirement. In Chapter 5 there was a discussion on increasing the withdrawal rate as a retiree gets older. That discussion may not seem consistent with this chapter. Actually, utilizing one unchanging withdrawal rate for 20 years or more is not realistic, but is a useful working tool. Showing the shift in withdrawal rates as people age as was done in the earlier chapter is also useful. Withdrawal planning is an exercise in dealing with probabilities, not certainties, and the information sources vary. As a result, continual fine-tuning and adjusting is essential. As noted, being off slightly (by as little as 0.5 percent annually) in an estimated annual withdrawal rate can create a serious condition if ignored for long. Generally, you can deal with this situation by regularly making adjustments, using the best information available at that time.

For most people there will not be one unchanging rate of withdrawal for the balance of their lives. People's spending patterns in their mid-eighties will not be the same as they were in their mid-sixties, but for peace of mind retirees will feel secure with the assurance that based on probabilities, their current spending patterns are affordable if sustained for the balance of their life spans. Prior to 1990 many advisers assumed that the cost of living for a person was 5 percent to 15 percent less after retirement, but generally this does not seem to be so.

A good part of this book is based on learning from experience; that is, what has happened before gives us guidance on what will happen in the future. The theory is usually helpful, but not always so. We do not know what economic conditions will be like during the next 10, 20, 30, or more years that will encompass your retirement years. We also do not know what personal events will happen to you that will affect your financial condition. A basic principle involved in this planning, or in planning in any field where the records of the past are regarded as significant to predicting future performance, is *regression to the mean*—the idea that things will basically return to normal. If a baseball player has a batting average for the prior five years of .250, but for the past 10 games his batting average is .550, regression to the mean dictates that trending toward maintaining .250 rather than .550 is more indicative of future performance. The "mean" is the average. For example, Bill's annual bonuses were $5,000, $3,000, zero, $6,000, and $6,000. Adding these figures together and dividing by five years equals $4,000 which is the mean or the average annual bonus that Bill received.

regression to the mean the likelihood that unusually high or low results will tend to return to normal or average over time.

Periodically, you will have to examine and adjust your portfolio to determine suitable withdrawal rates during retirement. You should not rely blindly on regression to the mean. For example, for the past 30 years, long-term interest rates have averaged almost half of what they averaged for the 150 years prior to 1970. Will regression to the mean take over, or will this be an exception? For portfolios with a time horizon of 20 years or less that are adequately diversified, it won't matter much. Regression to the mean can give us some guidance, but the shorter the time frame, the less you should rely on it. Without substantial reliance on regression to the mean, there would be a flood of optimists thinking that they had a sufficient portfolio at age 50, and a torrent of pessimists believing that they still did not have a sufficient portfolio at age 80. While not a perfect tool, it is the best one that we have; probability is as close to certainty as we can get.

In 1999 our firm and others began utilizing computer programs prepared by mathematicians and economists to calculate probabilities for withdrawal rates by retirees under various scenarios for portfolios containing stocks and bonds in different proportions. Versions of these programs are available to both individual investors and professional advisers. Withdrawal rates of more than 7 percent per year from a portfolio are not sustainable for periods of time over 25 years at a probability level that is comfortable for most retirees. Generally, retirees get more comfortable with the conclusion when the probability for success is determined to be 90 percent and higher.

Case Study—Rob and Elise

Rob and Elise are both 58 and thinking about retirement. We entered their spending, saving, and portfolio data into the probability program and the initial forecasts were not encouraging. They have a portfolio of $1,140,000; their annual expenses in today's dollars are $100,000 including income taxes at the federal and state levels; when they reach age 65, their combined Social Security and pension benefits will generate $35,000 per year; this leaves $65,000 per year to be generated by their portfolio in today's dollars. Rob is an executive making $125,000 per year, while Elise works part-time as a decorator and earns $40,000 per year. Rob invests $10,000 annually in his company's 401(k) plan, and Elise invests $4,000 per year of her salary. They wanted to retire in two years. They invest 60 percent of their portfolio in equities and 40 percent in fixed-income investments. This portfolio will generate an average of 9.3 percent per year in growth based on Standard & Poor's data for 1947 to 1990, but only 9.0 percent per year based on data used in the "Retirement Spending Planner" program that we utilize. (The inconsistency is a reminder of the limitation of the tools that are available.) The initial printout was not encouraging.

The Retirement Spending Planner program produces tables, graphs, and charts to deal with a number of investment and retirement planning concerns and is based on over 2,000 different economic scenarios utilizing historical data. We reran the report after discussing possible revisions with Rob and Elise, including postponing their retirement for three more years.

We are duplicating two schedules of their new report, which illustrates probabilities in terms of current (year 2000) dollars. Current dollar figures have been calculated by utilizing a 3 percent per year inflation rate.

First, Figure 6.2, "Portfolio Investment Strategies—Year 2000 Dollars," shows the probabilities of Rob and Elise having over $250,000, over $500,000, or over $1 million at different ages (75, 80, and 85) with different asset allocation ratios. For example, if a portfolio is invested in 60 percent equities and 40 percent fixed-income, there is a 100 percent chance you will have more than $250,000 when the older spouse (Rob is several months older) is age 75. There is an 89 percent chance that there will be more than $1 million at age 75. The chances of having more than $1 million at age 85 drops to 79 percent.

Additional Observations

Moving to a more aggressive portfolio—80 percent equities and 20 percent fixed-income—increases the probability of having more than $1 million at age 85 (slightly up from 79 percent to 84 percent), but it also increases the volatility of the portfolio during the period from age 58 to age 85. The increased volatility or risk of a more aggressive portfolio may not be justifiable in many cases. Generally, choosing a more conservative portfolio to reduce volatility is recommended for later years whenever possible.

Figure 6.3, "Spending Plan Strategies—Year 2000 Dollars," shows (in the middle column headed "Original Plan") the same probabilities as shown in the 60 percent–40 percent column in Figure 6.2, because it is based on the same factors.

Figure 6.2 is useful in comparing probabilities under different portfolio mixes, while Figure 6.3 compares probabilities under different budgets. Together these two tables give valuable, continuing guidance for investing and spending decisions. We thank Dr. Bernard McCabe and the staff at Wagner Associates, 40 Lloyd Avenue, Suite 200, Malvern, PA; 800-345-1252; e-mail: bmccabe@pa.wagner.com for their guidance in the preparation of this material.

Frequent reviews of performance are necessary so that adjustments can be made. Also, as you get older, different allocations of investments will become advisable. Age, health, market performance, unforeseen events, and inflation are factors that can affect both withdrawal rates and asset allocation. Diversifying broadly using stocks and bonds—both U.S. and international—greatly increases the probability that you will have

Name *Example* *Date* *3/7/00* *Case* *A*

Portfolio Investment Strategies—Year 2000 Dollars

Equity/Fixed Income Ratio	*Age of First*	*0%/100%*	*20%/80%*	*40%/60%*	*50%/50%*	*60%/40%*	*80%/20%*	*100%/0%*
Probability	*75*	1.00	1.00	1.00	1.00	1.00	0.99	0.99
Total Wealth	*80*	0.99	0.99	0.98	0.98	0.97	0.97	0.96
> *$250,000*	*85*	0.76	0.89	0.92	0.93	0.93	0.94	0.94
Probability	*75*	1.00	0.99	0.98	0.98	0.98	0.97	0.96
Total Wealth	*80*	0.88	0.93	0.94	0.94	0.94	0.94	0.94
> *$500,000*	*85*	0.42	0.77	0.86	0.88	0.89	0.90	0.91
Probability	*75*	0.66	0.83	0.87	0.88	0.89	0.90	0.90
Total Wealth	*80*	0.25	0.66	0.79	0.82	0.84	0.87	0.89
> *$1,000,000*	*85*	0.06	0.51	0.71	0.76	0.79	0.84	0.86

Example: *If you invest your portfolio in 60% Equities and 40% Fixed Income then there is a 100% chance you will have more than $250,000 at age 75.*

FIGURE 6.2 Portfolio investment strategies—year 2000 dollars.

Source: R&P—The Retirement Spending Planner, by Daniel H. Wagner Associates. Used with permission.

Name *Example* Date *3/7/00* Case *A*

Spending Plan Strategies—Year 2000 Dollars

Spending Plan Adjustment	*Age of First*	*25% Decrease*	*10% Decrease*	*5% Decrease*	*Original Plan*	*5% Increase*	*10% Increase*	*25% Increase*
Probability	*75*	1.00	1.00	1.00	1.00	0.99	0.99	0.96
Total Wealth	*80*	1.00	0.99	0.98	0.97	0.96	0.95	0.87
> $250,000	*85*	1.00	0.97	0.95	0.93	0.90	0.88	0.75
Probability	*75*	1.00	0.99	0.98	0.98	0.97	0.96	0.91
Total Wealth	*80*	0.99	0.97	0.96	0.94	0.92	0.90	0.80
> $500,000	*85*	0.99	0.94	0.92	0.89	0.86	0.82	0.68
Probability	*75*	0.96	0.93	0.91	0.89	0.87	0.85	0.76
Total Wealth	*80*	0.96	0.90	0.88	0.84	0.81	0.77	0.65
> $1,000,000	*85*	0.95	0.87	0.83	0.79	0.75	0.71	0.56

Example: If you increase your spending plan by 5% then there is a 99% chance you will have more than $250,000 at age 75.

FIGURE 6.3 Spending plan strategies—year 2000 dollars.

Source: R&P—The Retirement Spending Planner, by Daniel H. Wagner Associates. Used with permission.

enough capital to sustain you comfortably through retirement. However, unforeseen factors such as being sued and held liable for damages or having to help loved ones in financial trouble are examples of unexpected challenges.

By analyzing your withdrawal program realistically, postponing retirement, or cutting back to working on a part-time basis for a brief period can greatly increase the probability of a secure retirement. In 1995, my wife and I calculated that we would have enough to last us about 27 years. I was 63 and my wife was 56. We estimated that if I worked for four more years and she worked part-time during that period and our portfolio would hold its own, that she would be financially secure to age 90 or so.

We both happened to change jobs at that time, and we came up with an unexpected bonus—we each enjoyed what we were doing much more than before although we made less than we previously did. If our portfolios had hit some potholes, either or both of us could have undone at least part of the damage by extending our employment for a short period.

If you no longer enjoy your job, you may find that you can change positions and meet your financial goals with less stress. A former law client who was one of three partners in a service business came to dread the pressures at work. At age 64, he sold his business interest, invested the proceeds, and obtained a job at the township golf course working nine months a year. He has been with the parks and recreation department for several years with no thought of quitting. Working several years for $25,000 per year and enjoying it rather than working one or two years for $150,000 per year and being miserable will make sense for many people. After age 60, this kind of math can work.

Continuing to work on a part-time basis can make investment setbacks in your retirement years less of a burden. The added years of less stressful employment also give you an opportunity to assess your financial needs more accurately—to confirm that you have enough or to reveal that you may need more while you are in a position to do something about it. If your retirement is a comfortable one—replacing cars regularly, taking vacations, making substantial gifts to loved ones, maintaining a vacation home or boat—you have the opportunity to cut back to some degree if necessary. By tacking on several years of less stressful employment, you may not only keep your portfolio from disappearing but you may keep yourself around a little longer, too.

Tapping Your Home Equity

If you own your home, its equity may be a source of substantial funds. Generally, this would be a last source to tap, but it could be a psychological safety net for many retirees. To utilize the equity you could sell the home, refinance it, get a home equity loan, or secure a reverse mortgage. If you sell, you must buy another home or become a renter. If you refinance or get a home equity loan, generally you must satisfy the lender that you have income in order to make regular payments on your new loan. Remember the joke where the borrower answers the banker, "If I had income, I wouldn't need the loan." With a reverse mortgage you borrow against your home and do not have to make payments as long as you live there, so having income is not a consideration in qualifying.

Because the lender is concerned about the date of eventual payment, people seeking reverse mortgages generally must be 62 or older. When a borrower obtains a conventional mortgage loan, it is a personal loan and must be repaid in full even if the property substantially decreases in value. With a reverse mortgage, the loan is usually a nonrecourse loan, meaning that the obligation to the lender does not exceed the value of the mortgaged property (your home) when the loan is to be repaid. The lender has no recourse against any other cash or assets of yours or the assets of anyone else.

With a reverse mortgage, the lender usually takes your age and the age of your spouse into account. Generally, as the borrower, you will receive monthly installments based on life expectancy; or, you can withdraw amounts up to a set limit—your line of credit; or, you may be able to receive a lump sum.

As with conventional mortgage loans, the cost of the proposed loan should be analyzed and compared to other sources by the prospective borrower beforehand. Since death of the surviving spouse or other events—such as moving to a warmer climate or closer to family members, or to a long-term care facility—can trigger the obligation of sale of the home and repayment of the loan, there is no assurance that you are securing long-term benefits for the fees that will be paid. From the lender's point of view, it has no assurance that you or your spouse may not live far beyond the life expectancy of the survivor of the two of you.

Reverse mortgages are generally utilized by elderly people of moderate means—often a widow or widower. Fraud is a major concern, with the elderly being tempting targets to con artists. There have been suits against lending firms claiming abuses such as outrageously high fees and unconscionable terms such as the lending firm claiming half of the appreciation in the value of the property.

Reverse mortgages can be divided into three categories:

1. Home equity conversion mortgages (HECM loans) sponsored by the Federal Housing Administration (FHA). These are generally

the most modest reverse mortgages since the highest home value that is the base for these loans is the median cost of homes in the described area—generally around $200,000 for most areas.

2. Reverse mortgages supported by the Federal National Mortgage Association (Fannie Mae). The limit on home value as a base for these loans is currently $240,000. Generally the best terms for borrowers are found in the HECM loans sponsored by the FHA and the loans sponsored by Fannie Mae.
3. Reverse mortgage loans on expensive homes are available from few private lenders. Many firms have withdrawn from this market. Financial Freedom Senior Funding Corporation of Irvine, California, makes reverse mortgage loans for homes valued at up to $700,000.

For more general information, call Fannie Mae at 810-732-6643 for free facts and a list of both FHA and Fannie Mae reverse mortgage lenders. Also, the National Center for Home Equity Conversion in St. Paul, Minnesota, has a web site at www.reverse.org with information.

WITHDRAWALS FROM QUALIFIED RETIREMENT PLAN ACCOUNTS

A *qualified plan* is one that complies with complex governmental rules resulting in favorable tax treatment, such as tax-deductible contributions and tax-free accumulations prior to withdrawal. The terms of the plans are generally submitted to the Internal Revenue Service for advance approval before it is made available to participants.

qualified plan a retirement plan that complies with complex governmental rules resulting in favorable tax treatment.

There are a number of different types of qualified retirement plans. Many corporations offer 401(k), profit sharing, and pension plans to their employees. Governmental agencies offer 403(b) plans. Other plans are established by employers, the self-employed, or the participants themselves. Some examples are the individual retirement account (IRA),

Keogh plan, simplified employee pension (SEP), Simple IRA, Simple 401(k), and Roth IRA.

In this section we are concentrating on the withdrawals from the accounts. It is important for you and your adviser to review the literature about the plan or plans in which you participate. The employer, broker, or bank that is the sponsor may have included provisions that are unique to that particular plan.

A word about pension and other fixed-income payments: Upon retirement the payout of a pension is predictable, so taking the periodic payments that pensions provide and grouping them with Social Security and annuity payments, leaves a smaller burden for your other assets to cover. However, the longer the wait until your retirement date (or the date that the pension starts, if later), the more the uncertainty.

In recent years many companies have switched from traditional pension plans to cash balance plans. The traditional plan determines the pension by a formula that generally takes into account an employee's years of service with the company and his or her pay at or near retirement. The cash balance plan is more like a profit sharing plan since it credits an employee's pension account with a percentage of current pay—for example, 5 percent of annual salary. The company guarantees that these contributions will grow by a certain percentage each year.

With the traditional pension plan, the company is committed to funding a certain benefit by the worker's retirement age, and that commitment relates to a generally higher salary level than is the case with the cash balance plan, where the commitment is related to the current salary level.

The cash balance plan has become more popular with companies because of their reduced commitment for current years. When one Fortune 500 company initially considered switching, it estimated that the switch would save $200 million annually. The switch often comes at the expense of older workers who may have the value of their expected benefits drop by 30 percent to 50 percent—a huge blow to retirement expectations. A number of employers give employees who are within 10 years of retirement the option of remaining with the traditional plan. Generally, younger workers are favored with the cash balance plan, particularly if they change employers frequently, because they build up larger account balances earlier in their working years.

Withdrawals from 401(k), profit sharing, and other plans that are not pension plans are controlled primarily by the recipient. Withdrawals from these plans prior to age 59 are usually penalized, and by age 70½ certain minimum amounts must be taken.

Someone who is about to retire, or who has retired, must fit these rules into the overall withdrawal-during-retirement strategy. The following case histories will illustrate common problems and solutions. Since most retirement plan accounts are IRAs, including those accounts that were initially other types of retirement plan accounts and were rolled over or transferred into IRA accounts, they are emphasized. Other types of retirement plans have similar rules in some instances, and very different rules in others. The policy behind different treatments is often unclear. Again, the objective of this chapter is to make you more knowledgeable so that you can work with your tax adviser—not replace him or her. These rules are not only complex but are constantly changing.

Case Study—Mark

Mark was 54 when he decided to retire early from his management position and teach part-time at the local community college. He asked the trustee of the company pension plan to send him a check for the $350,000 balance in his retirement plan account. Instead, he was sent information about his options and realized how he nearly made a costly mistake. He learned that he could have his money rolled over into his personal IRA and avoid paying a 20 percent withholding tax, plus an 11 percent additional federal income tax (he was in the 31 percent bracket) and a 4.5 percent state income tax. There is generally also an additional 10 percent penalty tax on withdrawals from a qualified plan before 59½ years of age. But, if Mark waits until he is 55 and terminates his employment, withdrawal of his account would not then be subject to the 10 percent penalty tax.

What Could Have Happened to Mark

Retirement plan account balance	$350,000
20 percent withholding for federal income tax	–$70,000
11 percent balance of federal income tax	–$38,500
4.5 percent state income tax	–$15,750
10 percent penalty for early withdrawal	–$35,000
Balance after taxes	$190,750

By establishing an IRA account and rolling over the entire $350,000 balance, Mark could ensure no taxes or penalties would be assessed until he withdrew amounts from the IRA, and then only to the amounts withdrawn. The remaining monies could continue to accumulate tax-free. The penalty tax would apply to only amounts withdrawn before age 59½, and this penalty would be avoided if "substantially equal periodic payments" over Mark's life expectancy or over the joint life expectancy of Mark and a beneficiary were made. Avoiding the penalty requires utilizing Section 72(t)(A)(iv) of the Internal Revenue Code, and professional guidance should be secured. This payment schedule could be revised or discontinued after five years or when Mark turned 59½, whichever period is longer.

Mark could establish his rollover IRA account through either a direct or an indirect rollover. If he used a *direct rollover,* the transfer would be made directly into an IRA account that he would have his broker establish for him beforehand. The trustee of his prior employer's plan would transfer Mark's account balance directly to this new IRA rollover account. It is important to have the plan administrator issue the check directly payable to the broker for the benefit of the IRA. (This procedure is also used when a plan participant changes employers and the retirement plan account from the prior employer is transferred to the participant's plan account with the new employer.)

direct rollover the permitted transfer of a participant's account from the trustee or custodian of a qualified retirement plan to the custodian or trustee of another qualified plan. When legal requirements are met, there is no income tax on the transfer.

An *indirect rollover* is a payout made to the participant. Under this procedure, for tax purposes Mark would have 60 days to roll it over into an IRA or a qualified plan of a new employer. In this case, 20 percent would be withheld from the distribution made to Mark (even if it is eventually rolled over). Thus, Mark would have to dip into his own funds to make up for the 20 percent withheld by his prior plan if he wanted to roll over his entire balance within the 60-day period.

indirect rollover the distribution of a participant's account in a qualified plan to the participant for transfer by the participant to another qualified plan while meeting the legal requirements to avoid income tax on the transfer.

If Mark were at least 59½ and born before 1936, he could have qualified for a *forward averaging formula,* which would reduce the federal income tax exposure on a lump-sum distribution. Under the forward averaging formula, the tax is paid in one year but is calculated as if the distribution had been made evenly over 10 years. (Ten-year averaging is limited to people born before 1936; five-year averaging was phased out in 1999). To qualify for this treatment:

> **forward averaging formula** a method of calculating and minimizing taxes on a lump-sum distribution.

- ✔ The distribution must include the employer's entire balance from all qualified plans of his or her employer.
- ✔ The total balance must be received within one calendar year.
- ✔ The employee must be at least 59½.
- ✔ The employee must have been a plan participant for a minimum of five years.
- ✔ The distribution must have been made because of death, disability, or termination of employment.
- ✔ The employee can use forward averaging only once.

In some instances, if the employee was born before 1936 and was a plan participant before 1974, a portion of the distribution would be taxed at a 20 percent rate with the balance subject to forward averaging. In Mark's case, and in most cases, a rollover into an IRA or other qualified plan is preferable to forward averaging as long as the funds aren't needed immediately.

Case Study—Clark

Mark's friend Clark is 55 and works for Bubbly Cola, a Fortune 500 company. Clark wants to take early retirement and work part-time as a football coach at his son's high school. Mark has alerted Clark to the benefits of a direct rollover. Clark intends to execute a direct rollover of his $400,000 retirement plan account to an IRA that his broker is opening for him. Clark is discussing his plans one Saturday morning at the barbershop when Kent, another customer, overhears the story and asks Clark if he has Bubbly Cola stock in his plan account. (Actually, $50,000 of his account is in Bubbly

Cola stock.) Kent urges Clark to consider keeping the stock out of the IRA. This is a choice that one has with regard to company stock only.

This is good advice in Clark's case, since the value of the stock was $3,000 when it was added to his account. If Clark were under age 55 when his employment terminated, the 10 percent excise tax would apply to only the $3,000 *tax basis* of the stock, not its $50,000 value. The stock can continue to appreciate tax-free until sold. Dividends would be taxable (they would not be taxable if the stock were held in an IRA), but generally this would be a minor negative in deciding to keep the stock out of an IRA.

> **tax basis** the starting point in determining taxable gain or loss upon the sale or disposition of property. Often it is the cost of the property; for inherited property, generally it is the fair market value on the date of death.

Let's assume that Clark continues to hold the Bubbly Cola stock until he dies 30 years from now. By then, the stock is worth $700,000. Clark's heirs get a stepped-up basis for the stock (equal to its fair market value as of the date of Clark's death) and are able to sell it for $700,000 and pay no capital gain tax. On the other hand, if the stock were in his IRA, Clark would probably have liquidated all or most of it to take required taxable distributions from the IRA beginning at age 70½. To the extent that the stock was still in the IRA, it would be taxable for income tax purposes to his heirs. (The stock would be included in Clark's estate for federal estate tax purposes whether or not it was held in an IRA.)

Some Retirement Plan Transfer Considerations

If you are planning to change jobs or retire, you will have to repay amounts borrowed from the retirement plan or pay taxes on those amounts and possibly an additional 10 percent penalty tax. If you are rolling over your balance to a new employer's plan that allows loans, you may be able to repay the old loan and then borrow from the new plan. If you are going to roll over the account or transfer it to an IRA, you can't borrow from the IRA; *nor can you use your account as collateral for a loan.* You can withdraw funds and reinvest in an IRA account within 60 days without paying income tax or penalties, but see Figure 6.4, "Comparing the Direct and Indirect Rollover to an IRA."

If you are planning to withdraw part of your retirement plan account to start a new business or another project, note that there is a difference

Direct Rollover

1. If $350,000 is in the retirement account, the entire $350,000 is transferred to the new IRA.

Retirement Plan Account → IRA Account

$350,000 → $350,000

Net Effect:

1. Full balance transferred—no reduction.
2. Additional tax and penalty cost: 0.
3. Entire balance of $350,000 can continue to accumulate tax-free.

Indirect Rollover

1. Amount withheld from rollover for federal taxes $350,000 times 20 percent equals $70,000.
2. Since the $70,000 withheld is deemed to be a "taxable distribution," it is taxed at distributee's tax rate—assuming 31 percent: $70,000 times 31 percent equals $21,700.
3. Penalty of 10 percent on $70,000 taxable distribution: $70,000 times 10 percent equals $7,000.
4. Depending on state law, about 4.5 percent levied by state on taxable distribution: $70,000 times 4.5 equals $3,150.

Net Effect:

1. Instead of $350,000 in the IRA account, there is $280,000 ($350,000 minus $70,000).
2. Additional tax and penalty cost: $21,700 plus $7,000 plus $3,150 equals $31,850.

Lesson: It is better to go with the direct rollover.

FIGURE 6.4 Comparing the direct and indirect rollover to an IRA.

between withdrawing the money from the retirement plan account before rolling it over to an IRA and withdrawing money after it is rolled over into an IRA. Either way, the withdrawal is taxable. But if you are 55 or older, the 10 percent penalty tax won't apply if the withdrawal is made from the retirement plan after separation from service. To make a withdrawal from an IRA before age 59½, the penalty tax will apply unless you qualify under certain emergency situations discussed shortly. Also, if you follow rules requiring "substantially equal periodic payments" figured over your life expectancy and you keep up with these withdrawals for five years or until age 59½, the penalty tax will not apply.

Case Study—Rose

Rose is 52 and is leaving her job to open up her own consulting business. She has $500,000 in her retirement plan account. She doesn't need much capital to start the business but does need a steady income flow until the business is established. If she elects to receive "substantially equal periodic payments" to avoid the 10 percent penalty for withdrawals before age 59½, she would have more taxable income than necessary once the business is established. Her portfolio manager advises splitting the retirement account among several IRAs and taking "substantially equal periodic payments" from one of them. The additional IRAs provide flexibility.

Case Study—Lou and Beth

Lou has several IRAs that have a $300,000 total balance as of December 31, 2001. He is required to start taking a minimum distribution when he reaches 70½. If he doesn't take the minimum distribution each year, a penalty equal to 50 percent of the shortfall will be assessed. Lou was born in May 1931 and turned 70½ in November 2001. His first required minimum distribution (RMD) must be made by April 1 of the year following the year he turned 70½ (i.e., April 1, 2002). All subsequent distributions must be made by December 31 of each calendar year. Thus, by December 31, 2002, he has to take his next RMD. For 2002, he will have to take two distributions, although he could have taken his first distribution during November or December 2001 after he reached 70½.

There are several planning alternatives that a tax adviser could clarify. Lou needs to decide whether he should utilize his own life expectancy or the joint life expectancy with his wife, Beth, who will then be 67. She is the beneficiary of his IRAs. On the joint life expectancy table authorized by the Internal Revenue Service (IRS publication 590, Individual Retirement Arrangements; call the IRS at 800-829-3676 to order), their joint life expectancy is 22 years. To calculate the first required minimum distribution, he divides his IRA balance of $300,000 by 22 years for an RMD of $13,636.

This amount is calculated on the basis of all of Lou's IRAs and qualified plan accounts. Each year, reference must be made to the joint life expectancy table. (See Table 6.2) To locate the joint life expectancy, you find where "70" and "67" meet. Find "67" on the top of the chart and run down the left column where "70" is, and 22.0 is the factor. Or, you can lo-

TABLE 6.2 Excerpt from IRS Tables of Expected Return Multiples Ordinary Joint Life and Last Survivor Annuities Two Lives—Expected Return Multiples

Age	*65*	*66*	*67*	*68*	*69*	*70*	*71*	*72*	*73*	*74*
65	25.0	24.6	24.2	23.8	23.4	23.1	22.8	22.5	22.2	22.0
66	24.6	24.1	23.7	23.3	22.9	22.5	22.2	21.9	21.6	21.4
67	24.2	23.7	23.2	22.8	22.4	22.0	21.7	21.3	21.0	20.8
68	23.8	23.3	22.8	22.3	21.9	21.5	21.2	20.8	20.5	20.2
69	23.4	22.9	22.4	21.9	21.5	21.1	20.7	20.3	20.0	19.6
70	23.1	22.5	22.0	21.5	21.1	20.6	20.2	19.8	19.4	19.1
71	22.8	22.2	21.7	21.2	20.7	20.2	19.8	19.4	19.0	18.6
72	22.5	21.9	21.3	20.8	20.3	19.8	19.4	18.9	18.5	18.2
73	22.2	21.6	21.0	20.5	20.0	19.4	19.0	18.5	18.1	17.7
74	22.0	21.4	20.8	20.2	19.6	19.1	18.6	18.2	17.7	17.3
75	21.8	21.1	20.5	19.9	19.3	18.8	18.3	17.8	17.3	16.9
76	21.6	20.9	20.3	19.7	19.1	18.5	18.0	17.5	17.0	16.5
77	21.4	20.7	20.1	19.4	18.8	18.3	17.7	17.2	16.7	16.2
78	21.2	20.5	19.9	19.2	18.6	18.0	17.5	16.9	16.4	15.9
79	21.1	20.4	19.7	19.0	18.4	17.8	17.2	16.7	16.1	15.6
80	21.0	20.2	19.5	18.9	18.2	17.6	17.0	16.4	15.9	15.4
81	20.8	20.1	19.4	18.7	18.1	17.4	16.8	16.2	15.7	15.1
82	20.7	20.0	19.3	18.6	17.9	17.3	16.6	16.0	15.5	14.9
83	20.6	19.9	19.2	18.5	17.8	17.1	16.5	15.9	15.3	14.7
84	20.5	19.8	19.1	18.4	17.7	17.0	16.3	15.7	15.1	14.5
85	20.5	19.7	19.0	18.3	17.6	16.9	16.2	15.6	15.0	14.4
86	20.4	19.6	18.9	18.2	17.5	16.8	16.1	15.5	14.8	14.2
87	20.4	19.6	18.8	18.1	17.4	16.7	16.0	15.4	14.7	14.1
88	20.3	19.5	18.8	18.0	17.3	16.6	15.9	15.3	14.6	14.0
89	20.3	19.5	18.7	18.0	17.2	16.5	15.8	15.2	14.5	13.9

cate "70" at the top of the chart and run down the left column where "67" is, and again 22.0 is the factor. Now try it for the ages of you and your spouse.

Upon Lou's death, Beth has the option of treating his IRA as her own. She can name new beneficiaries, choose a new minimum distribution schedule, and, if she's under 70½, make additional contributions.

TABLE 6.2 *Continued*

Age	*65*	*66*	*67*	*68*	*69*	*70*	*71*	*72*	*73*	*74*
90	20.2	19.4	18.7	17.9	17.2	16.5	15.8	15.1	14.5	13.8
91	20.2	19.4	18.6	17.9	17.1	16.4	15.7	15.0	14.4	13.7
92	20.2	19.4	18.6	17.8	17.1	16.4	15.7	15.0	14.3	13.7
93	20.1	19.3	18.6	17.8	17.1	16.3	15.6	14.9	14.3	13.6
94	20.1	19.3	18.5	17.8	17.0	16.3	15.6	14.9	14.2	13.6
95	20.1	19.3	18.5	17.8	17.0	16.3	15.6	14.9	14.2	13.5
96	20.1	19.3	18.5	17.7	17.0	16.2	15.5	14.8	14.2	13.5
97	20.1	19.3	18.5	17.7	17.0	16.2	15.5	14.8	14.1	13.5
98	20.1	19.3	18.5	17.7	16.9	16.2	15.5	14.8	14.1	13.4
99	20.0	19.2	18.5	17.7	16.9	16.2	15.5	14.7	14.1	13.4
100	20.0	19.2	18.4	17.7	16.9	16.2	15.4	14.7	14.0	13.4
101	20.0	19.2	18.4	17.7	16.9	16.1	15.4	14.7	14.0	13.3
102	20.0	19.2	18.4	17.6	16.9	16.1	15.4	14.7	14.0	13.3
103	20.0	19.2	18.4	17.6	16.9	16.1	15.4	14.7	14.0	13.3
104	20.0	19.2	18.4	17.6	16.9	16.1	15.4	14.7	14.0	13.3
105	20.0	19.2	18.4	17.6	16.8	16.1	15.4	14.6	13.9	13.3
106	20.0	19.2	18.4	17.6	16.8	16.1	15.3	14.6	13.9	13.3
107	20.0	19.2	18.4	17.6	16.8	16.1	15.3	14.6	13.9	13.2
108	20.0	19.2	18.4	17.6	16.8	16.1	15.3	14.6	13.9	13.2
109	20.0	19.2	18.4	17.6	16.8	16.1	15.3	14.6	13.9	13.2
110	20.0	19.2	18.4	17.6	16.8	16.1	15.3	14.6	13.9	13.2
111	20.0	19.2	18.4	17.6	16.8	16.0	15.3	14.6	13.9	13.2
112	20.0	19.2	18.4	17.6	16.8	16.0	15.3	14.6	13.9	13.2
113	20.0	19.2	18.4	17.6	16.8	16.0	15.3	14.6	13.9	13.2
114	20.0	19.2	18.4	17.6	16.8	16.0	15.3	14.6	13.9	13.2
115	20.0	19.2	18.4	17.6	16.8	16.0	15.3	14.6	13.9	13.2

Caution: There are circumstances when quick action must be taken by the surviving spouse upon the death of the owner of an IRA account. In some cases a surviving spouse must act by December 31 of the year that a spouse dies. If an IRA owner dies in November, the surviving spouse may not think about looking into the status of the decedent's IRA for several months. If the decedent had reached age 70½ and had elected the single recalculation method and utilized only his life expectancy, severe problems could arise. Different rules apply if the decedent had elected to use the joint life expectancy of himself and his spouse or if the beneficiary is not the spouse. Certain trusts can also effectively act as recipients of distributions.

If Lou had named his son or anyone other than his spouse as a beneficiary and given that person or persons complete control of the account after his death, then:

- ✔ If Lou died *before* the required beginning date (April 1, 2002), either (1) the entire account must be distributed to the beneficiary by December 31 of the calendar year that includes the fifth anniversary of Lou's death, or (2) the beneficiary can take the distributions based on his or her life expectancy so long as they begin before the end of the calendar year after the year that Lou died.
- ✔ A nonspouse beneficiary may not roll over Lou's retirement account into his or her own IRA account.
- ✔ If Lou died *after* the required beginning date, distributions must continue at least as quickly as the payout period selected by Lou. The joint life expectancy table could not be used to the extent that a nonspouse beneficiary is more than 10 years younger than Lou. After Lou dies, the actual life expectancy of the beneficiary can be utilized.

Case Study—Nate, Dorothy, Jane, and Jean

Nate has $500,000 in his IRA and names his wife, Dorothy, as the beneficiary of 50 percent of the account and their two adult children as beneficiaries of the balance with 25 percent of the account for each of them. Dorothy is 70 and the two children, Jane and Jean, are 45 and 40 when Nate dies. If Nate had divided his IRA into separate IRA accounts for each of the beneficiaries before death, each child could use her own life expectancy instead of being limited to her mother's life expectancy. Jane would collect an additional $170,625 and Jean would collect an additional $209,349 with separate IRA accounts. (See Table 6.3.)

In all life expectancy calculations, either the recalculation method or the reduce-by-one method is used and, once selected, can't be changed. To assist you, the attorney who prepared your estate plan or your CPA is the best one to talk to if you have a substantial portfolio in IRA or retirement plan accounts. Also, it is most important to have the adviser review the retirement plan's agreement—particularly the terms of distributions. Because IRA and retirement plan accounts have their own rules, estate planners

TABLE 6.3 Case Study Illustration

	Deferral Period Allowed	*Amount Received*[1]	*Additional Benefits with Three Separate Accounts*
One $500,000 IRA Account			
Wife $250,000 initially	15 years	$404,478	
Child $125,000 initially	15 years	202,239	
Child $125,000 initially	15 years	202,239	
Total		$808,956	
If Three Separate IRA Accounts			
Wife $250,000	15 years	$ 404,478	$ 0
Child Jane $125,000	40 years	372,864	170,625
Child Jean $125,000	45 years	411,588	209,349
Total		$1,188,930	$379,974

[1]Assumes 7 percent annual return

should pay particular attention to the choice of beneficiary for these accounts. To give you a glimpse of some of the complexities in this area—particularly how IRA beneficiary designations interact with estate planning—here are some subtopics from an article written for tax lawyers by an expert:

- ✔ Features to include in a trust designated as an IRA beneficiary.
- ✔ Irrevocable retirement plan payment trusts.
- ✔ Postdeath channeling to the decedent's IRA.
- ✔ Loss of the marital deduction when a qualified terminable interest property (QTIP) marital trust is the designated beneficiary.
- ✔ Problems when reduce-to-zero marital trusts are designated as beneficiaries.

The following eight types of distributions from regular IRAs are not subject to the 10 percent penalty tax (the premature distribution penalty), although these distributions are taxable:

1. "Substantially equal periodic payments" as described earlier.
2. Distributions taken in order to pay for higher education expenses.

3. Qualified first-home purchase distribution.
4. Distributions to a beneficiary after the death of the participant.
5. Withdrawals made upon the disability of the participant as determined under IRS guidelines.
6. Distributions taken in order to pay medical expenses exceeding 7.5 percent of the participant's adjusted gross income.
7. Withdrawals made in order to pay health insurance premiums after the participant is separated from employment, has received unemployment compensation under federal or state law for at least 12 consecutive weeks, and meets other requirements.
8. Distributions after the participant is 59½.

Before age 59½, penalty-free withdrawals from other types of plans such as Keoghs, 401(k) plans, and 403(b) plans are subject to special rules. You can seek guidance from your employer or the administrator of the plan. Generally, versions of the regular IRA exceptions for medical expenses, higher education expenses for certain family members, or purchase of a home are available. In addition, most of these plans, *but not IRAs*, allow borrowing of up to the lesser of $50,000 or 50 percent of the participant's vested account balance, usually subject to repayment within five years.

A new type of IRA—the Roth IRA—became effective in 1998. A couple with an annual adjusted gross income of up to $150,000 (and an unmarried individual with income of up to $95,000) may deposit $2,000 each annually to his or her Roth IRA account. Although these contributions are not income tax deductible, they are not taxed as they grow nor upon withdrawal. Since withdrawals may begin as soon as five years later if you are then at least age 59½ (or to use the money to buy your first home), Roth IRAs may even be of interest to those who will retire shortly who may be reluctant to have the money unavailable for too long.

Case Study—Ross

Ross is 60 and has been making annual contributions to his Roth IRA for five years. He could begin making withdrawals but doesn't. At 70½ he has to begin withdrawals from his deductible IRA but does not have to withdraw any amount from his Roth IRA, which can continue to grow tax-free. In fact, being 70½ does not prevent Ross from making further contributions.

It is possible to convert a regular IRA, deductible or nondeductible,

SEP or SARSEP IRA, or Simple IRA into a Roth IRA if an individual's *adjusted gross income is less than $100,000*. To do so, you must pay income tax on all prior contributions and earnings that were not taxed. If the conversion had taken place before 1999, the tax bill could have been spread over four years. Is it worth converting? Here are some factors for you and your adviser to consider:

- ✔ What is today's deduction worth versus the tax rate you can expect to pay in retirement?
- ✔ What growth are you likely to achieve in the account that will eventually be withdrawn tax-free?
- ✔ Can you pay the income tax on converting without making a taxable withdrawal from the IRA to pay the tax?
- ✔ What are the state and local income tax consequences?

The following five rules should be noted relative to the Roth IRA:

1. Only upon death are distributions required.
2. The maximum contribution to the Roth IRA is coordinated with the contribution to the regular IRA so that the maximum annual IRA contribution level is not exceeded.
3. Just as with regular IRAs, there can be a rollover between Roth IRAs only once in 12 months.
4. No transfer can be made from a Roth IRA to a regular IRA, qualified plan, 403(b), Simple IRA, or Education IRA.
5. There cannot be a rollover from a qualified plan or 403(b) arrangement to a Roth IRA.

Currently there are: regular IRAs, Simple IRAs, Education IRAs, SEP-IRAs, and Roth IRAs. SARSEP IRAs still exist for those who adopted them before 1997. The Medical Savings Account (MSA) has some IRA-like features but should not be considered an IRA. There is a type of MSA designed for senior citizens, first available in 1999 relating to Medicare. It is described in Chapter 8. Because of differences in rules relative to contributions, transfer, rollovers, and distributions, none of these categories should be commingled. This is an area where Congress has made changes in the rules and is likely to continue to do so. Since many rules have changed recently and further changes are likely, decisions regarding your retirement program should be made only with the assistance of a professional adviser.

Here is the last case history in this chapter. Its message should be clear.

Case History—Hank, Junior, and Erin

Hank, a widower, died in 2000. His son, Junior, was the beneficiary of his IRA with a balance of $250,000. Hank's daughter, Erin, was a joint owner with rights of survivorship of his house, his only other asset. The value of the equity in the house was $250,000. At first, it seemed that Hank's plan for equal bequests would work out. There was no federal estate tax since the total estate was under $675,000, the maximum credit exclusion equivalent in the year of death. However, Junior's lawyer told him that Erin could sell the house with no income tax liability while Junior would eventually have to pay income tax on the entire $250,000 from the IRA—which would leave him with substantially less than what his father intended.

SOCIAL SECURITY DISTRIBUTIONS

In this section, we will concentrate on the Social Security retirement income distributions that will supplement the amounts that you will withdraw from your investment accounts. Much of the information in this part is contained in various Social Security pamphlets. This section brings the information together in an overview. You can check with Social Security and your advisers for updated details in areas of special concern.

To qualify for retirement benefits, the first reference is made to your date of birth. For those born after 1928, 40 credits are needed. Generally, four credits are earned for every year of work. One less credit is needed for every year of birth before 1929 (39 credits for those born in 1928, 38 credits for 1927, and so on). Most people earn many more credits than are required to qualify for benefits. But earning the required credits is only the beginning.

The more income that you earn while working increases your benefits. You may request a personalized estimate of benefits by filling out a Request for Earnings Benefit Estimate obtained by calling 800-772-1213. After you complete and send the form back, Social Security will send you your earnings history and estimates of retirement benefits. To aid your planning, the estimates will be for "early benefits" (as early as age 62), "full retirement" (as early as 65), and "maximum benefits" (age 70). There are automatic cost of living increases that will supplement these estimates. Full retirement age will be increased for those who are born after 1937 as shown in Table 6.4.

TABLE 6.4 Age to Receive Full Social Security Benefits

Year of Birth	*Full Retirement Age*
1937 or earlier	65
1938	65 and 2 months
1939	65 and 4 months
1940	65 and 6 months
1941	65 and 8 months
1942	65 and 10 months
1943–1954	66
1955	66 and 2 months
1956	66 and 4 months
1957	66 and 6 months
1958	66 and 8 months
1959	66 and 10 months
1960 or later	67

If you were born after 1937, you can qualify for benefits as early as age 62, but your benefit will be about 70 percent of the full benefit. For those born before 1938, the early benefit at age 62 will be about 80 percent of the full benefit. The law's objective is to provide about the same total Social Security benefits over one's entire lifetime even if one retires early. For every year before age 65, your benefit level is reduced by a little more than 6 percent.

Note: It is important to sign up for Medicare at age 65 even if you do not retire, because medical insurance may cost more if you apply for it later. Medicare covers people age 65 or older, disabled people, and people with permanent kidney failure. For more information call Social Security and ask for the pamphlet "Medicare" (Publication #05-10043).

If poor health caused your early retirement, contact Social Security about the Supplemental Security Income (SSI) program that Social Security administers, although it is a separately funded program. The Supplemental Security Income program provides payments to low-income individuals age 65 and over, blind persons, and the disabled. Widows and children of workers who have died, including those who have died before retirement, may receive Social Security survivor's benefits. Disability benefits under the Social Security Act may be paid to disabled workers before their retirement, and their dependents.

Spouses of retired workers are entitled to one-half of a retired worker's benefits unless the spouse begins collecting before age 65, in which case the spouse's benefit is permanently reduced by an amount that depends on how many months before he or she will be age 65.

There has been some confusion as to whether a spouse is eligible for retirement benefits based on his or her employment apart from spouse's benefits. Social Security pays a person's retirement benefits first, and if the spouse's benefit would be higher, an additional amount equal to the shortfall is paid so the spouse gets a combination of benefits.

The Social Security booklet "Retirement Benefits" provides an example: Mary Ann qualifies for a (monthly) retirement benefit of $250 and a wife's (monthly) benefit of $400. At age 65, she will receive her own $250 retirement benefit and Social Security will add $150 from her wife's benefit for a total of $400. If she takes her retirement benefit at any time before she turns 65, the payments will be reduced.

Under certain circumstances, a divorced spouse may be able to get benefits based on a former husband or wife's record. Benefit payments to a divorced spouse do not reduce the amount of benefits for which the current spouse can qualify. In order for a divorced spouse to qualify for these benefits, their marriage must have lasted for at least 10 years and the divorced spouse must be currently unmarried and age 62 or older. In addition, they must have been divorced for at least two years and the worker must also be 62 or older with enough credits to qualify for benefits.

If you are 70 or over, you collect your full Social Security benefits regardless of how much you earn during the year. Before age 70, earnings may reduce or eliminate Social Security benefits. Workers who are under 65 will have $1 in benefits held back for every $2 in earnings above the earnings limit set for that year. Before 2000 if you were 65 to 69, $1 of Social Security would be withheld for every $3 in earnings above the limit. The limit is increased every year. In 2000, the limit on earnings was $10,080 for workers under 65 and $17,000 for workers 65 through 69.

Early in the year 2000, a change in law became effective retroactive to January 1, 2000. Eligible people between the ages of 65 and 70 will now receive Social Security benefits without a reduction, regardless of the amount earned. People between 65 and 70 can elect not to receive special credit for each full month that they were eligible for, but did not receive, benefits before reaching age 70. This credit will increase the amount of the retirement benefit to be received and could also increase the benefit that a surviving spouse would receive. The amount of credit earned varies according to a person's year of birth. If a person chooses not to receive benefits for a partial year, partial credit will be given. For example, if you were born in late 1934 and retire at age 70, your benefit would be about 27.5% higher (5.5% × 5 years). (See Table 6.5.)

For those who are self-employed, the amount earned is not the

TABLE 6.5 Delayed Retirement Credits

Year of Birth	*Annual Percentage Rate*
1930	4.5%
1931–1932	5.0%
1933–1934	5.5%
1935–1936	6.0%

Caution: Don't jump to conclusions as to whether it is best to postpone receiving benefits to age 70. Collecting up to five years of benefits before age 70 will amount to more than many people will collect as a result of the special credit by waiting until age 70 to start receiving benefits. Among the factors to consider are health, life expectancy, and health and age of a person's spouse. For general information on the new law or Social Security benefits, visit the Social Security website at www.ssa.gov on the Internet or call 1-800-772-1213.

only factor. Generally, if you are engaged in self-employment activities for more than 45 hours a month, you are not retired. But you are retired if you work less than 15 hours a month. The rules get a little more technical if you are engaged between 15 and 45 hours per month in self-employment. If your business is sizable, or you are considered to be in an occupation requiring a lot of skill, working between 15 and 45 hours a month will probably mean that you are not retired.

Being self-employed, your earnings are considered for Social Security purposes when received by you rather than when you earned them. An exception is made for amounts earned before you became entitled to Social Security but received afterward. If you are self-employed and want further information on determining such questions as to whether your work is considered substantial, call Social Security and ask for the fact sheet "When You Retire from Your Own Business: What Social Security Needs to Know" (Publication # 05-10038).

Reporting Nonqualified Plan Earnings

Unlike self-employment, wages are counted for Social Security purposes when they are earned rather than when they are received. For example, you cannot expect to qualify for Social Security while working before you are 70 by postponing receipt of these earnings until after you reach 70. This type of deferral is categorized as nonqualified plan earnings and is required to be reported on the W-2 form in the year earned.

Other Considerations

There are retirees receiving Social Security who now live in another country. A number of Americans have chosen to retire to Mexico because it offers a lifestyle that is appealing for what appear to be lower prices. (*Caution*: Be careful about dealing with foreign currencies and foreign institutions. A few years ago, there was a devaluation of the Mexican currency that adversely affected a number of Americans living in Mexico with bank accounts in Mexican banks.) Others retire to their native lands. If you are not a U.S. citizen, or if you work outside of the United States, different rules apply in determining your qualification for Social Security.

If you are a U.S. citizen you can receive your Social Security checks in most countries, except Cambodia, Cuba, North Korea, Vietnam, and some of the former Soviet Republics. For more information on receiving Social Security while living in foreign countries, request the booklet "Your Social Security Payments While You Are Outside of the United States" (Publication #05-10137).

The Social Security Administration has a number of pamphlets that you can request related to such items as retirement benefits, Medicare, and the Supplemental Security Income program. The key telephone number is 800-772-1213 and the toll-free fax line is 888-475-7000. Sometimes you can get an answer to a fairly simple question by calling the 800 number. Otherwise, you should try to obtain the telephone number of your local office and, if necessary, schedule a face-to-face meeting with a claims representative.

There may be a Social Security office closer than the one you are initially referred to, so be sure to discuss location options. If you are still not satisfied after meeting with a claims representative, refer to your state office on aging. A schedule of telephone numbers of state offices on aging appears in Chapter 8. Other helpful sources may be the National Committee to Preserve Social Security and Medicare (800-966-1935) or the office of your U.S. senator or congressman. Your senator or congressman has a staffer assigned to help constituents who are having problems with Social Security or other federal programs.

If you disagree with any decision that Social Security makes in your case, you have a right to request reconsideration. Your request must be in writing and filed with any Social Security office within 60 days of the date that you receive a letter with an adverse finding. There are further steps in the review process, and they are explained in the fact sheet "The Appeals Process" (Publication #05-10041). If the matter is serious enough for you to seek the assistance of a lawyer or other representative, refer to the fact sheet "Your Right to Representation" (Publication #05-10075).

Chapter 7

Retirement and Preretirement—Even If You're under 50

With retirement, there are many varieties. You should not lock into a retirement picture that may be ideal for someone else but not for you—and economics is only a part of it. Here are some cases that we have run into that may give you some ideas.

RETIREMENT COMES IN MANY SHAPES AND SIZES

Herb is a doctor nearing age 70 and required to retire soon under his contract with his employer, a hospital. Carol, his wife, is a social worker who is in her early sixties, recently earned her PhD, and wants to work several more years. She is considerably younger than Herb and would like to put more money away since it is likely that she will outlive him by 10 years or more. Ideally, she also would like to be able to take time off during the year to travel with him. Her position with a university should work out well for both of them.

Erwin is a retired contractor. His wife, Barbara, is busy with tennis, bridge, and other social activities with her friends. Erwin plays golf in the summer but had time on his hands the rest of the year. His church has a program to deliver meals to shut-ins and a community college was looking for a part-time instructor to teach home modernization skills. Erwin is happier now with these activities.

What about Richard, the 90-year old cellist touring Asia with an orchestra made up of retirees—then coming home to join the fight for better municipal transportation for seniors?

Margo is 37 and Jerry is 40. They have three children, and the oldest is 5. Jerry is an unhappy lawyer, and previously he was an unhappy accountant. Margo was a successful executive with a mortgage company before quitting to have a family. But with three small children, Margo is tempted to go back to work, and her old company wants her badly. Jerry is very patient with the children. The mortgage company wants to hire Jerry as a part-time bookkeeper, which he could do primarily from their home. Their combined salaries would be more than half again as much as Jerry is making at present, and Jerry can take care of the children with part-time help. Has Jerry retired? When Margo left work to start her family, did she retire?

It's liberating to get past definitions. Whether you're younger or older, you should accommodate your changing needs and desires when possible. If you're over 50, you're allowed to explain yourself in terms of retirement. (What about the 32-year-old professional athlete who "retires" from playing a sport for four months per year to selling insurance for 12 months per year?)

The big key for many people in their forties and fifties is that they have created a financial engine to work for them—an investment portfolio that can generate $5,000, $20,000, or more per year. This may open up job opportunities that may be less stressful and more enjoyable that they couldn't consider before. They may prefer a different path than the conventional one of building a larger portfolio for a later different type of retirement.

Another version of retirement—not limited to people over 55—is for those who are not their own boss and would like to be. They're "retiring" from their current employer and "divorcing" themselves from an unhappy pattern of earning a living. Before making this move, there is the need for analysis and planning. Since self-discipline is critical if you're going to be your own boss, your first hurdle is taking the time to read up on self-employment and analyzing what you're going to do. Some questions to consider are:

- ✔ How much money is it going to take to get started, including starting costs and living expenses until the new venture generates income?
- ✔ Can you get started while still holding on to your old job? This will give you an opportunity to make a better assessment if you can make self-employment work to your satisfaction.

- ✔ Is there a better idea for a small business than you now have? Visits to local bookstores may be helpful. One useful book is *201 Ideas for Your Small Business* by Jane Applegate (Bloomberg Press, $14.95). Your opportunity may relate to the business you are in. If you are in a service business such as accounting, public relations, or sales, you may see an opportunity to offer your services without the need to put up with a boss or pay office rent or salaries for other workers. It may be an opportunity that requires a period of education and accreditation such as qualifying as an acupuncturist, personal exercise trainer, bookkeeper, or TV repairperson.
- ✔ If it doesn't work out, do you have a fallback strategy such as going back to work for the same company or in the same industry, or becoming qualified in a new industry as a result of your venture?
- ✔ Can you candidly evaluate your ability to stick it out, work harder than you ever have, and do the worst parts of the job in a timely fashion?
- ✔ Are there persons who can mentor you—answer questions and make suggestions because they're experienced? They've done it or something like it, or you have confidence in their judgment. It's a good idea to talk to them first.

Steve and Tina are in their thirties. He is an electrician, while she is a receptionist in a dental office but has a flair for home decorating. They bought a ranch-style home for $200,000 in a neighborhood with houses ranging up to $500,000 in value. The house is structurally sound but needs work. They plan to move in and devote a lot of energy and money into making it much more valuable. If they live in it for at least two years and sell it at a profit, they do not have to pay income tax on a gain of up to $500,000. Recent tax law changes allow couples to make up to $500,000 ($250,000 for individuals) in profit on the sale of their residences—provided that each house is their principal residence for at least two years before the sale. *One note of caution*: Buying a house for $200,000, adding capital improvements costing $50,000, and selling the house after two years for $750,000 seems to qualify to exclude the entire $500,00 gain from tax ($750,000 minus $200,000 minus $50,000). However, before buying the house you had a $100,000 gain on a prior house that you rolled over tax-free, you must subtract this gain from the cost so that the current house is considered to cost $100,000, not $200,000, and you have a $600,000 gain with $100,000 of it being taxable.

Alexa and Karl are in their forties and in the process of divorcing. They have $200,000 in net assets, including $100,000 in investments and $75,000 equity in their house. They have tentatively agreed that each of them will get $100,000 in assets, and Alexa wants to retain the house. Alexa has not worked for over 15 years. A friend of Alexa's who is a financial adviser has now pointed out that $100,000 in investments can generate much more income and security for her than the house would, and suggests that $50,000 of the investments that are held in a tax-sheltered plan account could be held for Alexa's benefit. A complicating factor is that the house could be sold tax-free, while there would be income tax plus a 10 percent penalty generally for withdrawals from the tax-sheltered account before age 59½. A more equitable property settlement is worked out that includes putting Alexa in a better position to support herself both initially and for the long term. Their respective long-term economic needs are now recognized on an equitable basis.

In divorce situations, particularly if the couple does not have a CPA or financial adviser to rely on, there are certified divorce planners who are called in, often by one or both divorce attorneys. The Institute for Certified Divorce Planners was formed in 1993, and referrals can be secured by calling 800-875-1760. CDPs may also be useful as expert witnesses. They are generally financial planners, CPAs, or attorneys with additional training.

Also, a word for those under 50 about Social Security. Until recently, those under 50 were advised not to count on Social Security benefits for their retirement. Now, with serious talk of paying off the national debt in less than 15 years, the survival of Social Security benefits, particularly for those now over 40, seems likely. Currently, many newly retired couples in their sixties receive $1,500 to $2,000 per month in retirement benefits, counting the benefits of both spouses. Even if equivalent benefits would start at age 70 for couples now in their forties, the benefits are substantial and would last for the balance of your respective lives.

Part Three

Preserving Your Wealth: Estate Planning

Chapter 8

Dealing with Potentially High Health Care Expenses

In planning for retirement, a logical starting point is figuring out how much it costs to live now. If your sources of retirement income can cover these expenses, are you prepared for retirement? Probably, but potential health care costs as you age are likely to be more than they were in your younger years. The costs and availability of adequate health insurance and related programs designed to meet these needs must be considered.

MANAGED PLANS AND INSURANCE PROTECTION

High medical expenses can destroy or severely damage most retirement portfolios. Health care costs have risen faster than the overall inflation rate for the past 15 years or longer. As a consequence, the cost of health insurance also continues to rise substantially. Adding a larger *deductible* feature (such as $1,000 instead of $200) will substantially reduce annual premiums. A comprehensive major medical policy should cover at least 80 percent of medical bills that are over and above the deductible so that your *copayment* is 20 percent or less. The policy should be guaranteed renewable and noncancelable.

Another area to explore in controlling health care costs are managed care plans such as health maintenance organizations (HMOs) and preferred provider organizations (PPOs). HMOs are supposed to control medical costs by adopting measures including dictating whom the insured and other family members may see for medical care. A PPO is usually formed by an insurer or a large business that negotiates with a group of doctors and hospitals to provide medical services at reduced prices. If the insured goes to an approved physician, the entire bill is paid for, but only a portion is paid if an outside physician is seen. Choosing an HMO or PPO is much like selecting any health insurer. The following suggestions for those who are over 65 and considering Medigap insurance will also apply if you're considering an HMO or a PPO.

deductible the amount you pay before an insurance policy will pay, generally an annual requirement.

With group health coverage the insurance premium will cover each individual in the group. Group coverage is estimated to be about 15 percent less expensive than the cost of purchasing the same coverage individually. Also, with group insurance, individuals who have serious chronic problems usually are not excluded. Large employers usually provide group health coverage. Sometimes professional organizations and fraternal groups provide group insurance. Check with any organizations and groups that you belong to about group coverage. It may even be worth joining a group for this coverage alone.

copayment after satisfying the annual health insurance deductible, the percentage of remaining fees or costs you must pay.

If you retire or are laid off and you have group coverage, COBRA provides that you can continue that coverage for at least another 18 months; COBRA is the Consolidated Omnibus Budget Reconciliation Act. You may be charged up to 102 percent of what the coverage costs the employer, but the cost is still less than an individual policy with the same coverage; if you are a dependent of a covered employee and are in danger of losing health coverage because the covered employee has died, is divorcing or separating from you, or has become eligible for Medicare, you can buy coverage for yourself through that covered employee's group for up to three years. There are exceptions from COBRA, such as when a company terminates the entire plan.

MEDICARE

Medicare coverage is available for those 65 or over who qualify for Social Security retirement benefits. Medicare benefits consist of Part A, basic hospital insurance, and Part B, supplementary medical insurance. Basic hospital insurance includes in-patient hospital care, some skilled nursing home care, and, under certain circumstances, hospice care. Most people do not have to pay monthly premiums for Part A because they paid Medicare expenses while they worked. Supplementary medical insurance covers physician services, outpatient hospital care, physical therapy, medical equipment, and certain other services not covered by basic hospital insurance. The participant pays only nominal monthly premiums with the major cost subsidized by the federal government. Supplementary medical insurance, Part B, is optional. Medicare Part B premiums were $45.50 per month in 1999 but can change yearly. Monthly premiums may be higher if you did not elect Part B when you first became eligible.

If you are not getting Social Security, you should sign up for Medicare as you approach your 65th birthday, even if you are not ready to retire. For those who receive Social Security benefits, Medicare (Part A) starts automatically at age 65. For those with limited resources, Medicaid is a joint federal and state program and under it some states will pay the Medicare premiums and certain other out-of-pocket Medicare expenses. Your state determines if you qualify under this low-income Medicare beneficiary program. For more information, contact Social Security (800-772-1213) and request a copy of "Medicare Savings for Qualified Beneficiaries" (Publication No, HCFA-02184, revised June 1999). Medicare does not cover prescription drugs and certain other medical costs. Also, Medicare often reimburses health care providers at rates below those charged to a patient. A number of HMOs cater to Medicare patients by offering broad coverage for an annual fee plus nominal copayments.

Medicare does not pay all of the costs of health care, so it is helpful if your doctor or supplier of health care equipment and supplies agrees to accept the Medicare-approved amount as payment in full. This is called "accepting assignment." If you have purchased a Medigap policy, it may pay part of the bill where the doctor or supplier has not accepted assignment.

Assignment does not pay for services covered by Part A (hospital insurance). Assignment applies to only the services and supplies covered by Part B (medical insurance). Assignment works with only "The Original Medicare Plan." In some areas of the country there are "Medicare Managed Care Plans." Assignment does not apply if you are in a Medicare Managed Care Plan.

Doctors and suppliers must accept assignment for lab tests covered by Medicare if you are enrolled in Medicaid and your state helps pay for your health care costs. For more information on assignment call 800-633-4227 and order Publication No. HCFA-10134, or look on the Internet at www.medicare.gov.

Medigap is Medicare supplemental insurance that pays for expenses not covered by Medicare such as deductibles and copayments. Since uncovered costs may be substantial, many retirees purchase this supplemental insurance. Medigap policies do not extend the coverage beyond the limits provided by Medicare. By law, insurance companies are required to offer Medigap policies in 10 different categories ranging from "A" (basic) through "J," which is the most comprehensive (see Figure 8.1). State law may limit the types of these policies that are available in your state.

NEW MEDICARE SAVINGS ACCOUNT PLAN

Another development is the Medical Savings Account (MSA). Initially, the latest version is to be made available for up to 390,000 senior citizens. The federal government provides a tax-free cash allowance for these Medical Savings Accounts based on age and other factors such as the cost of living. These cash allowances cover premiums for a health insurance policy with a high deductible amount as well as funding part of the deductible. To the extent that an individual's premiums and medical expenses do not use up this account, it accumulates. Once it reaches 60 percent of the deductible, the amount over that figure may be withdrawn and retained by the individual. The principal concern is that if you have substantial medical expenses, they could far exceed the balance that you have available to meet them. Under a non-Medicare version of MSAs, 95,000 policies were sold. At this time (January 2000), Medicare advises that no private insurance company provides a policy to pay medical bills after you meet your deductible. Updated information can be obtained by calling 800-633-4227, or contact www.medicare.gov on the Internet. If you are satisfied with your Medicare benefits, you do not have to do anything about the MSA plan.

Call your state insurance department (see the directory at the end of the chapter) to find out what Medigap policies are available in your area.

Basic Benefits: Included in All Plans

- [X] **Inpatient Hospital Care:**
  Coverage for the Part A coinsurance and for 365 additional days of hospital care during your lifetime after Medicare benefits end.
- [X] **Medical Costs:**
  Coverage for the Part B coinsurance (generally 20 percent of the Medicare-approved payment amount).
- [X] **Blood:**
  Coverage for the first three pints of blood each year.

Medigap Benefits	*A*	*B*	*C*	*D*	*E*	*F*[1]	*G*	*H*	*I*	*J*[1]
Basic Benefits	X	X	X	X	X	X	X	X	X	X
Part A: Inpatient Hospital Deductible		X	X	X	X	X	X	X	X	X
Part A: Skilled Nursing Facility Coinsurance			X	X	X	X	X	X	X	X
Part B: Deductible			X			X				X
Foreign Travel Emergency			X	X	X	X	X	X	X	X
At-Home Recovery				X			X		X	X
Part B: Excess Charges						100%	80%		100%	100%
Preventive Care					X					X
Prescription Drugs								Basic Coverage X	Basic Coverage X	Extended Coverage X

FIGURE 8.1 Medigap policies: chart of 10 standardized Medigap plans.

[1]Plans F and J also have a high deductible option.

Source: Chart used with permission from the United Seniors Health Cooperative.

Note: For more information on Medigap policies, call 800-MEDICARE (800-633-4227; TTY/TDD: 877-486-2048 for the hearing and speech impaired) and ask for a free copy of the "Guide to Health Insurance for People with Medicare."

New Medicare regulations went into effect in October 1997. There will be additional health plans owned and operated by doctors and hospitals that may be superior to the plans of some of the insurers, but we will have to wait to see whether this will be the case. Before these regulations, premiums were to rise to $51.50 per month by the year 2002. Under the new regulations, the increased benefits will cause these rates to rise to $67 per month by the year 2002.

Recently private insurers started offering Medicare-type coverage with more generous pay schedules than Medicare offers. These policies came about because of complaints that the low payments under Medicare resulted in less attention being given to Medicare patients. Of course, this more generous schedule will result in higher copayments and greater premiums. Under the new law, if the Medicare patient pays the entire bill and the doctor agrees not to accept any Medicare reimbursements for at least two years, the doctor is allowed to accept these private payments. However, since almost all doctors who treat the elderly receive a substantial portion of their income from Medicare payments, it is not likely that many doctors will enter into this agreement.

Health insurance, along with the complex rules for Medicare and Medicaid, can be confusing. Some of these coverages overlap into the area of long-term care insurance. If you believe that you may need more health insurance, review the following checklist. Also look to insurance counseling services (phone numbers are listed at the end of this chapter).

✔ ***Shop with care.*** Don't pay for more coverage than you need. One broad policy is better than several policies that may duplicate coverage in one area and omit coverage in another area. It is unlawful for an insurance company to sell you a Medigap policy unless you sign a statement that you intend to cancel the prior policy when the new policy becomes effective. It is unlawful to sell a policy that violates the antiduplication rules; the salesman, broker, or insurance company could be subject to criminal penalties, civil penalties, or both.

The federal toll-free telephone number to file Medigap complaints is 800-638-6833. Illegal market practices include high-pressure tactics to force or frighten a prospect into buying a Medigap policy or deceptive advertising such as mailings to those who may be particularly vulnerable to buying insurance. As with other expensive purchases, you should contact different companies and compare the costs and coverage. It is also helpful to ask friends, relatives, and acquaintances about particular companies to learn which ones are more cooperative.

- ✔ *Evaluate your existing coverage.* You should not retain inadequate coverage simply because you've had it for a long time. Unlike most other coverages, when you replace a Medigap policy, you must be given credit for the period you held the old policy in determining whether any restrictions for preexisting conditions apply under the new one. You have up to 30 days to decide whether to cancel the old policy and keep the new one or to return the new policy and retain the old policy. Delivery of the new policy or a refund if you decide not to purchase it should be within 30 days. Otherwise, contact the company, and if there will be a further delay, ask for a written explanation. If there is no response from the company, contact your state insurance department. A list of the telephone numbers of the state insurance departments is included at the end of this chapter.
- ✔ *Pay attention to maximum benefits.* A policy with lower premiums may offer reduced benefits. It may reduce the number of days of care or the dollar amount for the treatment of a particular condition. Some policies may eliminate certain coverages or provide less coverage.
- ✔ *Remember, neither the United States nor your state is in the insurance business.* Do not be misled! The insurance companies that are selling the policies are privately owned. "State approval" means only that a company has met legal requirements. Insurance that supplements Medicare is not government-sponsored. If a salesperson tells you that the insurer is connected with the government in order to sell you an insurance policy, that insurer should be reported to federal authorities (800-638-6833) or to your state insurance department.

  It is illegal to use names, symbols, and emblems of various government-supported programs including the Social Security Administration, the Health Care Financing Administration, and the U.S. Department of Health and Human Services. It is unlawful to mail solicitations that appear to be endorsed or in some way related to the U.S. government.
- ✔ *Utilize your state insurance department.* It should have a record of any company doing business in your state. Call the department to confirm that an insurer is in fact licensed to do business in your state. A salesperson contacting you should be able to give you confirmation of the name of the company that he or she represents and that that company is licensed. Be sure to get all sales-

persons' business cards and their addresses and telephone numbers and those of the insurance companies they represent.

If you do purchase a policy, make the check or money order payable to the insurance company, never the agent or anyone else. Get a receipt that acknowledges the insurance company, not the agent. Furthermore, it is a good idea to contact the insurance company to verify that the agent is affiliated with that company. Never pay cash.

Insurance policies are difficult to read. The salesperson is required to give you a summary that is easily understandable, and you should take the time to read and understand it.

- ✔ ***Check for exclusions for preexisting conditions.*** You may have an existing health condition that the policy will not cover, while your existing policy *does* cover it. Generally, these are problems that you saw a doctor about within the six-month period preceding the effective date of the policy. Medigap policies must cover preexisting conditions after the policies have been in effect for six months. Some companies may offer a shorter exclusion period for a particular preexisting condition.
- ✔ ***Consider alternatives.*** Rather than replacing a policy because it doesn't have long-term care with a new policy that does provide for long-term care, consider shopping for a long-term care policy that will *supplement* your coverage. Compute the cost and the coverage from this alternative with the cost of replacing your existing policy. Joining a managed care plan (HMO or PPO) may be preferable to a more costly alternative. Friends and relatives, particularly if they are health care professionals, may be very helpful.
- ✔ ***Be sure to compare rates among several insurance companies.***
- ✔ ***Get health insurance information from the Social Security Administration.*** Call the SSA (800-772-1213) to order "The Guide to Health Insurance for People with Medicare."
- ✔ ***Don't be rushed into making a decision, but recognize there is a time limit.*** If you are age 65 or older and qualify for Social Security benefits, you have a period of six months from the date that you meet both of these qualifications to buy a Medigap policy regardless of your health problems. If your birthday is on the first day of the month, your Part B coverage, if you buy it, starts on the first day of the previous month although you would still be 64 at that time, and your six-month Medigap open enrollment period also starts on that date. After that open enrollment periods ends,

a person is limited as to the Medigap policy that is available, particularly if he or she has a preexisting health condition.

- ✔ *Complete the application carefully.* Often an insurance salesperson is eager to complete the sale and may rush you to complete the application. Keep in mind that if you leave out any medical information, a later claim may be refused or delayed if you didn't specify a medical condition. The insurance company could also deny the claim completely or cancel the policy.

LONG-TERM CARE INSURANCE

Medicare and Medigap insurance may cover short-term periods in a nursing home when they are directly related to an illness or injury. Medicaid would pay additional amounts, but to qualify for Medicaid, personal assets must be substantially reduced. A long stay in a nursing home can be very costly. For those with more modest investment portfolios, long-term care insurance may be advisable. To determine whether you should insure against this type of risk, you or your adviser should do some projections. The potential annual expenses of $30,000 to $100,000 a year should be taken into account as well as the shorter life expectancy that may also be a consideration. The range of potential costs for extended long-term care varies greatly among the different sections of the country.

To purchase long-term care insurance you must be in reasonably good health. If you are not in good health but have life insurance coverage that you were about to cancel, you may decide to retain some life insurance coverage not as a complete substitute for long-term care coverage, but as a partial substitute. Life insurance won't give you money to pay for long-term care during life, but death benefits could replenish your estate for the benefit of a surviving spouse or other dependents. Its cash value could be borrowed and if your condition became terminal, access to death benefits may be possible. See "Viatical Settlements of Life Insurance Policies" at the end of Chapter 11.

Recently, some insurance companies have added a long-term care rider to a life insurance policy. For a $50,000 one-time premium, a 60-year-old woman in good health can purchase a $139,500 death benefit with a rider allowing the advance of up to the entire death benefit to pay for long-term care costs, and if it is completely utilized for long-term care, up to an additional like amount is provided for long-term care. It seems that the policy cost is too high for the benefits. Obtaining separate premium quotes for life insurance policies and for long-term care policies should make the analysis easier for anyone considering coverage. Also consider the other factors listed next in analyzing the coverage. Your insurance agent or CPA may be helpful in analyzing this alternative. As you get older, the annual premium rate increases. Here are some of the factors to consider in evaluating an adequate long-term care insurance policy.

"Qualified" or "Nonqualified" Policies

The Health Insurance Portability and Accountability Act was passed in 1996. It created a category of policies with assured tax benefits ("qualified"), while leaving the other policies in a state of uncertainty relative to tax benefits ("nonqualified"). The qualified policies allow owners to exclude policy benefit payments from taxable income and to deduct part of the costs under certain circumstances.

In determining whether to purchase a qualified or nonqualified policy, an update on the tax status of the nonqualified policies should be obtained. Check with a knowledgeable source such as an attorney specializing in either elder care or taxes, since the regulations are not always clear.

At this time, qualified policies appear to be inferior to nonqualified policies. For example, under the qualified policy, a health care professional must certify that the insured will have the disabilities for at least 90 days to be eligible for coverage. Thus, if you are recovering from a fall and need care for five or six weeks, you would not be eligible.

To collect benefits, you must be unable to care for yourself in at least two out of six (or sometimes two out of five) of the following "activities of daily living": bathing, dressing, eating, toileting, continence, and transferring (e.g., moving from a chair into your bed). Nonqualified policies don't have the 90-day restriction. You may qualify for benefits under many of these policies if a doctor determines that it is a "medical necessity" for you to have help in taking care of yourself. One example is with very old and frail people who need help in taking their medication or bathing, or who are so frail that the doctor determines that they can no longer live alone safely. It seems clear that there will be significantly fewer claims for both nursing home care and home care under qualified policies.

If you owned a long-term care policy before January 1, 1997, you have tax-favored status for your coverage; it is "qualified." You must be careful before replacing it or making any changes to the policy, such as increasing the benefit level, to avoid having it be considered the equivalent of a new policy. You should check on current tax status with both your tax adviser and the insurance company before making any replacements or revisions.

Coverage Details

- ✔ *The elimination period.* The choice of waiting periods is usually between 20 and 100 days. You have to decide whether the savings in premium costs justifies the need to self-insure for an additional period.
- ✔ *The amount of "daily benefits."* Nursing home facilities vary in different parts of the country. Paying for daily benefits of $80 per day may not be adequate protection if expenses are incurred at the rate of $200 per day or more.
- ✔ *"Inflation-adjusted" coverage.* If you are purchasing this policy at age 60 and you expect to need it at age 80 or 85, the cost of care will probably be considerably higher. Some insurers give you the choice of providing for an inflation adjustment when you initially buy the policy, while others periodically give you the opportunity to add inflation adjustment protection.
- ✔ *Time period for benefits.* Should you receive benefits for a maximum of two to five years or for life? The longer the period, the greater the cost.

Other considerations are nursing home benefits without prior hospitalization, home health benefits without prior hospitalization, restrictions on the number of days, coverage for Alzheimer's disease, some protection against rate increases, waiver of premium if you are in a nursing home, and restoration of benefits to the original maximum if after receiving benefits you go for a stated period without using further benefits.

Selection of Insurance Company

Select an insurer with care. Questions about the insurance company, the policies, and the agent should be directed to your state insurance department or insurance counseling program. (See the directory at the end of this chapter.) Certain companies may be easier to deal with when the time comes to put in your claim. Insurance agents with whom you have had prior favorable experience or who are recommended by trusted advisers, as well as nursing home administrators, may be helpful. Contact several companies and compare coverages and costs. Generally, it's not advisable to buy multiple long-term care policies.

Evaluate the financial strength of the insurance company. Any policy purchased from an unsound company is a poor choice. The opinions of rating agencies cannot be guaranteed, but the opinion of two or more agencies should be very useful. Each rating agency has its own rating scale, so make sure you understand the rating system of each agency. Some of this information is available at public libraries, or you can call the following numbers. These rating agencies can also be helping you when you're considering life insurance policies.

Names of Agencies and Telephone Numbers

A. M. Best Co., Oldwick, New Jersey	908-439-2200
Duff & Phelps Credit Rating Co., Chicago, Illinois	312-368-3198 (no charge)
Moody's Investors Service, New York, New York	212-553-0377 (no charge)
Standard & Poor's Ratings Group, New York, New York	212-438-2000 (no charge)
Weiss Ratings Inc., Palm Beach Gardens, Florida	800-289-9222

Both the insurance department of your state and the state insurance counseling program can provide you with information on long-term care coverage and other insurance. (See Table 8.1.)

TABLE 8.1 State Insurance Departments, Insurance Counseling Programs, and Agencies on Aging

Note: The 800 numbers shown can only be accessed by calls from within the respective state.

Insurance Departments	*Insurance Counseling*	*Agencies on Aging*
	Alabama	
Insurance Department Consumer Service 334-269-3550	800-243-5463 334-242-5743	Commission on Aging 800-243-5463 334-242-5743
	Alaska	
Division of Insurance 907-349-1230	800-478-6065 907-269-3680	Older Alaskans Commission 907-465-3250
	American Samoa	
Insurance Department Governor's Office 011-684/633-4116	800-586-7299	Territorial Administration on Aging 684-633-1252
	Arizona	
Insurance Department 602-912-8444	800-432-4040 602-542-6595	Department of Economic Security; Aging and Adult Administration 602-542-4446
	Arkansas	
Insurance Department Seniors Insurance Network 800-852-5494	800-852-5494 501-371-2785	Division of Aging and Adult Services 501-682-2441
	California	
Department of Insurance 800-927-4357 916-445-5544	800-434-0222 916-323-7315	Department of Aging Health Insurance Counseling and Advocacy Branch 916-332-5290
	Colorado	
Insurance Division 303-894-7499, ext. 356	800-544-9181 303-894-7499, ext. 356	Aging and Adult Services Department of Social Services 303-620-4147

(Continued)

TABLE 8.1 *Continued*

Insurance Departments	*Insurance Counseling*	*Agencies on Aging*
	Connecticut	
Insurance Department 860-297-3863	800-994-9422 860-994-9422	Elderly Services Division 800-994-9422 860-424-5277
	Delaware	
Insurance Department 800-282-8611 302-739-4251	800-336-9500 302-739-6266	Services for Aging and Adults Department of Health and Social Services 302-577-4791
	District of Columbia	
Insurance Department Consumer and Professional Services Bureau 202-727-8000	202-676-3900	Office on Aging 202-724-5626 202-724-5622
	Florida	
Department of Insurance 904-922-3100	800-963-5337 850-414-2060	Department of Elder Affairs 800-96ELDER 850-414-2000
	Georgia	
Insurance Department 404-656-2056	800-669-8387	Division of Aging Services Department of Human Resources 404-657-5258
	Guam	
Insurance Division Department of Revenue and Taxation 617-475-5000	808-586-7299	Division of Senior Citizens Department of Public Health and Social Services 617-477-2930
	Hawaii	
Department of Commerce and Consumer Affairs Insurance Division 808-586-2790	808-586-7299	Executive Office on Aging 808-586-0100

TABLE 8.1 *Continued*

Insurance Departments	*Insurance Counseling*	*Agencies on Aging*
	Idaho	
Insurance Department SHIBA Program 208-334-4350	S.W.—800-247-4422 N.—800-488-5725 S.E.—800-488-5764 Central—800-488-5731	Commission on Aging 208-334-3833
	Illinois	
Insurance Department 217-782-4515	800-548-9034 217-785-9021	Department on Aging 800-252-8966 217-785-2870
	Indiana	
Insurance Department 800-622-4461 317-232-2395	800-452-4800 317-233-3475	Division of Aging and Rehabilitative Services 800-545-7763 317-232-7020
	Iowa	
Insurance Division 515-281-5705	800-351-4664 515-281-5705	Department of Elder Affairs 515-281-5187
	Kansas	
Insurance Department 800-432-2484 913-296-3071	800-860-5260 316-337-7386	Department on Aging 785-296-4986
	Kentucky	
Insurance Department 502-564-3630	800-372-2973 502-564-7372	Division of Aging Services Cabinet for Human Resources 502-564-6930
	Louisiana	
Department of Insurance 800-259-5301 504-342-5301	800-259-5301 504-342-0825	Office of Elderly Affairs 225-342-7100
	Maine	
Bureau of Insurance 207-582-8707	800-750-5353 207-624-5335	Bureau of Elder and Adult Services 207-624-5335

(Continued)

TABLE 8.1 *Continued*

Insurance Departments	*Insurance Counseling*	*Agencies on Aging*
Marshall Islands, Republic of		
		State Agency on Aging Department of Social Services Republic of the Marshall Islands Marjuro, Marshall Islands 96960
Maryland		
Insurance Administration Complaints and Investigation Unit—Life and Health 410-333-2793 410-333-2770	800-243-3425 410-767-1100	Department on Aging 410-767-1100
Massachusetts		
Insurance Division 617-521-7777	800-882-2003 617-727-7750	Executive Office of Elder Affairs 800-882-2003 617-727-7750
Michigan		
Insurance Bureau 517-373-0240 (General Assistance) 517-335-1702 (Senior Issues)	800-803-7174 517-373-8230	Office of Services to the Aging 517-373-8230
Micronesia, Federated States of		
		State Agency on Aging Office of Health Services Federated States of Micronesia Ponape, E.C.I. 96941
Minnesota		
Insurance Department Department of Commerce 612-296-4026	800-333-2433	Board on Aging 651-296-2770

TABLE 8.1 *Continued*

Insurance Departments	*Insurance Counseling*	*Agencies on Aging*
	Mississippi	
Insurance Department Consumer Assistance Division 601-359-3569	800-948-3090 601-359-4929	Council on Aging Division of Aging and Adult Services 800-948-3090 601-359-4929
	Missouri	
Department of Insurance Consumer Assistance Division 800-726-7390 314-751-2640	800-390-3330 517-893-7900	Division of Aging Department of Social Services 573-751-3082
	Montana	
Insurance Department 406-444-2040	800-332-2272 406-444-7781	Division of Senior Long-Term Care 800-332-2272 406-444-4077
	Nebraska	
Insurance Department 402-471-2201	402-471-2201	Department on Aging 402-471-2306
	Nevada	
Department of Business and Industry Division of Insurance 800-992-0900	800-307-4444 702-486-4602	Department of Human Resources Division for Aging Services 702-486-3545
	New Hampshire	
Insurance Department Life and Health Division 800-852-3416 603-271-2261	800-852-3388 603-225-9000	Department of Health & Human Services Division of Elderly & Adult Services 603-271-4394
	New Jersey	
Insurance Department 609-292-5363	800-792-8820	Department of Community Affairs Division on Aging 800-792-8820 609-984-3951

(Continued)

TABLE 8.1 *Continued*

Insurance Departments	*Insurance Counseling*	*Agencies on Aging*
	New Mexico	
Insurance Department 505-827-4601	800-432-2080 505-827-7640	State Agency on Aging 800-432-2080 505-827-7640
	New York	
Insurance Department (Outside New York City) 800-342-3736 (NYC Area) 212-602-0203	800-333-4114 (Outside NYC) 212-869-3850 (NYC Area)	State Office for the Aging 800-342-9871 518-474-5731
	North Carolina	
Insurance Department Seniors' Health Insurance Information Program (SHIIP) 800-662-7777 (Consumer Services) 919-733-0111 (SHIIP)	800-443-9354 919-733-0111	Division of Aging 919-733-3983
	North Dakota	
Insurance Department Senior Health Insurance Counseling 800-247-0560 701-328-2440	800-247-0560 701-328-2977	Department of Human Services Aging Services Division 800-755-8521 701-328-8909
	Northern Mariana Islands, Commonwealth of	
		Department of Community and Cultural Affairs 607-234-6011
	Ohio	
Insurance Department Consumer Services Division 800-686-1526 614-644-2673	800-686-1578 614-644-3458	Department of Aging 800-282-1206 614-466-5500
	Oklahoma	
Insurance Department 800-522-0071 405-521-6628	800-763-2828 405-521-6628	Department of Human Services Aging Services Division 405-521-2327

TABLE 8.1 *Continued*

Insurance Departments	*Insurance Counseling*	*Agencies on Aging*
	Oregon	
Department of Consumer and Business Services Senior Health Insurance Benefits Assistance 800-722-4134 503-378-4484	800-722-4134 503-947-7250	Department of Human Resources Senior and Disabled Services Division 800-232-3020 503-945-5811
	Palau	
		State Agency on Aging Department of Social Services Republic of Palau P.O. Box 100 Koror, Palau 96940
	Pennsylvania	
Insurance Department Consumer Services Bureau 717-787-2317	800-783-7067 717-783-8975	Department of Aging "Apprise" Health Insurance Counseling and Assistance 800-783-7067
	Puerto Rico	
Office of the Commis-sioner of Insurance 809-722-8686	800-981-4355 787-721-8590	Governor's Office of Elderly Affairs 787-721-5710
	Rhode Island	
Insurance Division 401-277-2223	800-322-2880 401-222-2880	Department of Elderly Affairs 401-222-2858
	South Carolina	
Department of Insurance Consumer Affairs Section 800-768-3467 803-737-6180	800-868-9095 803-253-6177	Division on Aging 803-737-7500
	South Dakota	
Insurance Department 605-773-3563	800-822-8804 605-773-3656	Office of Adult Services and Aging 605-773-3656

(Continued)

TABLE 8.1 *Continued*

Insurance Departments	*Insurance Counseling*	*Agencies on Aging*
	Tennessee	
Department of Commerce and Insurance 800-525-2816 615-741-4955	800-525-2816 615-741-4955	Commission on Aging 615-741-2056
	Texas	
Department of Insurance Complaints Resolution (MC 111-1A) 800-252-3439 512-463-6515	800-252-9240 512-424-6840	Department on Aging 800-252-9240 512-424-6840
	Utah	
Insurance Department Consumer Services 800-429-3805 801-538-3805	800-439-3805 800-538-3910	Division of Aging and Adult Services 800-606-0608 801-538-3910
	Vermont	
Department of Banking and Insurance Consumer Complaint Division 802-828-3302	800-642-5119	Department of Aging and Disabilities 802-241-2325
	Virginia	
Bureau of Insurance 804-371-9691 800-552-7945	800-552-3402 804-662-9333	Department for the Aging 800-552-4464 804-662-9354
	Virgin Islands	
Insurance Department 809-774-2991	809-774-2991 340-778-6311 ext. 2338	Senior Citizen Affairs Division Department of Human Services 340-692-5950
	Washington	
Insurance Department 800-562-6900 360-753-7300	800-397-4422 206-654-1833	Aging and Adult Services Administration Department of Social and Health Services 360-902-7797

TABLE 8.1 *Continued*

Insurance Departments	*Insurance Counseling*	*Agencies on Aging*
	West Virginia	
Insurance Department Consumer Service 800-642-9004 800-435-7381 (Hearing-Impaired) 304-558-3386	800-642-9004 304-558-3317	West Virginia Bureau of Senior Services 304-558-0004
	Wisconsin	
Insurance Department Complaints Department 800-236-8517 608-266-0103	800-242-1060 608-267-3201	Board on Aging and Long-Term Care 800-242-1060 608-266-2536
	Wyoming	
Insurance Department 800-438-5768 307-777-7401	800-856-4398 307-856-6880	Division on Aging 800-442-2766 307-777-7986

Chapter 9

Protecting Your Portfolio from Creditors, Crooks, and Carelessness

While you're increasing your retirement assets or estate, you're like the rancher building his or her herd. The rancher improves the breeding methods used to increase the numbers and quality of the herd, but at the same time must be vigilant to protect it from disease, disasters, and attacks from wolves and other predators.

In this chapter, we deal with the protection of your "herd" from claims of creditors, losses to thieves, swindlers, and other varmints, as well as carelessness.

PROTECTION FROM LEGAL CLAIMS

Many of you who are reading this book are 50 or older. If you haven't had your second retirement eye-opener, this is it. The first retirement eye-opener probably occurred in your forties when you considered how much more you would have to accumulate in order to retire.

Your net worth is probably much more substantial than it was then. You are entitled to congratulate yourself—you have amounted to more than some neighbor or teacher would have predicted during your childhood. However, now you must be like a rancher with his or her herd—your protective instincts must be sharpened.

You must protect your portfolio against potential claims by others. Automobile accidents, household accidents, and malpractice claims are three major areas of concern that can damage or destroy an investment portfolio. Business owners have an extra area of concern: They can lose their businesses, which, for most of them, is their most valuable asset. If a person is highly compensated for his or her services, such as a doctor, dentist, or business executive, and his or her earning capacity is substantially reduced due to your act or failure to act, you may be legally liable for huge damages. Automobile and homeowners insurance policy protection may seem substantial but is probably limited to hundreds of thousands of dollars, while a skilled professional or executive in his or her early forties may have lost lifetime earning power valued at much more. A successful claim results in your becoming indebted to the other party—you could owe a sum of money to compensate for someone's injury and loss.

In order to increase your protection, you should consider adding to your current insurance coverage, buying personal umbrella insurance protection, or both. A knowledgeable insurance agent can be very helpful. Many accountants and attorneys can also be helpful. One million dollars' worth of personal umbrella coverage can be purchased for about $500 per year; $5 million of protection would cost about $1,000 per year. Expert advice is often needed to determine which policy should be purchased and the terms to elect. Policies issued by different companies vary so that you may have better protection for about the same cost by becoming knowledgeable or relying on a knowledgeable insurance adviser. Umbrella insurance adds a layer or layers of protection over existing specific policies by increasing policy limits on certain coverages or insuring against additional liabilities not covered by the basic policy or both. Generally, this additional protection is only offered by the insurer of the underlying automobile, homeowner, or other insurance policy.

In certain circumstances insurance may be too expensive or not adequately able to protect a portfolio and other assets from potential claims. Then, legal assistance may be needed. Only skilled, experienced attorneys with a thorough knowledge of creditors' rights should be relied on. If your attorney does not have this expertise, he or she should refer you to a specialist in this area. Again, probabilities must be considered. Protection may be costly or incomplete, and may introduce other risks. Individual accounts in qualified employer retirement plans will have substantial protection from creditor claim and to a lesser degree, IRAs and Keogh plans will often have a degree of protection from creditors that is based on the law of the state where the participant resides. Annuities, including variable annuities, are protected to a substantial degree in most states. Please see information on annuities later in this chapter under the heading "Carelessness."

In Chapters 10 and 11 covering estate planning, we describe certain trusts designed to accomplish estate planning objectives. Please look under the "Irrevocable Life Insurance Trust" heading in Chapter 11 for a brief discussion on the ability of the irrevocable life insurance trust (ILIT) to act as a shelter against creditor claims. Not only may the creator of the trust get a measure of protection, but his or her children, grandchildren, and other beneficiaries can receive a substantial degree of protection—possibly protection of the trust assets from the claims of existing creditors if certain distribution provisions are included in the ILIT. Other irrevocable trusts may also offer many of these benefits. See "Other Developments in Trusts" at the end of Chapter 10.

Protection from claims may also be available by establishing an offshore trust. All trusts are legal entities just as corporations are legal entities. Sometimes their independent status is successfully challenged if their creator directly or indirectly controls the trust by retaining the right to revoke the trust or amend its provisions. If the trust is established to operate outside of the United States, it is an offshore or a foreign trust. Offshore trusts are often designed to protect substantial assets from legal claims arising from professional malpractice, divorce claims, and other lawsuits. To be legally effective, the transfer of assets to an offshore trust cannot be in fraud of creditors. For example, transferring a vacation home to an offshore trust after your spouse files for divorce in order to remove it from consideration by the court for property settlement purposes is probably ineffective. A better case for a court upholding a transfer to a trust would be if the transfer took place long before there was any hint of a claim—particularly if a legitimate purpose such as tax planning could be used to justify the transfer.

Both the doctor who amputates the wrong limb and the billionaire who is sued for divorce are subject to having any transfers that he or she makes without getting something of equal value in return set aside as being a fraudulent conveyance. However, if there are no claims in process or imminent, the transfer of assets to an offshore trust may successfully insulate the assets from claims that could arise sometime in the future.

Many of those with concerns for the protection of their assets would not consider establishing an offshore trust because of the costs involved, which could be $15,000 or much more, and having to rely on the laws of remote jurisdictions such as the Isle of Man or the Cayman Islands. Alaska and Delaware have passed laws that may afford the same kind of protection at a lower cost. Alaska and Delaware adopted their statutes in

1997, so the statutes haven't had much chance to be tested. There was some talk that the Delaware statute could be improved by amending it to resemble the Alaska law more closely. Texas is also considering new legislation in this area. (Some Indian tribes have established banks and trust companies that *may* be beyond the reach of federal and state law but subject only to tribal law. At this early stage of development experts generally are not advising people to rely on these banks.)

It is likely that the Alaska and Delaware trusts will not offer as much asset protection as offshore trusts in most cases. However, there are estate planning advantages that may give these trusts more credibility as an asset protection device in other cases. The person establishing the trust may also be a "discretionary beneficiary" without having the trust assets included in his or her estate for federal estate tax purposes. However, the Internal Revenue Service (IRS) has not yet ruled on these new trusts.

It may take years before Alaska and Delaware trusts have their tax status and their usefulness as asset protection devices adequately clarified. At first, only the most adventurous and the most desperate are likely to utilize these devices. Just as offshore trusts often have been utilized together with such devices as family limited partnerships, it is likely that some of the earliest trusts established under these new state trust laws also will involve limited partnerships utilized by families. Please refer to Chapter 11 for more information relative to these limited partnerships. Remember to seek the guidance of an experienced attorney, who is knowledgeable in creditors' rights, if you are seeking to protect assets from substantial claims. The greatest value of these extreme asset protection strategies is to make the pursuit by creditors so difficult that a creditor will become willing to satisfy his or her claim for a fraction of its face value. There are many cases where a person has settled for a fraction of the claim rather than incur substantial costs, delays, and uncertainties in pursuing a full settlement. Keep in mind that generally fraudulent transfers will be ineffective.

FRAUD

Con artists and high-pressure salespeople seek to victimize the unsuspecting, and as people accumulate wealth, they are earmarked as targets. One tempting area for these predators is reverse mortgages. The use of reverse mortgages is discussed in Chapter 6 under the subheading "Tapping Your Home Equity." Many of the elderly are not as alert as they once were and, in addition are inexperienced in financial matters. This makes them targets for the predators. Another target group is people with terminal illnesses who may be eager to convert life insurance policies into cash under a procedure known as a viatical settlement. This topic is discussed at the end of Chapter 11.

Television ads and free seminars are used to peddle a variety of schemes, including wireless cable licenses, rare coins, commodities, and second mortgages. They may be categorized as long shots, near fraud, or full-blown fraud. Remember the old bromide that "if it sounds too good to be true it probably *is* too good to be true." Don't give out your Social Security number, credit card information, or other personal information to anyone unless you are convinced that the person has a legitimate need for it. If you specify that the information should not be retained where it is not necessary, such as credit card information incident to a purchase, you may be successful. It's worth a try.

Most of us assume that we are far too clever and wise in the ways of the world to be swindled. Yet newspapers frequently carry stories about "pigeon drop" or "bank examiner" scams. These frauds are usually perpetrated on the naive and the elderly. In the "bank examiner" fraud, the victim gets a call from someone claiming to be a bank official who requests the victim's help in order to trap a crooked bank teller at his or her bank. The victim is requested to make a "test withdrawal" of several thousand dollars and to meet the "investigator" outside of the bank, being sure not to tell anyone. After the withdrawal the victim meets the investigator and turns over the "evidence" that will be needed to expose the criminal. Of course, that is the last that the victim sees of the investigator or the money. In the "pigeon drop," the victim comes upon someone apparently in the process of finding a great deal of cash. The "finder" offers to split the prize with the victim but requires the victim to make a "good-faith deposit," with predictable results. Authorities believe that these con games are often not reported to authorities by the victims because of the pain of embarrassment. This leaves the crook free to repeat the crime.

The First Con Job on Manhattan Island

The story is told that the Dutch settlers bought Manhattan Island from the Manahata Indians for about $20 worth of trinkets in 1626. This has been regarded as one of history's great con jobs, and it was. Yet if the $20 or so in trinkets had been sold for their value and the proceeds invested by the seller for an average return of 7 percent per year for over 370 years, this investment would be worth more than $1 trillion today. The Indians could now repurchase Manhattan Island with all of its improvements and have a huge sum left over to purchase many other cities as well.

Ponzi and Other Schemes

The criminal can even be a trusted investment adviser. To protect yourself, keep investments in a custodial account with an established bank or brokerage firm. Your account should not be accessible to the adviser or anyone else. Generally bank and broker custody accounts are insured against fraud for millions of dollars, but you must not let your guard down. Monthly statements from the bank or broker that are mailed directly to you will help you keep track of your holdings, but always be alert. Consider the tale of Terrence Hansen.

Terrence Hansen of Salt Lake City confessed to stealing over $400,000 from his clients. Mr. Hansen was a broker for eight years before he was caught in 1995. He used his computer to reproduce the logos of reputable brokerage firms and mutual funds. He had his clients make checks payable jointly to a legitimate firm and to "Income 36 Funds," which was the name on his private account at the bank. His bank accepted these checks after he had printed the name of the legitimate firm as well as "Income 36 Funds" and endorsed them. If a client requested a distribution from the client's brokerage account, Mr. Hansen sent out redemption checks from his private account, but these checks had the logos of the mutual fund company or securities firm instead. This is a version of what is known as a Ponzi scheme. When the scheme was uncovered, his bank paid out a total of more than $400,000 to several of Mr. Hansen's victims.

Mr. Hansen's con game lasted as long as it did because he was trusted; more funds came into the account than went out. The father of this type of swindle was Charles Ponzi, who after World War I set up shop in Boston. He promised investors a $2,000 return in 90 days for an investment of $1,250. When the 90-day period was about to expire, he encouraged investors to renew. Those who did not renew received their money. In all, Mr. Ponzi received $15 million, but over $8 million of it was never accounted for. So great was the attraction and so skillful was Mr. Ponzi that when the con game was revealed and challenged, he had many supporters who refused to believe he was a crook. In fact, the publicity initially brought in huge amounts of additional cash to Mr. Ponzi.

What can we learn from Mr. Ponzi and Mr. Hansen? In Mr. Ponzi's case, a $750 return on $1,250 over a three-month period fails the smell test; it was just too good to be true. In Mr. Hansen's case, one of his clients happened to stop by the brokerage office where the client supposedly had an account. Of course, there was no record of the client's account, and that ended Mr. Hansen's Ponzi scheme. His clients learned that just relying on someone's good reputation was not enough to protect them.

Another common scam revolves around zero coupon municipal bonds. Bonds may sound safer than stocks and zero coupon bonds sound very attractive because they sell at a huge discount from their face value. The reason for the discount is that with legitimate zero coupon bonds, the interest is paid in full on the date of maturity. Because the zero coupon bond does not pay any interest until maturity, it is an ideal setup for swindlers. Remember, buying securities without using a reputable broker or buying real estate without utilizing the services of a qualified lawyer are dangerous practices.

Another popular field for the con artist is business ventures. Among these so-called opportunities are placing and servicing display racks for candy, greeting cards, and other items, and servicing vending machines and pay telephones. These schemes are bait for the unemployed or people fearful that their retirement income may not be enough. Often the ads in the newspapers hold out the promise of making full-time income with little or no work. Once again, don't let your fears or greed cause you to fall for these cons.

You should not consider any of these opportunities without examining the proposal with your lawyer or CPA. You should also take the time to discuss the proposal with someone who has knowledge of the business. Check references carefully. Be alert to the possibility that the "reference" may be part of the scheme. Ask to see accounting records to support the claims, and have your CPA carefully review these records. Be sure that all legal requirements have been met, and ask for the opportunity to have your lawyer talk to the lawyer for the promoter. Keep in mind that even if everything checks out, there is no guarantee that you will make money. You should plan on giving at least as much time and attention to investigating a business venture as you would when you would buy a car.

If you are computer literate, you may give the scam artist an additional path to fleece you, but you also have additional tools for protection. Harold Jones (not his real name) was looking at message boards relating to stock investing on his home computer. There were references to Uniprime Capital's announcement that it was achieving promising results in developing a cure for AIDS. In short order, over five million shares had been traded over the counter as the stock shot up from $1.50 a share to $8. Harold purchased 1,000 shares at $5 each. Uniprime turned out not to be a pharmaceutical company, but a car dealership. Currently civil and criminal charges are pending against Uniprime and its principals. Mr. Jones's shares were recently quoted at three cents each. He and hundreds of other investors are not likely to recover a significant part of what they lost.

It is no longer necessary for scam artists to limit themselves to cold calls on the phone to tout suspect stocks. Access to chat rooms and e-mail address lists are more efficient. Instead of swindlers making hundreds of calls to promote the sale of a phony stock, they leave the bait on web site message boards—it's much less costly and much more effective.

The advice about dealing with schemes like Mr. Ponzi's applies equally here. Some of the legal tools are discussed at the end of this chapter, but they probably won't help Mr. Jones and other trusting investors. If you get a hot stock tip whether online or otherwise, consider:

- ✔ Can you positively identify the source of the tip, and can you trust it? Mr. Jones thought that the statement about an AIDS cure could not have been made if it weren't true.
- ✔ Could you afford to lose all of the money that you are investing? Even an honest representation is not a sure thing. Harold probably felt that he could sell his Uniprime stock before it dropped 50 percent below his purchase price in any event.
- ✔ Can the stock be readily sold? Are there enough potential buyers? However, if a swindle is involved, this may be a case of a potential victim bailing out at the expense of someone else.
- ✔ Is the person recommending the stock a registered broker? This is no guarantee of safety, but not being a registered broker may earmark most scam artists. Check with the National Association of Securities Dealers at www.nasdr.com for the Central Registration Depository (CRD) records of the broker if he or she is registered. You can also contact the North American Securities Administrators Association web site at www.nasaa.org for your state's securities regulatory office.
- ✔ Again, as with the cases of Mr. Ponzi and Mr. Hansen, rely heavily on the smell test. Don't let your judgment be overcome by greed.

CARELESSNESS

Most of us will admit to having made some monumental financial blunders, and those who won't make this admission are probably worse off than the rest of us. Fear and greed can be blamed for legions of investment mistakes. Thinking that you know more than you do is also a likely contributing factor. The worst foul-ups and mistakes may not be the most obvious ones. Not acting on a favorable opportunity or acting on a poor one are common occurrences.

Probably more is lost through inertia or our own misguided efforts than is lost through fraud. Many people, young and not-so-young, add to their list of goof-ups such mistakes as not taking advantage of their employers' retirement plan programs, incurring credit card debt, and purchasing whole-life insurance when term insurance would be better for their needs.

Although losing money through a scam or to high pressure will hurt more, putting all of your money or too much of your money in Treasury bills, certificates of deposit, and/or money market funds for a long period of time can be more damaging. You want to be conservative and play it safe, but inflation can do more damage over several years than a stock investment that underperforms. According to figures from Charles Schwab and Company, Inc., for the 70-year period ending in 1994, the *real* rate of return—that is, the annual average return rate in excess of the inflation rate—for U.S. Treasury bills was 0.6 percent, and for long-term U.S. bonds it was 1.7 percent. The average annual real rate of return for common stock for the period was 7.1 percent.

In steering away from investing in equities, many retirees focus only on an investment yield or the dividend rate. You must also take into account potential price changes. Many investors have purchased long-term bonds without realizing that a substantial increase in interest rates will result in these bonds dropping substantially in value.

While considering long-term bonds, here's a reminder about U.S. savings bonds. Many holders of Series E bonds either don't know or have forgotten that these bonds stop paying interest after a number of years. Series E bonds issued before December 1965 earn interest for 40 years, and those issued after November 1965 earn interest for 30 years. See *Savings Bonds: When to Hold, When to Fold and Everything in Between* by Daniel J. Pederson (Sage Creek Press, fourth edition, $19.95). Since interest on these bonds can be deferred until they are cashed in, many people find these bonds easy to ignore, expecting to cash them only after their retirement when they expect to be in a lower tax bracket. It is estimated that over $6.5 billion in savings bonds have stopped earning interest and have never been cashed in.

The Series E bonds were followed by Series EE, which were first issued in 1980 and reach face value when they achieve "original maturity" (examples: $50 original maturity for $25 cost, up to $10,000 original maturity for $5,000 cost) and continue to earn interest until expiration but at various rates. Series EE bonds earn interest for 30 years from the issue date. The new Series I bond that is "inflation protected" by being linked to the consumer price index also earns interest for up to 30 years from the issue date.

Banks normally do not train their personnel to be knowledgeable about savings bonds, and the U.S. government does not send holders statements relative to their status—unlike the administration of the Social Security program.

Since it can be difficult to calculate how much interest is owed and banks generally lack expertise, cashing in bonds can be hazardous. Mr. Pederson has a service, the Savings Bond Informer (800-927-1901, www.bondhelp.com), that evaluates savings bond holdings for a nominal fee and includes advice on the best time to cash the bond in. For example, since interest payments on savings bonds are credited every six months, one can lose close to six months of interest by cashing in the bond in the fifth month of that six-month term. There is a government service available that is free on the Web but requires downloading and installing a program (www.savingsbond.gov).

A number of older people who grew up in the 1930s regard themselves as being very conservative when they limit their investments to money market funds, certificates of deposit, and fixed-income securities. Some of them may also add utility stocks. They believe that they are diversifying, because they do not have all of their holdings in one or two investments. But they're not recognizing that all of their investments are interest-sensitive; when interest rates shoot up, the value of their stocks and fixed-income securities will quickly drop.

Another generation of people without investment experience may be participants in company retirement plans. Unfortunately, they translate their fears into selecting money market funds as the sole or principal investment vehicle for their retirement plan account. Following this strategy prevents them from benefiting from diversification, and furthermore these investors don't realize that inflation will usually do more damage than market fluctuations.

Another common investment mistake is overinvesting in the stock of an employer. Although loyalty is commendable—and we know there are many cases where employees did very well as their companies' fortunes surged during their employment careers—diversification will usually do much more for an investment portfolio than investing in any one company. With diversification, if one stock out of many fails, the performance of the other stocks can offset the loss. If you have little choice during your working years or feel that showing company loyalty is critical to your career, you should diversify your portfolio at the earliest opportunity once you stop working for that company. With broad diversification, you will be able to sleep more soundly.

Many, if not most, purchasers of variable annuities have not made a wise choice. The principal advantage that a variable annuity has over comparable investments is favorable tax treatment. Many IRAs hold variable annuities. Since all qualified investments in an IRA are tax-free until withdrawal, there is no need for an IRA to hold a variable annuity that also is tax-free until withdrawal. If you hold a variable annuity in an IRA, you can cash in the annuity tax-free leaving the proceeds in the IRA for reinvestment, but check first if there is a penalty assessed by the insurance company. These penalties reduce and then disappear over the years. A knowledgeable adviser should be consulted. Generally, superior alternatives exist.

Insurance companies add features to their variable annuities such as limited death benefits, and recently some companies are offering guaranteed returns even if the market heads down and also money for nursing care. Still, fees for variable annuities average 50 percent more than comparable mutual funds. Investors who are interested in the add-on features can probably do better by separately shopping for such features as nursing care insurance.

Fee-only advisers, not those who sell variable annuities, will generally say that the added fringes are too costly so that if the tax shelter feature is important to an investor, the simplest variable annuity at the lowest cost should be the one that is bought. Variable annuities are a very profitable product, and competing companies even offer cash bonuses to attract business—3 percent or more. The insurance companies defend variable annuities by saying that many customers would not be in the equities market otherwise. The price seems too high in most cases, considering the alternatives. Until you have taken maximum advantage of your 401(k), IRA, or other tax-deferred plan, you shouldn't consider variable annuities.

More on Variable Annuities

In most states, annuities and other retirement payments generally are immune from the claims of creditors, so those who are fearful of lawsuits—such as professionals concerned with the possibility of huge malpractice judgments—would be interested. Keep in mind that the time to protect your assets is before a claim is likely to be made. O. J. Simpson's retirement payments were protected from the civil claims upheld against him under California law, but probably wouldn't have been if purchased subsequent to the start of legal actions against him. Anyone interested in protecting his or her assets with an annuity should first consult with competent legal counsel. For additional information on annuities online, contact www.annuities-online.com (and related www.variableannuityonline.com).

CHOOSING A FINANCIAL ADVISER

Clinging to an unsatisfactory investment in the hope that you will eventually break even can be costly. Someone who waits for months or years for a stock to return to its purchase price is guilty of foggy thinking. If there is a better investment, switch. It may be a signal that you need help if you are not aware of investment basics. For many of you, selecting a professional adviser could be the most important step in your investment education. Most of you will be pleased with the results that a competent adviser can achieve for you. Some of you not only will learn from what the adviser is doing for you but also will start to study independently and become knowledgeable about investing. Age, health, and other interests will be factored into your decisions. You will learn that the knowledgeable investor takes advantage of opportunities such as those that present themselves when there is a market correction of 10 percent or more.

The strong skepticism that we encourage when you are tempted by business opportunities or get-rich-quick schemes should carry over if you attend financial seminars. Let's distinguish these seminars from educational meetings at the workplace relative to your retirement plan. But, you should still be vigilant even during an educational meeting about your retirement plan account. If you are approaching retirement, the investment adviser for the plan may also be soliciting your business outside of the plan, particularly if you're rolling over a substantial retirement plan account balance into an IRA. If you have been impressed with the adviser's abilities for a period of time and if other employees, particularly ex-employees who have utilized his or her services, are satisfied, he or she may be a better choice than someone whom you do not know. But again, don't be too lazy to investigate. If you can devote five hours in deciding which refrigerator to buy, how much time and effort should you devote when the equivalent of 300 to 1,000 refrigerators is at stake?

Often financial seminars will convey useful information, but remember that they have been arranged to serve the needs of the brokers or financial planners who are the sponsors. Your needs are only incidental to their needs.

GOVERNMENT REGULATIONS

Beginning in 1933, Congress passed a series of acts that created and empowered the Securities and Exchange Commission (SEC). The effect on investment in all securities has been substantial. The SEC has been active in the supervision and regulation of the issuance of new securities and trading both on the various exchanges and over the counter, accounting practices relative to the preparation of financial statements of corporations, corporate reorganizations excepting those of railroads, key financial matters involving public utility holding company systems, the activities of insiders, the conduct of investment companies, and the conduct of investment advisers. (This list is not all-inclusive.)

Among the statutes that the SEC is concerned with are:

- ✔ The Securities Act of 1933, which deals with new issues of securities.
- ✔ The Securities Exchange Act of 1934, which covers trading on organized stock exchanges (expanded in 1938 to cover unlisted trading).
- ✔ The Public Utility Holding Company Act of 1935, which allows and regulates public utilities.
- ✔ The Trust Indenture Act of 1939, which deals with the responsibilities of corporate bond trustees.
- ✔ The Investment Company Act of 1940, which regulates publicly held investment funds (including investment companies such as mutual funds).
- ✔ The Investment Advisors Act of 1940, which requires registration of investment advisers and supervises their activities.

These statutes are credited with revolutionizing and purifying investment activities. However, not only are there continuing activities of fraud and misrepresentation, but some people design their activities to mislead and misrepresent by staying close enough to both sides of the boundaries of the law as to make them continuing problems for the uninformed and careless investor. Investors must keep in mind that the SEC's jurisdiction is limited. For example, relative to the regulation of new securities falling under its jurisdiction, it may refuse registration if there is not a "full and fair disclosure." If the offering is a bad investment because the underlying business activity is unprofitable or an unjustifiably high price is set, the SEC has no jurisdiction. Its activities are limited to the accuracy and adequacy of the disclosures, not the merits of the investment.

Securities Act of 1933

The 1933 Act requires companies to register stock offerings to the public with a detailed disclosure of important facts contained in a booklet for prospective investors called a "prospectus." The companies must also submit additional information to the SEC under this act.

Securities Exchange Act of 1934

The 1934 Act substantially ended manipulation of stock prices on the stock market. There are occasional attempts at manipulation of stock prices and more frequent accusations, but the ability to clearly identify price manipulation in recent years makes it a rare occurrence. One result has been a tremendous increase in activity over the years as evidenced by the huge increases in the number of stockholders, securities salespeople, and investment advisers.

Provisions of the 1934 Act, Section 16(a), require reports from insiders to be made to the SEC, detailing changes in their holdings of equity securities on a monthly basis. These activities are published in the financial press, which prevents unfair use of the information. A remedy is that profits realized by an insider from unfair use of information within a six-month period are forfeited to a corporation. Insiders are officers, directors, shareholders, and others who directly or indirectly own more than 10 percent of the voting securities of a company.

By making unfair profits of insiders forfeitable to a corporation, the 1934 Act generates the initiation of enforcement activity by the shareholders of the corporation and the corporation itself. The SEC does not have enforcement power relative to this provision. Section 16(b) has been criticized for not requiring proof of an abuse of trust. This can result in unfair litigation. For example, a director with other motives (such as to support the price of the shares for the benefit of the corporation and its shareholders) may be sued to return profits while not being able to utilize offsetting losses. Under current tax laws, wealthy directors would not be interested in taking short-term gains, so an improper motive is not likely.

The 1933 Act, the 1934 Act, the 1935 Act, and both 1940 Acts relate to providing requirements involving corporate statements and reports. Many of these requirements may be modified from time to time by the SEC. For example, registration statements for new securities must include financial information for the current year and the past three years. Form 10K requires figures for the registration of securities on a stock exchange.

Public Utility Holding Company Act of 1935

The 1935 Act was enacted to give the SEC a great deal of authority with regard to public utility companies because of prior improprieties and the opportunity for abuse. The SEC broke up systems of holding companies that were deemed to be harmful and unnecessary. At one time, there were more than 2,000 companies involved, but by the end of 1960 there were fewer than 200.

Trust Indenture Act of 1939

This act was designed to protect the interests of bondholders, generally by strengthening the enforcement of obligations of corporate trustees (banks and trust companies) acting under indentures (agreements) relative to the issuance of the securities. It requires the corporate trustees to be free of conflict of interest and to make periodic reports to the bondholders, and gives them authority to file suits and proof of claims on behalf of the bondholders. It also prohibits provisions in the indenture that would reduce or eliminate the liability of the corporate trustee to the bondholders and "to use the same degree of care and skill in their exercise [of duties] as a *prudent man* would use in the conduct of his own affairs," according to a description by the SEC of the objectives of the act (italics added).

Investment Company Act of 1940

Back in 1940, the mutual fund industry, which was generally referred to at that time as the "investment company industry," was a fraction of the size it is today. The Investment Company Act of 1940 requires registration of and regulates investment companies (mutual funds). It requires disclosure to afford investors full and complete information, prohibits the companies from changing the nature of their business or their investment policies without the approval of the stockholders, bars persons guilty of security frauds from serving as officers and directors, regulates the custody of assets, requires management contracts to initially be submitted to security holders for their approval, prohibits transactions between the companies and their officers and directors except on approval of the SEC, and prohibits pyramiding of such companies and cross-ownership of their securities.

Investment Advisors Act of 1940

This act requires the registration of persons engaged for compensation in the business of advising others with respect to securities. Registration can be denied or revoked by the SEC if an adviser has been convicted or enjoined because of misconduct in connection with securities transactions or for making false statements in registration applications.

A person who has fewer than 15 clients and generally is not presented to the public as an investment adviser is not considered to be an adviser under this act. Investment advisers may not engage in fraudulent or deceitful practices. They must disclose the nature of their interests in transactions that they execute for their clients. Profit-sharing arrangements are prohibited, and there are restrictions on the assignment of investment advisory contracts without the consent of the client. In 1960, the SEC's powers in the regulation of investment advisers were increased to include additional reasons for refusing, suspending, or canceling the registered status of an adviser.

Prudent Man Rule and Prudent Investor Rule

The Prudent Man Rule was established as a legal principle in 1830 in the case of *Harvard College vs. Amory*. It has been described as requiring trustees to manage as "men of prudence, discretion and intelligence manage their own affairs, not in regard to speculation, but in regard to the permanent disposition of their funds, considering the probable income as well as the probable safety of the capital to be invested."

Different states interpreted the Prudent Man Rule in different ways and adopted statutes describing in detail what that particular legislature considered to be permissible investments that could not be challenged as being improper. Over the years, most of the specific lists of permissible investments have disappeared, but there are a number of cases that have resulted in certain rules. Generally, speculation is not allowed. In addition, each investment must be judged separately as to whether it is appropriate for investment by the trust.

Concepts relative to safety through diversification are still in the process of being recognized. There are still places and situations where the trustee of a properly diversified portfolio may be successfully challenged because of the underperformance of an investment in a portfolio.

Fortunately, the law that governs qualified retirement plans—the Employee Retirement Income Security Act of 1974 (ERISA)—abandons the limitations of the more rigid versions of the Prudent Man Rule. This is doubly fortunate because ERISA, and not state law, is controlling in the area of qualified retirement plans. If qualified retirement plans were prevented from providing broad diversification because of the limitations of the Prudent Man Rule, millions of participants could be adversely affected. Which trustees would want to run the risk of having a particular mutual fund or a particular stock substantially underperform, although the overall performance could be substantially above average? The point of true diversification is that there will be underperformers at most, if not all, stages of the investment cycle. But the overall long-term performance will substantially benefit as a result of the diversification.

Before we summarize the Prudent Investor Rule, it should be pointed out that although forms of it have been passed in over half of the states in the past few years, the Prudent Man Rule is still a powerful influence. Just as the Prudent Man Rule took a number of years to develop, it may take a number of years before the Prudent Investor Rule substantially replaces the Prudent Man Rule. In the 150 years that the Prudent Man Rule was being developed and adopted, it was also being bent into different shapes for different areas.

For example, some courts and state legislatures have determined that a more restrictive list of permissible investments should be available for guardians appointed by the courts to look after the affairs of minors and legally disabled persons. If this rationale would continue, the benefits of more recent investment thinking may not be available in all cases where it should be and some fiduciaries may be penalized for following sound investment policies. Updating the investment knowledge of judges and state legislators is essential.

The Prudent Investor Rule was first set forth by the American Law Institute (ALI), which is a nonprofit group of legal scholars who are dedicated to developing statements of legal principles in efforts to improve the laws. Their proposals have been adopted by state legislatures and courts in a number of legal areas over the years. Their work in developing the Prudent Investor Rule filled almost 300 pages when it was published in 1992. The fact that the Prudent Investor Rule has been adopted in one form or another in over half of the states in less than 10 years as the Uniform Prudent Investor Act indicates the respect for the continuing work of the ALI.

The Prudent Investor Rule, as adopted in 1990 by the ALI, is lengthy. The heart of it is contained in Sections 227 and 228 of the ALI's Restatement (3d) of trusts:

> §227. **General Standard of Prudent Investment**
>
> The trustee is under a duty to the beneficiaries to invest and manage the funds of the trust as a prudent investor would, in light of the purposes, terms, distribution requirements and other circumstances of the trust.
>
> (a) This standard requires the exercise of reasonable care, skill, and caution and is to be applied to investments not in isolation but in the context of the trust portfolio and as a part of an overall investment strategy, which should incorporate risk and return objectives reasonably suitable to the trust.
>
> (b) In making and implementing investment decisions, the trustee has a duty to diversify the investments of the trust unless, under the circumstances, it is prudent not to do so.
>
> (c) In addition, the trustee must:
>
> (1) conform to fundamental fiduciary duties of loyalty (§170) and impartiality (§183);

(2) act with prudence in deciding whether and how to delegate authority and in the selection and supervision of agents (§171); and

(3) incur only costs that are reasonable in amount and appropriate to the investment responsibilities of the trusteeship (§188).

(d) The trustee's duties under this Section are subject to the rule of §228, dealing primarily with contrary investment provisions of a trust or statute.

§228. **Investment Provisions of Statute or Trust**

In investing the funds of the trust, the trustee

(a) has a duty to the beneficiaries to conform to any applicable statutory provisions governing investment by trustees; and

(b) has the powers expressly or impliedly granted by the terms of the trust and, except as provided in §§165 through 168, has a duty to the beneficiaries to conform to the terms of the trust directing or restricting investments by the trustee.

More detailed definitions of some of the terms contained in Sections 227 and 228 are contained in other sections of the proposed Act. Section 227(b) states that there can be an affirmative duty to diversify the investments of the trust, while Section 228(a) points out that the trustee has a duty to "conform to any applicable statutory provisions governing investment by trustees." Thus, the trustees should consult with their lawyers periodically since what has been true over most of the past 150 years is in the process of being changed. Incidentally, the reference in Section 227(b) to possible circumstances where it may not be prudent to diversify would cover such situations as tax planning by a terminally ill beneficiary or a beneficiary with controlling stock in a company where he or she has a high-paying position to defend.

It should be appreciated that the ALI, in its studies and preparation of the volume relating to the Prudent Investor Rule, did the intellectual work in understanding modern financial concepts. This is clear when the note and commentary in the volume are studied. Section 227(a) states that the evaluation of an investment is to be done on the basis of an overall investment plan that has risk and return objectives appropriate for the particular trust. There is neither approval nor disapproval with regard to any single investment. The trustee must be able to justify the role each investment plays in the overall investment program that is followed by the trust. Under these circumstances, it is necessary that a precise written investment strategy be adopted.

Unlike the Prudent Man Rule, the new standard does not prohibit speculation but recognizes that more speculative investments can play an important part in the overall investment strategy. The Prudent Investor Rule expressly negates a lack of care, indifference, or recklessness and requires a trustee of ordinary intelligence, but, to the extent that greater skills are possessed, then the trustee must utilize these abilities.

The degree of care that is required is for the trustee to seek the twin goals of obtaining a reasonable return while protecting the capital. Generally, the trustees' reasonable efforts are what investors require of their investment managers. That is, after a risk level has been determined, it must be continually monitored. There is a duty to diversify under the Prudent Investor Rule. However, the trust agreement may provide certain standards that may limit or eliminate the rule to diversify. Retention of control of a family business is one example.

An important departure from the old Prudent Man Rule is that the Prudent Investor Rule requires the effects of inflation to be recognized. This was one of the great weaknesses under the old Prudent Man Rule, which often led to an overemphasis on investments in certificates of deposit and fixed-income instruments in much larger proportions than were advisable. A continuing problem will be trust agreements that require the trustees to use fixed-income investments exclusively while their terms may extend over many years in order to cover minor grandchildren or great-grandchildren. It will be helpful if lawyers preparing trust agreements for their clients will be able to advise them of the best provisions to protect the interests of the clients' loved ones.

Even clients who seek to have control of a family business retained may be making a big mistake. For every successful long-term business such as the Ford Motor Company, there are hundreds of manufacturers of outdated products such as buggy whips and hula hoops that would have been better off sold than hung onto. Picking wise trustees and empowering them to be responsive to circumstances will usually be the best trust policy.

Part Four

Enjoying the Good Life

Chapter 10

Estate Planning—Arranging to Help Your Loved Ones after Your Death

Chapters 10 and 11 are the only chapters not focused solely on the well-being of you and your spouse. Estate planning is concerned with providing a substantial sum to help your children or other loved ones after you and your spouse are gone. During your lives tax planning is devoted to reducing income taxes and other taxes that are currently payable. When the first spouse dies, there is usually little estate tax impact because all of the taxable estate or almost all of it is left to the surviving spouse and will not be subject to tax until he or she dies. The estate tax impacts most heavily when the surviving spouse dies so that the children and other loved ones are most affected. This chapter is primarily concerned with the heirs and other remaining loved ones. With estate tax rates reaching 55 percent of the taxable estate, the effect of the federal estate tax can be enormous. The benefits of life insurance have grown as a result of the tax laws. Types of life insurance policies are summarized in Chapter 11.

Estate planning is the preparation of an individual's instructions about the disposition of his or her assets upon death. If the instructions are not left in proper legal form, state law dictates who gets your assets and how, probably not in a way you would choose. Furthermore, state laws generally do not provide the most favorable tax consequences. A well-thought-out estate plan can substantially reduce and, in many cases, eliminate estate taxes. The written instructions may be in the form of a combination of several of the following: a will, trust agreement, durable power of attorney, death beneficiary designation of an individual retirement account (IRA), life insurance benefits, medical instructions, and other documents.

In this and the succeeding chapter, you will examine ideas on how to design a program that will satisfy your wishes for your beneficiaries following your death at the least tax cost. There are about 15 serious concerns including how spouses should own their own assets, what probate is and when is it required, how to avoid having your portfolio mismanaged after death, how to use estate planning tools, and when it pays not to give.

This book concentrates on the financial needs of couples during their retirement years. We haven't addressed leaving an estate for loved ones; but, for many couples, that is an important issue, and for some, it is a necessity. Some parents want to leave a family farm or business to succeeding generations of family members; some may want to leave a home or investments; and others will create or supplement an estate with life insurance for the needs and enjoyment of loved ones.

With estate tax rates reaching a maximum of over one-half of the taxable estate and other federal and state taxes also being applicable at times, advanced estate planning can save hundreds of thousands of dollars, which can be the difference between success and failure.

To avoid marital disputes, many people simply do no estate planning, assuming they will "get around to it" or with a vague thought that "things will work out" after they die. Estate planning can put a greater strain on marriage than football on TV. What is logical to one spouse may not be logical to the other. The great difficulty that men and women have in understanding each other's thought processes is the basis for this story: A man spots a bottle on a California beach and removes the cork. A genie emerges in a cloud of steam and says, "You have one wish and make it quick. I know that you are expecting three wishes but that's not how I work."

The man replies: "I've always wanted to visit Hawaii but I'm afraid to fly and I get seasick. I want a bridge to Hawaii."

The genie responds: "That's out of the question. Consider how much steel and concrete would be needed plus permits and licenses. Pick something else."

"Okay, I want to understand women. I've been married and divorced three times. I want to understand what makes them moody, playful, sad. I have never been able to fathom what they are thinking. It's as if we don't speak the same language." (Many men experience this when discussing estate planning with their wives. Many women are no better off when trying to understand their husbands' planning priorities.)

The genie ponders awhile and then says, "Should that bridge be two lanes or four lanes?" (For that joke we thank our cousin and niece, Dr. Heather Wittenberg, and her husband, Dr. David Wittenberg, psychologists who do understand men and women much better than most of us.)

The first step in estate planning is for you and your spouse to discuss your respective concerns. Then, an inventory should be prepared. (See Figure 10.1) If, for example, your wife has few assets in her name, your attorney will usually advise you to transfer ownership of sufficient assets to her in order to take as much advantage as possible of her Unified Credit against federal estate tax. Before 1998, the Unified Credit available to each spouse was $192,800. This meant that up to $192,800 of estate and gift taxes could be offset by applying this credit, equal to the estate (or gift) tax due on assets of $600,000. The Unified Credit provision has been revised to increase gradually from 1998 to 2006, when it will reach the equivalent of sheltering $1 million in assets in an individual's estate. More information on the Unified Credit is presented later in this chapter.

You should prepare a descriptive inventory of your assets and liabilities and details of the legal ownership of all assets. Is the asset individually held or held jointly with one or more people? Also prepare a schedule of life insurance policies listing the owner of each policy, the beneficiary, and the face amount. Often overlooked is the face amount of life insurance policies. If the policy on you or your spouse is owned by the insured at the time of death, the face amount of the policy will be taxable for federal estate tax purposes. Better ways of owning insurance are covered in the next chapter. Many people are not aware that someone other than the insured may own a life insurance policy. The advice of a knowledgeable tax attorney is recommended before transfers are made or policies are purchased, however, since mistakes can be costly.

Retirement plan accounts, Keogh plans, and IRAs should be listed. Copies of death beneficiary designations that are in effect for these plans should also be located. If you cannot find these beneficiary designations, ask your employer or plan sponsor (a broker, insurance company, or bank) for a copy. In addition, substantial expectancies should be considered. An expectancy is a property interest that you anticipate receiving as a gift or inheritance at some future date, usually from a parent or other close relative.

The mortgage balance on your home and any other debts that you may have should also be separately listed. Separately note your concerns

	Current Value[1]		
	Husband	Wife	Joint
Assets			
Bank accounts (checking and savings)	$	$	$
Other cash accounts (money market funds, cash accounts at brokers, etc.)			
Stocks, bonds, and mutual funds			
Retirement plan (profit sharing, pension) 401(k) Keogh SEP Other			
Annuities			
Business partnership interests			
Paintings, other art			
Other personal property (autos, furniture, and furnishings)			
Life Insurance (face value)			
Home value			
Other real estate			
Total assets	$	$	$
Liabilities			
Mortgages and other debts	$	$	$
Loans on life insurance			
Other loans			
Total liabilities	$	$	$
Estimated taxable estate[2]	$	$	$
Federal estate tax (see Figure 10.2)	$	$	$
Amount available for your beneficiaries (net worth less federal estate tax)	$	$	$

FIGURE 10.1 Estate inventory.

[1]List amounts in the proper columns to show ownership.

[2]The exact value of the taxable estate will be reduced by funeral expenses and legal, probate, and other related expenses. Make copies of this blank form so that you and your spouse can make alternative calculations under different scenarios, varying the order of death and such factors as increases or decreases in values, the effect of an inheritance from a relative or friend, and so on.

and desires as well as the ages of family members and other beneficiaries. If you're worried that a spouse or child may be a spendthrift or have special care or financial needs, this should be noted. You and your spouse should give thought to what you consider to be appropriate provisions for these circumstances. Your attorney may also offer alternatives for you to consider.

Don't underestimate the importance of preparing this information before consulting an estate attorney. Not only will it help you clarify your wishes, but also the savings in time and cost for prior preparation and thought make the effort worthwhile. You can refer to Table 10.1 and Figure 10.2 in estimating your federal estate tax.

TABLE 10.1 Unified Federal Gift and Estate Tax Schedule

Taxable Gift or Estate		*Tentative Tax*	
From	*To*	*Tax on Column 1*	*Rate on Excess*
$ 0	$ 10,000	$ 0	18%
10,000	20,000	1,800	20
20,000	40,000	3,800	22
40,000	60,000	8,200	24
60,000	80,000	13,000	26
80,000	100,000	18,200	28
100,000	150,000	23,800	30
150,000	250,000	38,800	32
250,000	500,000	70,800	34
500,000	750,000	155,800	37
750,000	1,000,000	248,300	39
1,000,000	1,250,000	345,800	41
1,250,000	1,500,000	448,300	43
1,500,000	2,000,000	555,800	45
2,000,000	2,500,000	780,000	49
2,500,000	3,000,000	1,025,000	53
3,000,000	—	1,290,800	55

Note: This schedule is for gifts made after 1983 and estates of persons dying after 1983.

1. Taxable estate[1]	$
2. Total of all post-1976 adjusted taxable gifts[2]	
3. Sum of #1 and #2	
4. Tentative estate tax on #3 (from Table 10.1)	
5. Total of all gift taxes paid on post-1976 gifts	
6. Net tentative estate tax (#4 less #5)	
7. Estate tax credit[3]	
8. Estimated estate tax	$

FIGURE 10.2 Estimating federal estate tax.

Note: This computation provides only an estimate. For example, the state death tax credit and other credits are not taken into consideration. We again give notice that we are not supplying legal advice. You must review your plans with a competent adviser before acting. Further detail is beyond the scope of this book.

[1]"Taxable estate" is the gross estate less all available deductions, including the estate tax marital deduction and charitable deduction subject to certain other qualifications.

[2]"Total of all post-1976 adjusted taxable gifts" means total amount of post-1976 taxable gifts [gross gifts less deductions including $10,000 annual exclusion per donee ($20,000 if spouse joins in gift), gift tax marital deduction, and charitable gifts] other than adjustments relating to certain gifts.

[3]The maximum estate tax credit (the Unified Credit) is $202,050 for 1998; $211,300 for 1999; $220,550 for 2000 and 2001; $229,800 for 2002 and 2003; $287,300 for 2004; $326,300 for 2005; and $345,800 for 2006 and thereafter.

SELECTING AN ATTORNEY

It is important to select a competent attorney who is experienced and trained in estate planning to advise you and prepare the appropriate documents. You can get referrals from a friend or an acquaintance who is an attorney or certified public accountant. CPAs and attorneys with a more general practice often have the opportunity to work with estate planning attorneys.

Shopping for an estate planning attorney is similar to other types of shopping in many ways. If you are impatient, you are probably a poor shopper, and enlisting assistance would be a smart move.

It is strongly recommended that you receive a letter of understanding from your attorney at the beginning that describes what will be done and the costs involved. This is for both of your benefits. Also, detailed monthly statements from your attorney are generally recommended. This will reduce the chance of costs getting out of hand. Depending on the degree of service involved, it is not unusual for an estate plan (including a revocable trust, pour-over will, durable powers of attorney, and transfers) to exceed $1,500. Where a married couple is involved, the cost for estate plans for both spouses is little more than for one spouse, since the provisions for the survivor of the two of them and for the children of their marriage usually will be identical. However, this is not the case where one or both spouses have children by a prior marriage.

Technically, there is a conflict of interest when both spouses have the same lawyer. This is clearly the case if either or both spouses have children from a prior marriage. On occasion, even with first marriages, there may be disputes where one spouse claims that the attorney favored the other spouse. If you feel that your spouse is being unduly restrictive, raise this issue and consider hiring independent counsel to review drafts of the proposed documents before they are signed. Obviously, this is a very difficult thing to do.

Most couples and their attorneys believe that they are reasonable people who can resolve conflicts without the need for separate counsel, but this possibility should be kept in mind.

NONCITIZEN ISSUES

If you or your spouse is not a U.S. citizen, the unlimited marital deduction is not available for property transferred to that individual. The unlimited marital deduction generally results in no estate tax being charged on the amount that is left to a surviving spouse, so not having this deduction could be a major problem. The tax exposure can be huge. If a decedent has left his or her spouse $1 million in excess of the credit exclusion amount, the estate tax on that million dollars could be as much as $550,000. (The theory behind the unlimited marital deduction is that federal estate tax will be collected when the surviving spouse dies.)

When the law was passed in 1988 to limit the use of the unlimited marital deduction to surviving spouses who are U.S. citizens, the objective was to give the Internal Revenue Service (IRS) the same opportunity to tax the estate of a surviving spouse upon his or her death regardless of whether that spouse was a U.S. citizen. This opportunity could be lost if a noncitizen surviving spouse returned to his or her native land with the untaxed portion of the decedent's estate.

In the case of a noncitizen spouse, this problem can be solved through the use of a qualified domestic trust (QDOT). At least one of the trustees of a QDOT must be a U.S. corporation or a U.S. citizen. The withdrawal of principal from the QDOT is taxed as if it had been part of the taxable estate of the deceased spouse. It is taxed on a cumulative basis so that successive distributions to the surviving spouse could be taxed at higher estate tax levels.

Again, the advice of an experienced attorney is necessary in this area. Transferring assets to the noncitizen spouse during his or her lifetime (a nontaxable event if both spouses are U.S. citizens) contains a limitation in that gifts above $100,000 per year to a noncitizen spouse trigger the gift tax. Still, much can be accomplished by giving less than $100,000 a year. Note that other gifts made to a spouse during the year are taken into account. A gift of $100,000 to the noncitizen spouse could be added to a birthday, anniversary, or other gift made during the calendar year that will trigger the gift tax. If the noncitizen spouse becomes a citizen prior to the spouse's death or within nine months of the spouse's death, there is no need for a QDOT.

The noncitizen spouse may initiate proceedings within nine months of the death of his or her spouse by requesting permission to set up a QDOT. Then, the noncitizen spouse could begin proceedings to become a U.S. citizen and avoid the estate tax problem. Retirement plans, IRAs, and life insurance owned by the decedent generally pass to the noncitizen surviving spouse apart from probate proceedings and may fall outside of QDOT protection unless specific action is taken to modify the beneficiary designation.

Also, jointly held property should not be overlooked. Although owned in both names, jointly held assets are treated as owned solely by the first spouse to die if the contribution of the surviving spouse is not proved.

ALMOST MARRIAGES

Long-term heterosexual relationships without the formality of marriage are more prevalent now than ever before in our country's history. Avoiding the potential legal hassles such as divorce and alimony are key considerations in many cases. However, the tax costs that could be involved may make many couples in these relationships change their minds about marriage. Consider:

Jim and Jane have lived together for 10 years and each has a child by a prior relationship who lives with them. Jim has a net worth of $850,000 and Jane has a net worth of less than $25,000. They live in Jim's home. If Jim's will states that upon his death Jane is provided for by a trust and then the balance is to be split between the two children, there appears to be no tax advantage in having Jim and Jane marry. However:

- ✔ If Jim dies in late 2003 and his estate has increased to $1 million since the year 2000, his federal estate tax could be over $100,000. Jane and the children would lose 10 percent of Jim's estate to taxes, and none of it would have to be lost if Jim and Jane married. If Jim's net worth at the time of death was $2 million, the federal estate tax could be over $500,000 (all of which could be eliminated if they were married).
- ✔ If Jim and Jane were married, Jim could make tax-free gifts to Jane that could eliminate all estate tax for both of them on $2 million even if Jane died first. Generally, this could not be done if they remained single.

Other tax planning advantages are available to married couples that are not available to unmarried couples.

THE DO-IT-YOURSELFER

We suspect that many of you who are reading this book are do-it-yourself investors. The temptation also to be a do-it-yourself estate planner is great. An apparent savings of as much as $1,500 (or more) in legal fees is a strong incentive.

However, disastrous consequences may occur years later after the do-it-yourselfer dies. Serious errors by an attorney will usually result in his or her legal liability. Most attorneys carry professional liability insurance, but this relief is not available to the do-it-yourselfer or his or her loved ones.

Tax law related to estates can be convoluted. The potential do-it-yourselfer should be particularly aware of the need to regularly review case law and tax documents, since the law may have changed even if personal conditions have not. When the Tax Relief Act of 1997 was adopted, it made material changes in the gift and estate tax laws. The 1997 Act created potentially serious problems for many individuals with estate plans that were satisfactory immediately prior to its passage. For example, if Bill had a $2 million estate and his wife, Barbara, had a $600,000 estate, should he transfer up to $400,000 more in assets to her because the exemption equivalent has been increased? If Bill's living trust provided that his bypass or credit shelter trust should be of a size to maximize the tax savings—a common provision—the change in law would seem to increase its potential size automatically by $400,000 by the year 2006 (from $600,000 to $1 million).

Would Barbara like the idea of Bill's potential marital trust for her benefit being reduced by $400,000 in order to shift this account to the bypass trust? If Bill should die without reviewing his estate plan with his attorney, could Barbara successfully challenge the shift of $400,000 from the marital to the bypass trust as not being what Bill intended?

Be aware of the need to contact your attorney periodically to discuss the status of your estate plan. If nothing of a substantial nature is needed, little or no cost should be involved. Don't be tempted to make legal determinations by yourself. Most attorneys, including tax attorneys, are honest and fair-minded. We've discussed the methods to find these advisers earlier.

Here is another story. Chuck and his wife Laura have combined assets exceeding $2 million in value. After being quoted a fee in excess of $1,700 to prepare an estate plan for himself and Laura, Chuck, a do-it-yourself investor, goes to his local bookstore and finds an estate planning book. He prepares documents for Laura and himself that paragraph-for-paragraph and page-for-page look every bit as impressive as the documents churned out by an estate lawyer's office. The documents are appropriately signed and witnessed, and the trust agreements are even notarized.

Upon Chuck's death after 2005, his loved ones discover that, although no federal estate tax is then owed since all of the assets were held jointly by Chuck and Laura, under state law the assets then become the sole property of Laura, and Chuck's trust is wholly ineffective. The eventual tax bill after Laura's death will probably be over $340,000 more than it would have been with correct planning. Attempts at corrective planning after Chuck's death are likely to be inadequate.

The trust agreement contained the appropriate language, but Chuck's failure to revise ownership properly before his death leaves a substantial problem. There are tax planning tools for corrective planning that may reduce or eliminate this additional tax exposure. However, it will involve transfers and expenditures by Laura that she may not feel comfortable doing, such as disclaimers of ownership, substantial gifts to the children during her lifetime, the purchase of life insurance policies, or a combination of all of these activities, plus the legal expenses involved.

It is very important to promptly review the estate plan if you change legal residence to another state. In addition to changes in the law, changes in both personal and financial circumstances may make revisions necessary. Often, a call to your attorney and a brief telephone discussion will be all that is required. Do not count on your attorney to call you.

Because of the unlimited marital deduction, it is not unusual to have no federal estate tax owed upon death of the first spouse. The cases of Barbara and Bill as well as Chuck and Laura deal with situations involving the death of the first spouse with no federal estate tax owed, but difficult tax problems can still be present.

When initial estate planning has been inadequate, various planning devices may be available to undo the damage at least partially. Factors such as the life expectancy of a surviving spouse, the type or types of assets involved, and the financial needs of the surviving spouse and other beneficiaries have to be considered. Gifts of up to $10,000 per year (the annual exclusion amount) can be given to each donee by the surviving spouse without adverse tax consequences.

Perhaps the surviving spouse cannot afford to give substantial sums to the children and still meet possible emergencies and maintain the same standard of living. Prompt action is often necessary; a delay of several years in implementing a program can be costly. Proper planning can avoid these tax problems.

One more story about a do-it-yourselfer: Tom and his wife Helen have over $2 million in assets. Tom buys an estate-planning program and prepares an impressive living trust agreement and will for himself and Helen. Other than their home, nothing is held jointly, and almost all of the assets are in Tom's name. Upon Tom's death, everything would work out nicely. However, Helen dies first—with only $5,000 in assets solely in her name. As a result, her bypass (or credit shelter) trust created under the living trust agreement that is equipped to initially shelter up to $1 million in assets from taxation will shelter no more than $5,000. This probably will cost Tom's estate over $340,000 in estate tax. This amount could have been saved if Tom had transferred assets to Helen to bring her holdings up to at least $1 million at the time of her death. The added tax cost will occur upon Tom's subsequent death. (The bypass or credit shelter trust could generate a Unified Credit of as much as $345,800 if Helen had died after 2005.)

There are other ways to qualify for a maximum deduction than direct transfers to a spouse during life or upon death. These include: (1) adding your spouse as a joint tenant with right of survivorship or as a tenant by the entireties; (2) directly or indirectly designating the spouse as the beneficiary on a life insurance policy; (3) placing property in a marital trust for the sole benefit of the surviving spouse if certain requirements such as giving control over disposition of the remaining trust property after his or her death are met; and (4) placing property in a qualified terminable interest property (QTIP) trust.

A QTIP trust is unusual in that it enables an estate to obtain a marital deduction although it does not give the surviving spouse full control of the trust principal. The QTIP trust is often utilized when someone has remarried and wants the second spouse to be provided for but that the principal of the

QTIP trust will be preserved for the children of the first marriage. When there is a second marriage under these circumstances, a written agreement describing this arrangement should be entered into by the couple prior to marriage. Otherwise, if the second spouse survives, this spouse may have the right to claim a larger portion of the estate under state law. The premarital or antenuptial agreement is a technical document, and before it is adopted, each party should obtain a lawyer's advice—preferably well before their wedding. There have been challenges to signed marital agreements based on claims of duress because they were signed shortly before the wedding.

How property is held can be very important to estate planning. As the case of Chuck and Laura shows, joint tenancy with right of survivorship can be disastrous. Yet, in other circumstances it may be helpful. Joint tenancy with right of survivorship between a husband and wife is referred to in most states as tenancy by the entireties. The survivor becomes the sole owner without any probate procedure. In very modest estates, it may serve as a substitute for more sophisticated estate planning. Even in large and complex estates, tenancy by the entireties or joint tenancy with right of survivorship can play an important part, particularly with regard to ownership of the personal residence.

Tenancy in common is another form of joint ownership. It does not involve the right of survivorship. When a tenant in common dies, the decedent's share of the ownership becomes part of the estate and subject to probate.

Community property law applies in Arizona, California, Idaho, Louisiana, Nevada, New Mexico, Texas, Washington, and Wisconsin. In these states, community property is property acquired during the marriage by either spouse. If a spouse dies during the marriage or the couple divorces, each spouse has a half interest in the property that is community property. There are variations in the law from state to state. Any person relocating to another state should have his or her estate plan documents carefully reviewed by a lawyer in the new home state. Moving to or from a community property state, even to another community property state, increases the likelihood that changes will have to be made to the estate plan documents. Changes often are advisable even where community property law is not involved. A review of your documents should not be a costly process, but you should establish the fee beforehand in writing.

BEQUESTS

In almost all cases where there is a reasonable degree of family harmony, parents provide that upon the death of the surviving parent, the balance of the estate should be shared equally by their children. However, it may make more sense to spell out in the will or trust agreement that the children were loved equally but that their needs were unequal and that provisions were being made accordingly.

The documents should also provide that the surviving parent could make further adjustments to their children's shares as conditions warranted. One further point: If a surviving parent is considering remarriage, he or she may want to have a premarital agreement to deal fairly with all parties, including the children of the first marriage. The effectiveness of premarital agreements is controlled by state law, and its requirements may be technical. Last-minute arrangements or agreements entered into after remarriage may be ineffective in certain states.

Concerns may arise when some of the children are active in a family business or where all the children may be active in the business, but one or more of them show a much greater management ability than the others. What is fair treatment? These concerns should be discussed with your estate planning attorney and your CPA or other family adviser.

Maximum flexibility in dealing with alternatives must be preserved so revisions in your plans can be made later if expectations change. For example, the child or grandchild who decides to go into the family business after all instead of going to professional school, or the child or grandchild who, after being groomed to take over the family business, decides to do something else instead can raise problems. Usually it is best to get the opinions of several family members along with those of your advisers.

PROBATE

Probate is the legal procedure whereby the provisions of an estate plan are administered under a branch of the state court system. It covers the orderly valuation of a decedent's assets, the settlement of debts owed, and the payment of applicable taxes. The procedure is concluded by the distribution of the remaining assets. Completion of probate can take two years or more.

Depending substantially on the type of assets involved and the total value of your estate, certain delays may be unavoidable. If the probate procedure can be substantially reduced or eliminated, you will have substantial savings in time and money. If you have minor children at the time of your death and your spouse does not survive you, your will should designate your choice of a guardian. If your will does not provide for the naming of a suitable guardian, a judge will name the guardian, who may not be someone you would have chosen.

A will that is admitted to probate is part of the public record and is open to examination by anyone. A revocable trust, however, is not a public document. If there are matters that you want to keep private, such as provisions relative to the care of certain beneficiaries, these matters should be covered in a living trust agreement. If a competent trustee and successor trustee are picked, administration of more detailed wishes over a period of time can be accomplished most efficiently by a trust. If you feel that there may be family disagreements, or that probate court supervision to protect the interests of certain loved ones is desirable, you should discuss these concerns with your attorney. Under these conditions it may be preferable to have all or part of the estate subject to probate procedures.

BYPASS (CREDIT SHELTER) TRUST

In most estates, the bypass or credit shelter trust is the planning tool that results in the greatest estate tax saving. Generally, the marital trust will postpone the estate tax until the surviving spouse dies. But the assets held in the bypass or credit shelter trust of the spouse who is the first to die will escape estate tax in both spouses' estates even though the surviving spouse can be protected as the primary beneficiary during his or her lifetime.

Here are two examples to illustrate how a bypass (credit shelter) trust reduces estate taxes.

Estate Planning: Utilizing a Bypass (Credit Shelter) Trust Can Reduce Estate Taxes

Background

1. In Example A, Paul leaves his entire $2 million estate to his wife, Betty. Probate fees, legal fees, and other administrative expenses are not shown in any of these examples and vary substantially between states. They will generally run from less than 1 percent to as high as 5 percent of the assets in the probate estate. The expenses of administering a living trust are generally less but depend greatly on who the trustees are and the complexity of the trust.
2. Example B uses the same facts as Example A but assumes that Paul has a revocable living trust agreement which establishes a bypass or credit shelter trust.
3. Probate fees are incurred under Example A and normally not under Example B. The combined costs incurred in Example B will

usually be much less than the combined fees and costs under Example A.

4. Example C uses the same facts as Example B but assumes that during Betty's life, but after Paul's death, the assets in the bypass trust grow in value by $1 million. The point is that not only is $1 million sheltered from taxation initially, but also the growth in value is sheltered from federal estate tax in the surviving spouse's estate. (Annual income of the bypass trust is subject to federal income tax laws, however.)

5. If Example A, using the simple will, was changed to show growth in value from $2 million to $3 million in Betty's estate after Paul's death as in Example C, then the federal estate tax that would have been charged to the estate of Betty as the surviving spouse would be $945,000 ($1,290,800 minus $345,800 Unified Credit). This would leave Betty's beneficiaries with $2,055,000 rather than $3 million as shown in Example C.

Example A	*Example B*	
Paul has a will with bequest of all assets to Betty, his surviving spouse.	Paul has a revocable trust agreement with bypass and marital trust provisions created in the trust agreement. Will "pours" all assets not already subject to terms of the trust agreement "over" to it.	
Paul's Estate	*Bypass Trust*	*Marital Trust*
$2,000,000	$1,000,000	$1,000,000
Death of Paul Federal estate tax: $0	Death of Paul after 2005 Federal estate tax : $0	
Amount to Surviving Spouse, Betty	*Provisions*	
$2,000,000	*Bypass Trust* In trust for surviving spouse: with limitations on access to principal; then to children when surviving spouse dies:	*Marital Trust* Outright or in trust for surviving spouse:
	$1,000,000	$1,000,000

(Continued)

Death of Surviving Spouse, Betty, after 2005 Federal estate tax: $434,200 (Tax of $780,000 minus Unified Credit of $345,800)	Death of Surviving Spouse, Betty, after 2005 Federal estate tax: $0
Amount to Beneficiaries $1,565,800 ($2,000,000 minus $434,200)	Amount to Beneficiaries $2,000,000
	Savings over Example A: $434,200

Example C

This example is the same as Example B, except assets in the bypass trust increase in value during the period beginning with Paul's death and ending with surviving spouse Betty's death.

Bypass Trust	*Marital Trust*
$1,000,000	$1,000,000

Death of Paul after 2005

Provisions

Bypass Trust	*Marital Trust*
In trust for surviving spouse, then surviving children	Outright or in trust for surviving spouse:
$1,000,000 +$1,000,000 increase $2,000,000	$1,000,000

Death of Surviving Spouse, Betty

Federal estate tax: $0

Amount to Beneficiaries

$2,000,000 + $1,000,000 = $3,000,000

THE TRUSTEE

In most instances, estate planning involving more than $1 million in assets should involve the establishment of one or more trusts, whether subject to probate or not, that will be revocable during the lifetime of the creator of the trust (legally designated as the *grantor* or the *settlor*) and will become irrevocable upon the grantor's death or incompetency. A revocable trust is normally ignored for income tax purposes during the grantor's life. In many estates of less than $1 million, trusts can be beneficial for probate avoidance even if tax savings is not involved.

grantor an individual providing assets under written terms to be utilized for the benefit of one or more others.

The trustee or trustees that the grantor appoints are required under state law to carry out the grantor's wishes as provided in the trust document. Confidence in the trustee's integrity and ability is a critical element in a solid estate plan. Generally, the grantor names himself or herself as the trustee during his or her lifetime, and upon death or incompetency, an individual or a bank and trust company is named as the successor trustee or trustees. The advantage in using a corporate trustee such as a bank or trust company as your trustee or cotrustee is that there is continuity. That is, the bank will not become ill or die, and it does not have any relationship with a beneficiary that could cause tax or other legal problems.

settlor same as grantor

For example, the portion of your estate that will be held in a bypass or credit shelter trust so that it will be taxed in neither your estate nor your spouse's estate can be defeated if the IRS could show that your spouse had full control of that trust. With the phased-in increase in the credit shelter amount (based on the Unified Credit) that will reach $1 million by the year 2006, an erroneous trustee provision or designation could be costly. Hundreds of thousands or even millions of dollars could be lost in additional estate taxes, since the surviving spouse may live many more years and the initial credit shelter amount may grow in value to many times its original size.

The major drawbacks in utilizing a corporate trustee or a corporate cotrustee can be both real and imagined. You may have a fine relationship with the people at the bank or trust company that you deal with, but in all likelihood these are not the people that your loved ones will work with after you die. Also, the costs that are charged by a corporate trustee are usually set by a schedule (subject to negotiation) and are often steep.

If the trust officers of the bank or trust company are competent and the fees are commensurate with the services and the responsibilities involved, the best interests of the trust beneficiaries may be served by the bank acting as the trustee or successor trustee. However, some banks and trust companies, because of the substantial turnover of personnel, lack experience as trustees.

In addition, the performance records of most banks and trust companies as asset managers and investment advisers are poor. Even when mutual funds are utilized as the primary or sole investment medium, banks sometimes rely heavily on their own mutual funds, which do not compare favorably with mutual funds that are managed by the most skilled advisers in the investment industry. Our experience is that a replacement of about 20 percent of the mutual funds during a 12-month period that is based on management performance is not unusual. You want to avoid being locked into a portfolio by a bank or other adviser.

In recent years, fewer prospective grantors have wanted to use a corporate trustee. Our experience is that in most cases where a bank or trust company was named in the original agreement as a trustee, periodic review of the trust agreement will result in the grantor naming an individual to be the trustee instead. However, even when an individual trustee or trustees are used, it is a good idea to have a mechanism for the use of a substitute corporate trustee if it is possible that all individual trustee candidates could die or be incapacitated before the trust would terminate. In almost all instances, trust agreements can be prepared to accommodate a grantor's first choice of a trustee. However, extreme care must be exercised when relatives are named as trustees or cotrustees.

For example, if your spouse is to be a trustee over that portion of your estate that is to be excluded from your taxable estate, your spouse should not exercise that degree of authority that will allow the IRS to successfully challenge the exclusion from his or her estate. It may be necessary to give the power of removal of a trustee to one person and the power of appointment of a successor trustee to another person. Otherwise the IRS may argue that having the power to both remove and replace a trustee should be considered the same as possessing sufficient powers that would make the assets includable in that person's estate, although the decided cases are favorable to the taxpayer.

HOW SHOULD INVESTMENTS BE MANAGED AFTER DEATH?

An important point to discuss with your estate planning attorney is the management of your investments if you either are incapacitated during the term of the trust or die. Many people are unable to decide on a qualified individual they are comfortable to name as trustee. Still others are unable to choose a qualified individual as a successor trustee should the original trustee die or become incapacitated or resign. For this reason, a bank or trust company is often named as the trustee or the successor trustee.

In the absence of appropriate provisions, the bank or trust company will want to utilize its own investment department to manage the trust assets despite there being hundreds of better choices available. If you are satisfied with your current investment adviser, that adviser should be initially retained. To substitute unacceptable performance for acceptable performance, usually at a greater cost, does not make sense. On the other hand, if an investment adviser should underperform in the judgment of a majority of the adult beneficiaries, that adviser should be able to be replaced. These terms should be provided in your trust agreement, although most attorneys fail to include them unless requested to do so by their clients.

There are independent trust companies that offer "unbundled" services and seem to have gained a degree of acceptance in several states; but in most areas local banks and trust companies are utilized heavily. In recent years several large brokerage houses have formed or acquired trust companies and have made their services available as an alternative to the established local bank trust departments. The broker's objective is to retain more of the business that was lost when a trust department or trust company took over investment management upon the death of one of its customers. "Unbundling" trust department services means that a trust can choose to utilize certain trust department services such as administering the trust's payout and reporting provisions without having to utilize other services such as investment management that could be more satisfactorily provided elsewhere.

OTHER DEVELOPMENTS IN TRUSTS

In Chapter 9 the Prudent Man Rule and the Prudent Investor Rule are discussed. Many people put more emphasis than they should on preserving principal. In this book we discuss the advantages of utilizing total available assets in distributions, which would include recognizing that with appreciation in value of principal, utilizing this growth in distributions is permissible and usually necessary. This distinction underlies what is called Modern Portfolio Theory and the replacement of the Prudent Man Rule with the Prudent Investor Rule. Most attorneys are still dealing with older investment concepts because of their acceptance by clients and probably more because of inertia.

However, as attorneys have become aware of updated investment management concepts with the increasing flow of investment information and adoption of local versions of the Prudent Investor Rule, trusts are being prepared to give the trustees total discretion over all distributions. Additional reasons for this are to protect trust assets from the claims of creditors of the trust beneficiaries and to reduce or eliminate the effect of the generation-skipping transfer (GST) tax. If children of the decedent are trust beneficiaries, complete trustee discretion on distributions could protect them from having the trustee compelled to turn over distributions to satisfy the claims of their creditors. These creditors could include holders of substantial obligations arising from divorce, malpractice claims, or other legal proceedings. Under these conditions a creditor will be more willing to settle its claim for a reduced amount. Because of GST and other tax considerations, planning to postpone distributions to a later generation will require the input of the tax lawyer. Under these conditions the financial adviser to the trust and the trustee also have increased responsibilities, and consultations with beneficiaries (and the grantors of the trust if they are still alive) can be very important to all parties.

For hundreds of years the English common law has been the basis for the laws of most states as well as U.S. federal law, and it includes a rule against perpetuities. This rule limits the length of time that a trust can exist. As a result, all trusts created in these jurisdictions provide for winding up and distributing all principal at a certain point of time such as upon the death of the survivor of a designated group of people living at the time that the trust agreement is prepared plus 26 years. Alaska, South Dakota, and Delaware have eliminated the rule, and it is expected that other states will follow, particularly when banks and trust companies lose business to competitors in states that have abolished the rule. Of course, additional problems arise when a trust can go on for a very long time or forever, and the trust terms must cover the grantor's wishes under these circumstances. Generally, trust attorneys recommend that very broad authority be given to trustees and their successors. Then, the key issue becomes how these trustees and successors are selected, when are they replaced, and how are they replaced.

Chapter 11

More Estate Planning—Additional Tools

In this chapter, more complex estate planning problems and solutions are covered.

IRREVOCABLE LIFE INSURANCE TRUST

The irrevocable life insurance trust (ILIT) is a specialized type of trust that is created to be both owner and beneficiary of one or more life insurance policies. When the trust is used to purchase a life insurance policy or to be the transferee of ownership of existing life insurance, substantial estate tax savings can result. Upon death, the insurance proceeds are paid to the trustees of this trust. The trust agreement goes on to provide details for utilizing the policy proceeds for the benefit of loved ones of the insured.

When existing life insurance policies are transferred to an ILIT, the policy proceeds will be removed from your potential taxable estate if you survive for at least three years (the three-year rule). The most immediate benefit can be secured when the ILIT is utilized to apply for and purchase a new life insurance policy. When properly accomplished under the careful supervision of an estate planning attorney, although you are the insured, you will never be the owner or beneficiary of the policy and the three-year rule would not apply. Under certain circumstances it is advisable to have children of the insured or others purchase policies on the insured's life rather than the ILIT arrangement and still achieve substantial tax benefits. Generally, the ILIT arrangement is preferred.

Why would a person with substantial assets purchase life insurance coverage using an ILIT? If you own a business or undeveloped real estate, the purchase of life insurance may be a means to provide cash to pay all or a substantial part of the estate taxes and related expenses; otherwise, your heirs and beneficiaries might be forced to sell valuable assets at distress prices. By utilizing an ILIT properly, the proceeds of the policies can be utilized for this purpose without being included in your estate for federal estate tax purposes.

The trust agreement will provide that funds can be lent by the trust to your estate to pay taxes. In addition, it will provide that nonliquid assets may be purchased from your estate with these funds. In this way, the trust can transfer cash to your estate that can be used for tax payments, and the family business or other nonliquid assets will move from your estate to the ILIT. The ILIT will then transfer the business or other assets to the beneficiaries tax-free. The agreement establishing this trust cannot be revoked or amended or it will lose its tax-preferred status.

The experienced estate planning attorney will include some escape hatches to cover certain situations. For example, if cash contributions to pay annual insurance premiums are discontinued, the insurance policies owned by the ILIT may be able to be converted to paid-up policies with reduced face amounts. If the grantor is still insurable, a new ILIT with newly purchased policies can then be established with terms that will take the prior ILIT's terms and insurance policies into account.

A second-to-die life insurance policy on the lives of you and your spouse is often utilized under these circumstances. The premium on this type of policy will be less than the premium on the life of either one of you. If one of you is uninsurable, this policy may provide the ideal solution. It should usually be purchased through an ILIT. Maximum utilization of the marital deduction will postpone taxes upon the death of the first spouse to die. The proceeds from this type of policy will be paid to the ILIT when the surviving spouse dies so that cash will be available for estate tax payments and other needs at that time.

An additional advantage of an irrevocable life insurance trust is that its assets generally are protected from the claims of creditors of the insured when the beneficiaries that are named in the ILIT do not include the estate of the insured or a corporation. If the insurance policies have substantial cash value, cash may be available to trust beneficiaries even while the insured lives, if permitted by the terms of the trust agreement. Utilizing these funds to indirectly assist the insured or the spouse of the insured should not be attempted before consulting with an attorney on the availability of this approach. After the death of the insured (the "insured" may include both spouses if a second-to-die policy is involved), the policy proceeds generally would not be subject to other creditor claims against the decedents or federal estate tax claims against them.

Case Study—The Greens

Mr. and Mrs. Green established an ILIT to purchase a second-to-die policy on their lives for $5 million. Upon the death of the survivor, their two children, Lillian and Philip, acting as ILIT trustees, are advised to use $4 million to buy controlling stock in the family business from the estate of Mrs. Green, who had survived Mr. Green.

Now, the trust has the controlling stock, free of tax claims and other creditor claims against the Greens, and the $4 million in cash paid to the estate can be utilized to pay the estate tax of Mrs. Green. If Mrs. Green had directly owned the insurance policy instead, the $4 million of insurance proceeds would have been part of her taxable estate and the estate's tax bill would have increased by as much as $2.2 million (55 percent of $4 million) to $6.2 million. Details on the different types of life insurance policies that are sold are summarized at the end of this chapter.

PARTNERSHIPS AND BUSINESS INTERESTS

Putting business assets, investment assets, or both into a newly formed entity could enable you to retain control of assets while removing a substantial part of their value from your taxable estate. Limited liability companies (LLCs) and limited liability partnerships (LLPs) are recent additions to the laws of many states. They are hybrid entities that combine some of the characteristics of corporations with some of the characteristics of partnerships. Limited partnerships are not new. They also combine some of the characteristics of corporations with those of partnerships. We're discussing only those attributes that enable someone to retain control while establishing potential tax benefits by reducing the value of one's interest to a substantial degree.

Ignoring gift tax consequences for a moment, if you transferred your solely owned business to a partnership in which you retained a 52 percent interest, and your two sons each received a 24 percent interest, your interest in the business would be substantially reduced. If the business as a whole were worth $1 million, what would your 52 percent partnership interest be worth? The sum of $520,000 may not be the right answer. What would your sons' interests be worth? An amount of $240,000 each is probably not the right answer. What would an interested buyer of the business be willing to pay for your interest if your sons were not willing to sell—or pay them for their interests if you were not willing to sell? Lack of marketability of a business interest and minority interest ownership are both factors that reduce value.

Lack of marketability is not only looking for a buyer of a grocery store in a high-crime area, but also seeking a buyer for a 52 percent interest in a business where the balance is owned by two brothers who seem difficult to deal with. Justification for a discount for a minority interest can be given to you by an interested potential buyer for a 24 percent interest in a business when the remaining interests are owned by strangers who would retain the power to control decisions. Lack of control could mean that: (1) one's share of the profits could be held back rather than distributed; (2) one would not be employed by the business; or (3) if employed, one would not determine anyone's salary. Discounts in value of 25 percent to 50 percent are often justified for the combination of a lack of marketability of an interest as well as it being a minority interest with little or no decision-making authority.

Case Study—Jer-Jan, a Family Limited Partnership

Substantial advantages can be obtained by utilizing valuation rules. Jerry and his wife, Jan, have built a business with a value of over $3 million. Their adult children play important management roles in the business. Jerry and Jan consulted with their tax advisers to establish a comprehensive program that will keep control of the business in their family after they die while substantially reducing potential estate and gift taxes.

The plan that was adopted will utilize the principles of creating minority interests with reduced market values so that these interests can be used to transfer ownership from Jerry and Jan to their two adult children and their five grandchildren. Jerry and Jan can each give a $10,000 per year gift, tax-free, to each child and grandchild. That would be $20,000 per year of interest in Jer-Jan, the new family limited partnership, to be given to each child and grandchild, or $140,000 per year given to the seven donees.

If valuation discounts for lack of marketability and for minority interests were supportable at a combined 33⅓ percent rate, $210,000, not $140,000, would be removed from Jerry and Jan's taxable estates each year. Over 10 years, $2,100,000 would be removed, saving more than $1 million in potential federal estate tax.

What if Jerry and Jan are not in good health or their assets still have the potential of growing rapidly so that, in several years, their estates are still likely to increase greatly? Under these circumstances they don't have 10 years to achieve their goal of passing on their business to their loved ones instead of having it burdened with debt or sold in order to pay estate taxes. But Jerry and Jan each has a Unified Credit that can shelter up to $1 million in gifts beginning in the year 2006.

Most estates have applied the Unified Credit in full when calculating federal estate tax liability after the death of the individual. However, in large estates it is more effective when it is utilized to shelter gifts during life. Jerry and Jan also have $2 million in other assets. If they each give $1 million in partnership interests in 2006, the $2 million in gifts can remove $3 million from their potential estates because of the valuation discounts. If the $3 million in Jer-Jan doubled in value by the time that both Jerry and Jan died, the use of their federal gift tax and estate tax credit (the Unified Credit), instead of being worth $1 million in exclusions to each of their estates, has become worth $3 million of exclusions to each of their estates.

Note: This example does not cover all the technical problems that the competent attorney will have to deal with. For example, there is the generation-skipping transfer (GST) tax to discourage gifts that skip a generation such as the gifts to Jerry and Jan's grandchildren, but there are also cumulative $1 million GST exclusions for each of the grandparents.

If certain requirements are followed, everyone has the right to give up to $10,000 per year to anyone they wish to without incurring a gift tax or using up any portion of the Unified Credit. The primary requirement is that the gift is of a "present interest" rather than a "future interest." Generally, if there are restrictions on the donee's right to control the gift, it may be a gift of a future interest and the gift may not qualify for the $10,000 annual exclusion. How it can be used is shown in this tale of Jerry and Jan. Since 1998, the annual exclusion is indexed for inflation by a formula that will increase it in $1,000 intervals from time to time.

Taxpayer Relief

There may be additional estate tax relief under the Taxpayer Relief Act of 1997 where over 50 percent of a decedent's estate is the value of a qualified family-owned business. As the exemption equivalent of the Unified Credit increases from $625,000 in 1998 to $1 million in 2006, the combined Unified Credit and qualified business exclusion is capped at $1,300,000.

The rules under the 1997 Act are complicated and include provisions if one, two, or three families control the business. There may be situations where nonbusiness assets rather than business assets should be given during life in order for the estate to qualify for this limited relief. Failure to maintain family participation for at least 10 years after death can result in giving back the estate tax benefits. The complexity of this provision makes professional assistance necessary. Nontax problems such as the child who is not active in the business and the grandchild who should not be trusted with substantial assets are beyond the scope of this book. But, competent advisers can be helpful since they deal with these situations regularly.

To this point, we have discussed federal estate taxes. Since 1976, the estate tax and gift tax has been integrated into a Unified Transfer Tax so that the IRS can have a measure of control relative to avoidance of taxes on transfers at death by those who make substantial transfers during life. Generally, the tax on gifts during life and transfers at death are taxed at similar rates. A principal difference is that a gift received during life is considered to have the same income tax basis as it had in the hands of the donor. As discussed, a transfer upon death receives a step-up in basis—that is, an income tax basis equal to the value of the property as of the date of death or as of an alternate valuation date thereafter.

The gift and estate tax rules are integrated to an extent to make them more effective, but there are still great potential advantages in gifts during life. As shown in the stories of Jerry and Jan and George and Martha, if the gifts substantially increase in value, substantial tax savings can result. Assistance of a qualified attorney is advised when considering a program of gifts.

Case Study—George and Martha

George and Martha have three married children and five grandchildren. Annual qualifying tax-free gifts of up to $10,000 each to these donees by George would remove $80,000 per year (as well as the subsequent appreciation and income from these gifts) from George's estate. If George and Martha properly elect to treat the gifts as made equally by the two of them, the annual tax-free qualifying gifts can be increased up to $20,000 per donee. If George and Martha want to add their children's spouses to the donee list, or anyone else, they can. Where the donee is a minor, the establishment of a qualifying trust should be considered.

Let's suppose George and Martha give $160,000 per year ($20,000 times 8 donees) for four years by using both of their annual exemptions. These gifts would remove $640,000 ($160,000 times 4 years) from their combined estates. If the date of death of the survivor of the two of them is 10 years hence, these gifts would have appreciated in value by $700,000. The result would be that $1,340,000 ($640,000 plus $700,000) had been eliminated from the survivor's estate for a tax saving of $737,000 ($1,340,000 times 55 percent.) Also note that, if desired, George and Martha could have used some or all of their Unified Credits for additional gifts.

ESTATE TAX BENEFITS FROM CHARITABLE GIFTS

There are a variety of charitable trust arrangements that can be established to benefit the qualified charity of your choice and result in significant tax benefits for you and your loved ones. There are different forms of charitable trusts, including a charitable lead trust, which will pay income to a charity for a specific period and then distribute the trust principal to your beneficiaries.

Another variation is the charitable remainder annuity or unitrust, which pays a set dollar amount or a percentage of the trust assets to you or your beneficiaries, and then, after your death or after a specific period of time, the principal is donated to a charity. There are other variations, too. These are irrevocable arrangements that are generally utilized by the very wealthy who have a strong desire to assist a particular charity, coupled with a desire to obtain substantial tax benefits for their beneficiaries. Universities, religious institutions, and other charities maintain charitable giving departments that provide detailed information and assistance to potential donors.

DEATHBED PLANNING

Although it is a very difficult time, the terminally ill person should try some meaningful planning. Annual tax-free gifts of up to $10,000 per donee can be made without using any of the individual donor's Unified Credit. If it is late in the year, additional gifts of up to $10,000 per donee could be made for the new calendar year. Under these conditions, it usually does not make sense to make gifts of more than the annual tax-free amount to any donee since the gift tax amount paid within three years of death is added back into the taxable estate.

Also, the annual exclusion amount will increase from time to time after 1999. Generally, cash or assets that have not appreciated substantially in value should be used for these gifts. Assets that have appreciated greatly achieve a stepped-up basis at death, which can save substantial income tax for the donor's loved ones. It is important to keep in mind that all gifts and other transfers by check are not complete unless the checks are deposited and cleared before the donor's death.

Because of the unique nature of life insurance, there is an exception relative to deathbed planning: Gifts of life insurance made during the three years prior to death will *not* remove the policy proceeds from the estate. In the past, there was a question whether the policy was still includable in the estate if the insured continued to pay the premiums after the gift of the policy. The transfer is complete for the purpose of starting the three years prior to death period if other rights aren't retained. The assignment must cover all rights under the policy, and it must be a policy that automatically continues without the need to reapply. If a right is retained such as the right to change the beneficiary, the right to borrow on it, or any other right, the proceeds will be includable in the estate of the transferor.

Also, if the terminally ill person is married, the potential Unified Credit should not be wasted as they were in the cases of Chuck and Laura and Tom and Helen in the previous chapter. The schedule in Table 11.1 sets out the amount that should be held by a terminally ill spouse at the time of death in order to maximize the tax benefits of the bypass or credit shelter trust.

A special alert should also be given to those terminally ill spouses who had credit shelter trusts with up to $600,000 in their names pursuant to pre-1998 conditions. Their planning should be reexamined to take into consideration the phasing in of additional potential benefits for the 1998

TABLE 11.1 Maximum Asset Value Exempted from Tax Using the Unified Credit

Year	*Amount Excluded*
1998	$ 625,000
1999	650,000
2000	675,000
2001	675,000
2002	700,000
2003	700,000
2004	850,000
2005	950,000
2006 and thereafter	1,000,000

Note: Prior to 1998, full use of the Unified Credit could exempt $600,000 in value from federal gift and estate taxes. From 1998 to 2006, a higher exempt amount is being phased in as shown above.

to 2006 period. There is a requirement that the recipient of any transfers must live for at least a year and a day for the transfer to be effective. There is no penalty if the recipient does not survive that long, so it should be tried if the tax saving is desired, whether it is additional funding for an existing credit shelter trust or to establish a new credit shelter trust.

If a terminally ill person is not married but in a relationship where he or she wants to provide a substantial amount for the benefit of the other party, a substantial increase in the amount that will be available may result if the two of them are able to marry. The law favors spouses.

Transfers of greatly appreciated assets to a terminally ill person may make sense even with the year and a day rule to cope with to achieve a step-up in basis of the assets that will reduce future taxes of surviving loved ones. In some cases, it is possible that the year and a day rule can be bypassed by utilizing certain trusts. This transfer planning makes sense if the potential savings in capital gains taxes of loved ones is substantial when compared to the potential increased estate tax of the terminally ill person.

Another area of deathbed planning to consider is IRAs and other retirement plans where the terminally ill person is a participant. The beneficiary designation and the distribution election should be reviewed for each account. Potential errors can be corrected. Also, it may be advisable to roll a retirement plan account into an IRA before death so that substantial income tax liabilities can be postponed for the benefit of the ill person's loved ones. Depending on who the beneficiary is and his or her age, income tax liability may be delayed for many years.

Tuition payments and medical care payments, even if they cause the annual per-donee gift limit (currently $10,000) to be exceeded, are removed from the donor's estate if the checks are directly payable to a school, hospital, or physician.

If charitable gifts are contemplated, making the gifts before death will create an income tax deduction as well as remove the amount from the terminally ill person's estate.

Next, the disclaimer is an example of a postdeathbed device that a surviving spouse, heir, or beneficiary will sometimes find helpful.

Case Study—Sol and Sandy

Sol died leaving his wife, Sandy, with all $2 million of his assets. Sandy is a U.S. citizen, so there is an unlimited marital deduction, and no estate taxes are due. If Sandy should then die with $2 million in her estate, only the Unified Credit amount applicable to her estate (varying from $675,000 to $1 million depending on the year of her death) would be excluded from estate tax. But, if Sandy disclaimed a large sum from Sol's estate within nine months of his death, then that portion would go to Sol's next of kin, who would be their children, and to the extent that this sum would be less than the Unified Credit amount applicable to his estate, it would be excluded from estate tax.

Sandy could even eliminate the entire estate tax that would be due on her death if she disclaimed $1 million and died after 2005. Sandy would be reluctant to disclaim an amount that she felt she might need to meet her financial needs, including potential emergencies. If Sol had had an estate plan with a properly prepared credit shelter trust, Sandy still could have had the protection of the principal in that trust as well as the income. The children could have benefited by having the principal in the credit shelter trust excluded from the taxable estates of both of their parents. By her disclaimer, Sandy is rescuing some of the tax benefits that would be lost by Sol having failed to include a credit shelter trust in his estate plan. There are precise disclaimer rules that the knowledgeable tax adviser will utilize.

Case Study—Mr. Socrates

To illustrate how the step-up in basis rule works, let's take the case of Mr. Socrates on his deathbed on December 10. Mr. Socrates is a widower with a $5 million estate and 5 children and 10 grandchildren. Being able to give the annual exclusion amount (currently $10,000) to each of these potential beneficiaries would remove $150,000 from his taxable estate. If he survives to January 1, he can repeat the gifts for the new year, too. He is thinking of giving them either cash or common stock.

The stock is in Compu.com. Bought for $1 per share many years ago, it is now worth $100 per share. If Mr. Socrates makes $150,000 in gifts of the stock (1,500 shares valued at $100 per share), when the children and grandchildren as donees sell the shares they will have a taxable gain of $99 per share ($100 minus $1 cost). Using the capital gain rate of 20 percent for assets with a holding period of more than 12 months results in a capital gain tax of $29,700 when these donees sell the stock for $150,000. If Mr. Socrates gave $150,000 in cash instead, leaving the stock to be distributed after his death, this tax would be avoided entirely.

Upon receiving the stock after Mr. Socrates' death, the children and grandchildren could sell the shares. If the shares were worth $100 each on the date of his death, the children and grandchildren as new owners could use $100 per share as their own cost basis—the step-up from $1 per share to $100 per share. Note that Mr. Socrates also owns securities that have dropped in value. They should be quickly sold so the losses can be claimed on his income tax return. The opportunity to claim these losses ends at death.

PROTECTION FOR THE SURVIVORS—LIFE INSURANCE

Generally, if you have an adequate investment portfolio to fund retirement for yourself and your spouse, you do not need life insurance protection. The usual life insurance question is, "Who would suffer financially if I died?" But careful analysis may be necessary. A couple may conclude that they do not have enough saved to retire but that if an insured spouse is the first to die, his or her life insurance (perhaps acquired as an employee fringe benefit) will be an important source of funds for the surviving spouse.

Consider the example of a couple who believe that they have enough to retire on. However, they do not have long-term care insurance, and the husband has had health problems and can't purchase long-term care insurance without paying excessive premiums. From time to time, they've considered cashing in a life insurance policy on his life.

In this case, it may make sense for the couple to review the policy provisions with their agent and determine whether that policy could serve as a surrogate for a long-term care policy for the husband. According to one 1993 study, the average cost of a year in a nursing home is about $38,000, and this cost varies widely in different parts of the country. The life insurance policy could serve to replenish the portfolio for the spouse's benefit if the husband should die after an extended period in a nursing home. An alternative, if there is substantial cash value, would be to cash in the policy to utilize its cash value either to help fund long-term care insurance costs or to increase the investment portfolio so that the couple can better cope with long-term care costs if they are incurred. If there is little cash value, maintaining the policy for its death benefit may make sense if the premiums are not too high.

TYPES OF LIFE INSURANCE POLICIES

Here is a brief description of most, but not all, life insurance policies. (The summaries do not cover all policy features.) A decision to retain a policy to tie into retirement objectives will be based not only on the amount of insurance but the future cost of carrying it and certain features such as access to cash value.

Term Insurance

These policies provide insurance protection only. If the insured dies, the beneficiary is paid. Generally there is no cash value to the policy and there is no borrowing against the policy.

Level Renewable Term Insurance

The term, usually one year or five years, is covered by a fixed annual premium and a fixed face amount. Generally term policies are renewable; as long as you pay your premiums the insurance company will renew your coverage even if your health or occupational status has changed. Upon renewal, the annual premium is increased taking your age into account. Usually the insurance contract will allow you to reduce the amount of coverage, thereby reducing your premiums as well, but if you want to increase the coverage you will probably have to undergo a medical examination. This coverage may serve a temporary role depending on future circumstances, such as success in saving and investing when coverage may be cut back or dropped.

Level Nonrenewable Term Insurance

Usually this policy is not offered after you reach age 65 or age 70. You may have a limited time period when you can convert it to a cash value policy despite changes in health or occupation.

Decreasing Term Insurance

The annual premiums remain fixed, but the face amount gradually decreases. This type of policy is often used as mortgage life insurance so that the balance owed on your mortgage is paid upon death. Generally this type of insurance is not as good as a term policy that is large enough to cover your family's housing and other needs. Mortgage insurance must be used to pay off the mortgage, but if you have a favorable mortgage with low interest rates, your family may be better off not paying it off and utilizing insurance proceeds in another way. Credit life insurance is another kind of decreasing term insurance and is generally not advisable for the same reason.

Cash Value (Whole-Life) Insurance

This coverage is not limited to a certain term. Even if you don't die, it can build up cash value and act like a savings account. It is a form of forced savings. It costs more than term insurance in the early years of the policy, so there will be a fund to help offset the cost in later years. As you and the policy get older, a more substantial portion of the death benefit consists of the cash value in the policy.

For example, if you take out a whole-life policy with a face amount of $100,000, the death benefit remains constant while the cash value of the policy gradually builds up. If the cash value of the policy has built up to a level of, say, $20,000, you can cash in that policy and take the money, but you no longer have life insurance coverage. If the cash value of the policy is $80,000 when you die, the insurance company only has to come up with an additional $20,000 to equal the $100,000 death benefit. The cash value of the policy is for the benefit of the insured, who can borrow on it or cash it in. Whole-life insurance is not a good buy if you plan to keep your policy for only a few years. Little if any cash value would be built up in that period. It usually takes about 10 years for cash values to build up substantially.

Universal Life Insurance

This policy is similar to whole-life in that it builds up cash value. While whole-life policies do not inform the holder about the effective rate of return being paid through accumulated cash value in the policy, universal life increases the rates of return on cash value accumulations. However, in recent years universal life policies have provided for a surrender charge, and this reduces the cash value accumulations available if you drop the policy or borrow against it. Usually surrender charges gradually diminish and disappear sometime after the tenth year.

The policy may guarantee a certain minimum interest rate on your cash value, and in recent years the actual rate has been higher than the stated minimum. The interest rate fluctuates with prevailing interest rates.

Variable Life Insurance

This is a wrinkle on the regular universal life policy. The insured chooses an investment or investments from stocks, bonds, money market funds, mutual funds, or a combination of the vehicles. The insurance company deducts the cost of insurance protection and expense fees from the cash value, usually done monthly. However, if your cash value dips too low because you have not kept up premium payments, you may have to invest more money in order to keep your policy in effect.

"Final Expense" Policies

These policies, aimed at senior citizens and sold through television advertising and by direct mail, have become popular in recent years. Although they seem attractive because they promise "guaranteed acceptance" regardless of the health of the insured, they're not good buys. Generally, the insurance does not provide full benefits if the insured dies from an illness within the first two years after purchase of the policy, and illness is the usual cause of death for the elderly.

Second-to-Die Policies

This type of policy is usually issued to a married couple. The face amount is paid when the surviving insured dies. Because the policy requires two people to die before payment, the annual premiums are less than if either spouse were the sole insured. Because the estate tax provides an unlimited marital deduction, most taxable estates are created at the time that the surviving spouse dies. Where insurance proceeds can pay all or a substantial part of estate taxes, the need to sell the family business and/or valuable property is avoided. When one spouse is otherwise uninsurable, this type of policy may still be available. Often, it pays to talk to your attorney before signing an application for life insurance. Substantial estate taxes can be avoided where adult children or an irrevocable trust (often quickly created by the attorney for this purpose) is the policy applicant even if the insured are the husband and wife.

An Alternative to Life Insurance?

There may be an alternative for those who rankle at the thought of buying life insurance. Annual cash gifts to children or to an irrevocable trust for the benefit of the children, with the gifts being invested to develop a diversified portfolio, may be preferable under certain circumstances. For potential estates that would not be in difficulty by having to pay substantial estate taxes before the portfolio grew sufficiently, it may be a workable alternative. Perhaps a combination of both approaches could be used. The life insurance purchased by an irrevocable insurance trust could be converted to paid-up policies when the investment portfolio in the irrevocable investment trust grew sufficiently. A number of practical problems are involved, and your attorney can tell you whether a version of this alternative is workable for you.

ESTATE TAX CONSIDERATIONS

Generally, life insurance is seen as providing protection for the spouse and children of the insured to meet the cost of living such as mortgage payments, college costs, medical expenses, and so on. If you're retired or nearing retirement, life insurance policy proceeds may be used to pay all or part of estate taxes, thereby avoiding selling a home or closely held business in order to pay taxes. How life insurance is purchased and held can make a substantial difference relative to estate taxes.

Purchase of life insurance policies by children of the insured or through an irrevocable insurance trust can result in some interesting mathematics. For example, if Franklin has a $10 million estate and has his attorney prepare an irrevocable insurance trust that acquires a $2 million life insurance policy on Franklin's life, the proceeds of the $2 million policy will not be included in Franklin's taxable estate nor in his wife Elinor's taxable estate if the legal requirements for this treatment are met. Even if $1 million of premiums are paid over the years and this $1 million would have grown to $3 million if it had been invested, the adoption of this strategy could still prove very valuable to the trust's beneficiaries. The substitution of $2 million of insurance proceeds that is not subject to federal estate tax for $3 million that would have been included in the surviving spouse's estate is a good trade-off, because the $3 million would have been only $1.35 million after federal estate taxes applied at the 55 percent rate. Thus $650,000 ($2 million minus $1.35 million) would be gained.

Again, you must review the stability of the insurance company. Contact one or more of the five rating agencies (listed in Chapter 8) to get the ratings on the prospective insurer or insurers. Where very substantial sums are involved, it may be wise to split the coverage over two or more insurance companies.

VIATICAL SETTLEMENTS OF LIFE INSURANCE POLICIES

In addition to access to cash value of a seasoned life insurance policy, limited access to the death benefits before the insured dies may preserve more of the investment portfolio for the survivor.

Certain life insurance policyholders are able to receive accelerated death benefits on a tax-free basis. These proceeds would be received from a licensed settlement provider or individuals who meet insurance regulation requirements, and these proceeds would be tax-free. Policyholders who could qualify to sell or assign their life insurance for these benefits are terminally ill patients and chronically ill individuals. These provisions were enacted as part of the Insurance Portability and Accountability Act of 1996. "Terminally ill patients" are defined as physician-certified that their illness is reasonably expected to cause death within two years.

"Chronically ill individuals" are generally individuals who cannot perform at least two activities of daily living—eating, toileting, transferring, bathing, dressing, and continence.

For the terminally ill or chronically ill, such an arrangement may provide funds when needed. Since payout rates vary greatly depending on the circumstances as well as who the provider may be, several proposals should be secured. The Viatical Association of America (800-842-9811), a nonprofit group, will provide a list of its members. Gloria Wolf, a consumer advocate active in viaticals, can be reached at www.viatical-expert.net. Evaluate the proposal by asking whether the policy can be sold (the permission of the insurance company may be needed) and considering the life expectancy of the insured based on his or her medical records. The longer the life expectancy, the larger the discount on the face value of the policy. In other words, the longer the period that the provider will have to maintain the policy and wait for its money, the less it will be willing to advance.

Viatical settlements are fairly new and the opportunity for unscrupulous providers exists, in part because most states do not regulate settlement providers adequately. In 1994, CNA became the first large insurer to enter the viatical business. There are less than 100 firms providing viatical settlements. Fewer than 20 are firms with substantial funds for the purpose of funding benefits, while the others are brokers that charge a true provider a fee or commission, typically about 6 percent of the face value of the policy. Usually, there is no legal requirement that this fee be disclosed to the insured. Generally, the broker places the business where the broker will get the highest fee, rather than getting the best deal for the insured individual. Even a hospital, clinic, or doctor may be an undisclosed broker.

Make certain that the insured can receive the funds at the time that the policy is surrendered. After all, the point is to secure funds promptly from a nonliquid policy. Before entering into a viatical settlement, the insured should have a tax adviser establish whether the transaction will qualify for tax-free treatment under the Insurance Portability and Accountability Act of 1996.

A great deal of fraud has been present in the viatical settlement industry. The terminally ill insured may be underpaid for his or her policy, persons investing through a promoter of viatical settlements may be offered life insurance policies that have been fraudulently issued, or the insured may have a longer life expectancy that can reduce or eliminate the value of the policy. The North American Securities Administrators Association lists viatical fraud as one of the top 10 financial scams. A Texas viatical company has been accused of soliciting HIV-positive patients to lie about their condition on insurance company policy applications in order to buy many small policies for the purpose of having the viatical company then resell them. These small policies usually do not require a medical exam and would not be payable because of the fraud involved. Another scam is raising money from individual investors by promising them large annual returns from investing in viatical settlements, and then defaulting on the policies after a few quarterly payments.

Chapter 12

Putting It All Together: Your Comprehensive, Multigenerational Wealth Management Plan

As someone from Disney once said, "Now it's time to say goodbye." Empowerment comes from the knowledge that you now have in your hands (this book) and in your mind. You have all of the information that you will need to work effectively with your financial professionals: your investment adviser, accountant, attorney, and insurance broker. Perhaps more importantly, you should by now at least have started to have some peace of mind from knowing that you have the tools to get your financial life in order.

Complete peace of mind will come when you have implemented all aspects of your wealth management plan.

We sincerely hope that we have done our job well—namely, that we have thoroughly documented, in plain English, all of the financial principles that can help you achieve the best possible results and peace of mind. If we have done this, then our faith in the effectiveness of these principles will ultimately replace any fear that you have of financial planning. Then once your fear is gone you will feel better able to get the most out of your life. And, after all, isn't that what financial planning is all about? Money is not an end in itself, but rather is a means to help you both enjoy your life and do the things that are fulfilling in your life.

The best way to view your relationship with your financial professionals is to think of your financial life as a corporation. You (and your spouse) are the chief executive officer (CEO) of your financial life, and you're hiring your various financial professionals to be your senior officers or executive vice presidents in each of their areas of specialization. As good executive vice presidents they must report in a clear and concise fashion to you, and they must help execute your best strategy while keeping you fully informed.

You can think of your investment adviser as your chief financial officer, your attorney as your chief legal counsel, your CPA as your tax counsel, and your insurance broker as your risk management adviser. Your advisers should be encouraged to communicate with each other, and the ultimate result will be a well-coordinated financial plan for you that will provide you with as much financial freedom and independence at as early an age as is possible, regardless of whether you ever decide to formally retire.

As CEO of your financial life there's no time to waste, so write down three key action steps for either you or your advisory team to get started on today, and you'll be well on your way to financial success.

Glossary

AARP formerly known as the American Association of Retired Persons, AARP is now an acronym that just represents a nonprofit group of vibrant people over 50.

annual review a financial checkup equivalent to an annual physical.

annuity contract between an individual and an insurance company, providing lifetime income to the person on whose life the contract is based in return for either a lump-sum or periodic payment to the insurance company.

asset allocation how investment dollars are divided between the three major asset categories: stocks, bonds, and cash.

consumer price index (CPI) describes price increases for goods and services that the average consumer purchases.

copayment after satisfying the annual health insurance deductible, the percentage of remaining fees or costs you must pay.

correlation coefficient a measure that shows the relationship between two asset classes.

deductible the amount you pay before an insurance policy will pay, generally an annual requirement.

depreciation the deduction allowed annually for federal income tax purposes as a reasonable allowance for the exhaustion and wear and tear of property held for the production of income. Rules as to reasonableness and other qualifying requirements are prescribed by laws, rulings, and regulations.

direct rollover the permitted transfer of a participant's account from the trustee or custodian of a qualified retirement plan to the custodian or trustee of another qualified plan. When legal requirements are met, there is no income tax on the transfer. *See also* **indirect rollover.**

disability insurance provides coverage if an accident or illness renders you fully or partially unable to work.

dispersion degree to which a return in any single year is likely to vary from the average annual return.

efficient market line a series of points on a risk/reward graph which shows optimal portfolios for given levels of risk.

emergency fund six months' worth of living expenses kept in a money market account to guard against the unexpected.

estate plan designed to provide funds for the individual's dependents upon the death of the individual, but also to conserve the personal assets to be bequeathed to the heirs.

family limited partnership (FLP) a limited partnership where all partnership interests, both general and limited, are owned by members of the same family. *See also* **limited partnership.**

financial economics the scholarly study of investment principles and facts.

financial independence when work is no longer a necessity, but rather a choice.

financial inventory an exhaustive list of all key financial documents and advisers.

financial plan a written blueprint for achieving goals while taking into account all issues and contingencies.

financial planning team consists of your attorney, CPA, investment adviser, and insurance broker.

5 percent endowment spending rule by law an endowment must distribute 5 percent of its principal each year to various charities. This gives us a good estimate of a sustainable withdrawal rate for individual portfolios.

forward averaging formula a method of calculating and minimizing taxes on a lump-sum distribution.

401(k) plan a defined contribution plan offered by a corporation to its employees, which allows employees to set aside tax-deferred income for retirement purposes.

403(b) plan a tax-deferred savings plan for public employees including educators, health care workers, and professionals.

gerontologist one who studies aging and all the ramifications of aging.

grantor an individual providing assets under written terms to be utilized for the benefit of one or more others.

index fund tracks and measures the value and performance of a given group of stocks and/or bonds.

indirect rollover the distribution of a participant's account in a qualified plan to the participant for transfer by the participant to another qualified plan while meeting the legal requirements to avoid income tax on the transfer.

institutional investors corporations, pensions, endowments, and wealthy families.

lifeboat drill a rehearsal where you explore how you will react under a variety of adverse financial market conditions.

limited partnership a partnership that has at least one general partner and at least one limited partner. General partners have broad management powers and limited partners have very limited management powers. General partners have unlimited exposure to claims against the limited partnership; limited partners' exposure is limited to the value of their partnership interest.

long-term care insurance coverage if you require either an extended stay in a nursing home or at-home nursing care.

market timing futilely trying to be in the stock market only when it is rising.

mental accounting setting the sell target for a stock based on the original purchase price.

mutual fund an investment company that provides professional management and research of stock and bond portfolios.

no-load refers to a product that is bought directly without a commission (load).

personal inflation rate defines annual price increases in items that *you* purchase.

preretirement sabbatical taking a break from work for a period of time to embark on fulfilling activities, often followed by a healthy and enjoyable return to work at a later time.

probability the concept that nothing in this world is certain.

qualified plan a retirement plan that complies with complex governmental rules resulting in favorable tax treatment.

regression to the mean the likelihood that unusually high or low results will tend to return to normal or average over time.

Russell 3000 a broad index, covering over 3,000 common stocks. This gives an accurate idea of how the stock market is performing.

self-directed investors those who prefer to manage their own investments, in contrast to delegators.

settlor same as grantor.

Standard & Poor's 500 Index fund an index fund that contains 500 of the largest industrial companies in the United States.

standard deviation a statistical measure of volatility.

strategic consultants investment firms that provide state-of-the art investment designs typically for wealthy investors.

take-home pay the net amount of your paycheck after all taxes and deductions are withheld.

tax basis the starting point in determining taxable gain or loss upon the sale or disposition of property. Often it is the cost of the property; for inherited property, generally it is the fair market value on the date of death.

tax-deferred income whose taxes can be postponed until a later date.

total return dividends plus capital appreciation.

trust something (as property) held by one party (the trustee) for the benefit of another (the beneficiary).

umbrella insurance adds a layer of protection over existing policies by increasing policy limits on certain coverages or insuring against additional liabilities not covered by the basic policy. Provides coverage if your personal negligence causes an injury to another (e.g., car accidents or not cleaning the ice off your porch).

will a legal declaration of how a person wishes his or her possessions to be disposed of after death.

Wilshire 5000 an index of approximately the 5,000 largest U.S. companies.

Index